D0024909

TO WIRE THE WORLD

TO WIRE THE WORLD

PERRY M. COLLINS AND THE NORTH PACIFIC TELEGRAPH EXPEDITION

JOHN B. DWYER

Westport, Connecticut
London

Library of Congress Cataloging-in-Publication Data

Dwyer, John B., 1944–
To wire the world : Perry M. Collins and the North Pacific telegraph expedition / by John B. Dwyer.
p. cm.
Includes bibliographical references and index.
ISBN 0-275-96755-7 (alk. paper)
1. Telegraph—Russia—Siberia—History—19th century. 2. Telegraph—North America—History—19th century. 3. Collins, Perry McDonough, 1814?–1900. I. Title.
HE8219.S55 D95 2001
384.1'0979—dc21 00-023941

British Library Cataloguing in Publication Data is available.

Library of Congress Catalog Card Number: 00-023941
ISBN: 0-275-96755-7

First published in 2001

Praeger Publishers, 88 Post Road West, Westport, CT 06881
An imprint of Greenwood Publishing Group, Inc.
www.praeger.com

Printed in the United States of America

The paper used in this book complies with the Permanent Paper Standard issued by the National Information Standards Organization (Z39.48–1984).

10 9 8 7 6 5 4 3 2 1

Copyright Acknowledgments

The author and publisher gratefully acknowledge permission for use of the following material:

Excerpts from George R. Adams, *Life on the Yukon, 1865–1867*. Kingston, Ontario, Canada: The Limestone Press, 1982.

Excerpts from various documents in the Charles M. Scammon Papers, The Bancroft Library, University of California, Berkeley, BANC MSS P-K 200-207.

Excerpts from letter from James Wickersham to Newcomb Carlton (March 26, 1925), Wickersham Historical Site Collection Papers, Alaska State Library, MS 107, Box 73, Folder 2.

Excerpts from Record Unit 7073. William H. Dall Papers, *circa* 1839–1858, 1862–1927; and Record Unit 7098. Biographical Information File. Used by permission of the Smithsonian Institution Archives.

Excerpts from "Report of the British Columbian and Stekene Exploration Party to Colonel S. Bulkley" [UW #31]; and "Report on the Exploration of British Columbia from Victoria and Vancouver to the Stekene River" [UW #36] in the Wemple Papers Relating to the Russian-American Telegraph Project 1865–1867, Special Collections, University Libraries, University of Washington, Seattle.

This book is dedicated to the staff of the Dayton-Montgomery County Public Library, especially those at the inter-library loan desk, whose hard work and patience made it all possible.

And to those who persevere, transforming dreams into reality.

CONTENTS

ILLUSTRATIONS

PHOTOS

FIGURES

MAPS

Preface

I was sitting there, minding my own business, reading Walter McDougall's epic history of the North Pacific, *Let the Sea Make a Noise*, when I came to the part about Perry M. Collins and his North Pacific telegraph scheme. Hmmm. Interesting. Here was a subject with sufficient scope and drama and adventure to warrant a book. Besides, my mother's maiden name is Collins. More than enough motive to proceed. And that's pretty much how it began.

My goal was to tell the story of this nineteenth-century multicountry, trans-Pacific adventure in its entirety, with a primary focus on first-hand accounts of experiences in British Columbia, Russian America, Siberia, and at sea, by those who participated in exploring, surveying, and building Western Union's North Pacific telegraph line.

What intrigued me, among other things, was the fact that quite a few of these men were fresh from Civil War battlefields. Having survived, what would prompt them to reenlist in the "telegraph army" being organized in San Francisco; to board ships for a potentially dangerous sea voyage; to deploy to the wilds of British Columbia, Russian America, and eastern Siberia and their remote, sometimes hostile environments? I found the answer in *Reindeer, Dogs, and Snowshoes*, expedition veteran Richard J. Bush's book about his service with the telegraph army in Siberia. "What man has endured," we thought, "he can endure again. . . . [W]e were all young, stout, healthy and ambitious, and the enterprise one . . . worthy to chance one's life upon." Bush and the others saw the telegraph expedition not only as a great and challenging adventure, but as an important national undertaking, with Western Union carrying the flag to farflung lands with the solid backing of the United States government.

Then there was the compelling aspect of sailing the North Pacific in the brigs, barks, and one clipper ship of the telegraph navy. What must that have been like? Thanks to the well-written diaries, or logs, kept by the navy's commodore, Captain Charles M. Scammon, while commanding flagships *Golden Gate* and *Nightingale*, we know exactly what it was like. In regards to this aspect of the story I freely admit being inspired by the majestic seafaring novels of Patrick O'Brian.

But all of this—the men, the ships, the equipment, the deployments to distant outposts and arctic climes—was the result of one man's global vision. Perry MacDonough Collins was a no-boundaries entrepreneur who would not settle for dreams alone. He made the telegraph line happen, almost, through hard work and perseverance. In the end, however, another equally determined continent-linker, Cyrus Field, succeeded with his Atlantic cable, and the men of the telegraph army were called home.

Those who performed their duties in British Columbia, Russian America, and eastern Siberia trying to make the overland line a reality, who persevered mightily in the face of setbacks, delays, meager rations, deep snows, arctic storms, and angry seas never knew the meaning of failure or quitting. Their heroic endeavors stand as tributes to man's undying willingness to accept challenges, to face the unknown and endure its hardships for a noble cause, or simply to fulfill the pure spirit of adventure, whether it be journeying to the source of a huge river, scaling towering mountains, or exploring beyond our solar system.

For Collins and the men of Western Union's telegraph army and navy, the adventure was the attempt to build a line across the North Pacific's terrestrial dome in an effort to wire the world. This is their story.

ACKNOWLEDGMENTS

Researching this book took me to many different places that had one thing in common—hard-working, dedicated people who provided invaluable assistance and vital materials. Let me start by thanking, again, the staff of the Dayton-Montgomery County Public Library; up in Alaska, Gladi Kulp at the State Library's Historical Collections; Donna Darbyshire at the Yukon Archives in Whitehorse; at the B. C. Archives, David Mattison; Carla Rickerson, Manuscripts, Special Collections, University Archives, University of Washington; Patricia Keats at the California Historical Society; David Kessler and Susan Snyder at the Bancroft Library, Berkeley; Irene Stachura at the San Francisco Maritime Museum and its J. Porter Shaw Library. Thanks to Nancy Courtney for sending those missing pages from the Vevier book from the Ohio State University Library; to Debora Cheney at the Penn State University Library; to Henry Timmran, Trustee-Archivist at the Firelands Historical Society for that material on George Kennan; at the University of Rochester's Rush Rhees Library Rare Books and Special Collections, Karl Kabelac; the New York University Library's Archives; to Bill Cox and Bruce Kirby at the Smithsonian Institution Archives; to Bob Hoe for his research donation and friendship. And heartfelt thanks to my editors, Heather Ruland Staines, Marcia Goldstein, and Lisa Webber for their professionalism and patience. And, first, last, and always, to you, Mom.

Chapter One

Birth of a Vision

At 10 A.M. on Thursday, June 4, 1857, Perry MacDonough Collins stood on a small point of land in southeastern Siberia. Fifteen thousand miles outbound from New York and 5,000 rugged, overland miles from St. Petersburg, he was the first American to see the Amur River. Now the bearded Yankee, recently appointed U.S. commercial agent for the Amur River, prepared to embark a Russian vessel at its headwaters for a 2,750-mile journey down the "Mississippi of eastern Siberia," having sailed into latitudes and longitudes where American and Russian manifest destinies converged.[1]

Siberia, bordered on the north, south, east, and west by the Arctic Ocean, Mongolia, and the Amur, the North Pacific and the Urals, derived its name from Mongol and Tartar words meaning "beautiful sleeping land." It was awakened to exploration and exploitation following the death of the last great Cossack leader, Yermak, in 1585. Sixty-five years later, intrepid *promyshlenniki* (Russian fur trappers and traders) and Cossack explorers such as Ivan Moskvitin had extended imperial Russian sovereignty "east of the sun" to the Sea of Okhotsk.[2]

Beginning in 1724, Peter the Great inaugurated what might be termed officially sanctioned manifest destiny with a program of profit-motivated commercial expansion and scientific exploration which resulted in his

Left to right: D. I. Romanoff, Hiram Sibley, Perry MacDonough Collins, 1865. Used by permission of Hiram Sibley Papers, Department of Rare Books and Special Collections, Rush Rhees Library, University of Rochester.

successor, Empress Anna, launching the 1733 Great Northern Expedition. Two of its master mariners, Danish-born Vitus Bering and Alexei Chirikov, undertook the task of finding America's northwest coast and contacting natives for the collection of fur tribute. In 1740 Bering founded Petropavlosk at the tip of the Kamchatka Peninsula. A year later, sailing on an easterly course along 52 degrees north latitude, Bering and his men sighted Alaska. With the old Dane dying of scurvy, it was left to Chirikov to discover the Aleutians. Then came entrepreneurial fur trader Grigori Shelikov and Russia's first base in the region on Kodiak Island, followed by the establishment of the Russian-American colony and its fur trading company.[3]

To reach that point in time and history, to have expanded east of the sun and beyond, the Russians had to navigate and portage the massive riverine network that veined Siberia: the Ob, Taz, Tunguska, Iana, Lena,

Aldan, Yenisey, Kolyma, Indirka, and the major artery of its northeast sector, the Anadyr.

Central to that advance in trade and commerce was the Amur River, along whose shores Russia had riparian contact with Mongolia and China, a geographical reality which generated a politically and militarily fluid situation that continued until the 1858 signing of the Treaty of Aigun, which ceded all lands north of the river to Russia and guaranteed free navigation. One of the men most responsible for that significant agreement was Nikolai Muraviev. A Russian officer with a fine war record for action in Poland and Turkey, the hard-charging, no-nonsense Muraviev was appointed governor general of eastern Siberia by Tsar Nicholas I in 1848. He envisioned a Siberia that would rival America and Western Europe in commerce and development, with extensive transportation and communications networks. Key to making his dreams a reality was the Amur. "Whoever controls the mouth of the Amur," wrote Muraviev in 1849, "would dominate all Siberia." This belief explains why he and like-minded officials promoted and enacted policies and tactics that led, eventually, to the Treaty of Aigun. The very same year this man, later honored with the title Count Amursky, was appointed, an energetic young lawyer named Collins was preparing to sail for California.[4]

Born in 1813 to one of the founding families of Hyde Park, New York, Perry MacDonough Collins was named after two naval heroes of the War of 1812. After studying law in New York City, he traveled to New Orleans, where he found employment in a branch office of the Edward Knight Collins Steamship Company. Working for the fourth-generation Cape Cod entrepreneur whose ships were the fastest transatlantic steamers and having occasion to meet and talk with expansionists such as future California Senator William Gwin must have fired his imagination; going to the Gold Rush State was inevitable. His personal voyage along the course of manifest destiny had begun.[5]

It was the Renaissance man of founding fathers, Thomas Jefferson, who generated the manifest destiny concept, though the term itself wasn't coined until the 1840s. As early as 1786, Jefferson's concerns about Britain's Hudson's Bay Company, the Russian-American Company's *promyshlenniki*, and Spain's Commercial Company for the Discovery of the Nations of the Upper Missouri, plus his insatiable scientific curiosity, prompted him to encourage such men as adventurer John Ledyard and French scientist Andre Michaux to explore the continental Northwest. Ledyard attempted the journey backwards, overland, foreshadowing the Collins trek through Siberia. He never made it to the Bering Strait, having been arrested in Siberia and returned to America. Michaux's plan to ascend the Missouri, "cross the Stony Mountains and descend the nearest river to the Pacific," came to grief with revelations of his involvement in the Citizen Genet Affair.[6]

As had been the case in Russia, it was a riverine path that was followed to the North Pacific. In this instance, for a country about to double in size, the path followed the Missouri, all the way to its headwaters at Three Forks, Montana, over the Rockies to the Columbia, and then descent into the Great Western Ocean.

As was also the case in Russia, it was commerce that drove Jefferson's interest. When he sent Lewis and Clark's Corps of Discovery on their historic expedition in 1803, his principal motivation was securing likely new sources for American fur trappers. Scientific knowledge was important, but secondary.

Manuel Lisa, master of the Missouri Fur Company, had never heard of manifest destiny, nor had John Jacob Astor, but both assisted its realization with their Missouri Fur Trading Company and American Fur Company competition that invigorated Upper Missouri post building and potential profit increases following Lewis and Clark's return. Astor's idea was nothing less than putting the Hudson Bay and Northwest Fur Companies out of business. How? By establishing a chain of trading posts from the Great Lakes to the Pacific in 1810. Lisa had already set up several in Montana. Eventually, his company retreated to Lower Missouri trade, while Astor's maritime and overland expeditions led to the founding of Astoria, to the blazing of the Oregon Trail, and ultimately to the settling of the U.S.-Canadian boundary that added Washington and Oregon to the Union. California beat them to the punch, joining in 1850, giving geographical dimension to the rhetorical architecture of manifest destiny voiced by John Quincy Adams as early as 1812: "A nation coextensive with the North American continent, destined by God and nature to be the most populous and powerful people ever combined under one social compact."[7]

Drawn inexorably to a place awash in gold dust coated dreams and visions, of endless possibilities, bordering an ocean blooming with clouds of sails of clipper ships plying the China trade, Perry M. Collins sailed for California in 1849. Settling in Tuolumne County, 125 miles west of San Francisco, he immersed himself in Sonora politics, business, and real estate and became a member of the California bar. One of those business interests was the Tuolumne Telegraph Company, organized in 1854 to build a line from Stockton through Sonora to Columbia, center of local gold mining activity. A year later he went into the banking business with Ulysses S. Grant's brother-in-law, George W. Dent. Looking for other areas to exert his entrepreneurial skills, Collins became associated with the American-Russian Company.[8]

Organized in 1851 by Beverly C. Sanders, the company had varied interests. Its first operation was shipping ice from Sitka to San Francisco's hotels and bars. Then, with Russia engaged in the Crimean War, it undertook contracts to provide that country with beef and whiskey, and to procure Alaskan fish, timber, coal, and ice for them. This trans-North Pacific activity appealed to Collins, whose mind soon amplified and transmogrified it through his almost preternatural ability to conceive possibilities and ventures on a global political scale. Under sail, his imagination was propelled by the inspirational winds of recent maritime achievements.

From 1838 to 1841, Commander Charles Wilkes led an exploring expedition that surveyed much of the South Pacific and northern Antarctic coastal sectors. Commodore Perry opened Japan in 1854. Yankee whalers roamed abroad in search of cetaceans and their oil. And in 1855, Commodore John Rodgers returned to San Francisco.

The former commander of America's Mediterranean Squadron had been surveying the North Pacific littoral for his government and had returned with information on the Aleutians, coastal British Columbia, Russian-America, and the Sea of Okhotsk. He also brought news of the Amur, having studied, with Muraviev's assistance, the hydrography of areas adjacent to its mouth. He rated the river "one of the greatest in the world." Six years later Collins would petition Congress to fund a similar survey in connection with a project of his. But in 1855 he was thinking deeply about another matter.[9]

"For several years previous to 1855 . . . I had given much study to the commercial resources of the Pacific side of the United States, especially in connection with the opposite coast of Asia. I had already fixed in my mind upon the river Amur as the destined channel by which American commercial enterprise was to penetrate the obscure depths of Northern Asia and open a new world to trade and civilization, when news arrived in 1855 that the Russians had taken possession of the Amur country and formed a settlement at the mouth of the river. Greatly interested by this event, the important consequences of which my previous speculations enabled me to fully comprehend, I proceeded to Washington in search of accurate information on the subject.

"What I chiefly desired was to examine the whole length of the Amur and ascertain its fitness for steamboat navigation. That point settled in the affirmative, everything else was sure to follow as a matter of course. [In an 1865 lecture Collins stated that his secondary purpose was "to test by actual contact with the climate and country the practicability of an Overland Telegraph through Asiatic Russia to Europe."]

"At Washington I had conferences with President Pierce, Secretary of State [William] Marcy and the Russian ambassador, which resulted in my appointment, March 24, 1856, as Commercial Agent of the United States for the Amur River.

"Armed with this commission, and with letters to influential personages at St. Petersburg, I started without delay for the Russian capital, resolved to traverse the empire from west to east, across Siberia, enter Tartary and, if possible, descend the Amur River from its source to its mouth."[10]

And so began one of the great adventures of the nineteenth century, described by Collins in his 1860 book, *A Voyage down the Amur*. The first meeting between Collins and Muraviev in St. Petersburg must have been fascinating, the two kindred minds recognizing instantly the mirror images of their visions. They saw eye to eye on the matter of mutually beneficial trade and commerce centered on the Amur region as well as the need to build transportation and communications networks. By the time Collins departed Moscow, December 3, 1855, where he had since traveled, he had the full support of Muraviev and his tsar.

Collins was not the only American on the trip. He was accompanied most of the way by John L. Peyton, a thirty-two-year-old Virginia lawyer whose background included service as a secret diplomatic agent to Europe for the Fillmore administration. A boon companion, he returned to St. Petersburg before reaching the Amur.

Collins's point of departure was Irkutsk, near the shores of Lake Baikal in south-central Siberia. Upon reaching it, Collins wrote: "In an atmosphere ranging from 50 below to 10 above zero, Peyton and I have changed horses 210 times, had 200 (coach) drivers, 25 postilions (coach team guide horse riders) while being on the road 28 days and nights."

Throughout his travels Collins made detailed notes on the geography, natural resources, waterways, and transportation networks of various regions. He was keenly aware of how those networks connected and what that meant for the country. He wrote of roads and railroads under construction, their completion meaning that "commerce will be expedited and increased to a wonderful extent."[11] One of the maps he drew of the TransBaikal Province indicates deposits of gold, silver, coal, lead, copper, and iron.

Merely observing or describing was never Collins's style, however, so, on reaching Chetah, east of Lake Baikal astride the Yablonovii Mountains, he suggested the building of a rail-road from there, west-northwest, to Irkutsk. This would unite the Amur by rail and connect the two existing internal waterway systems to create a line of transit to Siberia's heartland. Local officials liked his proposal and Muraviev gave it his blessing. By the time Sergei Witte's trans-Siberian engineering masterpiece was completed, Chetah and Irkutsk were connected by rail.

During his voyage down the Amur, Collins was awed by the sight of ancient Tartar stone monuments built atop steep banks. Six to ten feet tall, they were believed to have been sacrifical altars. The nineteenth-century commercial Marco Polo was moved to write: "Standing upon this remote wild spot, where more than six hundred years previous, the agents of Genghis Khan had stood, or perhaps himself, calling upon God to 'give grace to his empire'—I could not but reflect upon the westward progress of the vast Tartar horde for many centuries afterward, until finally, the grandson of the Great Mogul himself made the very heart of Russia bleed, cities to smoke in ruin, whole districts to be laid waste, men by the tens of thousands to be dragged in chains to slavery and death."[12]

On July 11, 1857, Collins reached Nikolaevsk at the mouth of the Amur on the Okhotsk Sea's Gulf of Sakhalin. By the fall of that year he was back in America, reporting to congressional commerce committees and Secretary of State William Cass.

"Russia," he told them, "with giant strides approaching from the North, while England and France are pushing from the South, must soon meet in China." This confluence would, he asserted, generate "a new order of civilization, with European trade, commerce, manners and customs."[13]

When the Treaty of Aigun, which ceded all lands north of the Amur to Russia, was signed, Collins was sent back to St. Petersburg to assess the situation. Returning in the fall of 1858, he found another kindred mind in the person of American minister Francis W. Pickens, who listened as the man he considered expert on the subject described his ideas on east Asian policy.

Lest the reader think Collins was overstepping his bounds here, let us look at an excerpt from a letter written by Secretary of State William Seward in 1864 to Senate Commerce Committee Chairman Chandler: "During all the time that Mr. Collins has been engaged in maturing and developing it [the enterprise] . . . he has been acting under the instructions and with the approbation of the Department of State, and knowledge of that fact has not been withheld from Congress."

The "Collins Policy" was based on three interrelated points: the Europeanization of China financed by its trade with the Powers (England, France, and Russia); resultant commercial benefits for the United States; and economic advantages deriving from that situation via-a-vis American and Russian political friendship.

In terms of the post-Aigun Treaty situation, Collins stated that "the United States was no longer to the west of Russia or of Europe, but to the east, by way of the Amur River to California, Oregon, Washington, New York, New Orleans, Boston, Philadelphia and Baltimore."[14]

Commerce and communication have always been inextricably linked, so it was no surprise that in 1859 Collins refocused his protean mind on a project stemming from his telegraph interests. He was undoubtedly inspired by translations of articles by D. I. Romanoff in the journal *Russian Voice* and the *St. Petersburg Gazette* titled "Project of a Russian-American International Telegraph" and "The Siberian Telegraph." The

Russian engineer wasn't just theorizing, having supervised the initial surveys of the route and recently having been designated constructor of the Amur River telegraph line.[15]

Collins, who appreciated a great idea when he saw one, envisioned a line running across the terrestrial dome of the North Pacific, through British Columbia, Russian America, across the Bering Strait, and down through eastern Siberia, connecting America with Russia and Europe. He later wrote in a speech delivered to travelers clubs and other organizations across the country: "There has been nothing in the domain of scientific discovery more remarkable than the telegraph. The progress of telegraphy within the last twenty years has been gigantic. . . . May we not claim that we have discovered what the early philosophers and sages sought so industriously, and contend that electricity is the emanation of spirit, or the essence of the soul of the world? That this essence pervades all nature; guides the mariner over the dark and stormy fluid that envelops the earth to its center activity by gravitation—the two forces, positive and negative, holding the balance?"

The speech continued: "The demands of science and international intercourse, as well as the necessities of commerce, press the extension of the telegraph on all sides; transient wars, barbarous tribes and semicivilized nations delay its progress in one direction or another, but all these impediments will be overcome, and wherever there are great centers of commerce, the telegraph will penetrate."[16]

To wire the world was an undertaking that would require careful planning, all possible pertinent information, solid organization, and the support of several governments. For Collins, this meant securing U.S. government backing; his entrepreneurial instincts told him the private sector must also play a role.

Because part of the continent-linking line would be a submarine cable beneath the Bering Strait and perhaps elsewhere (the Sea of Okhotsk), and because the enterprise depended on seaborne support, Collins decided the first order of business ought to be a survey of the littoral areas of the North Pacific's terrestrial dome. He petitioned Congress for fifty thousand dollars to finance it. Employing his considerable persuasive skills, he elicited entirely favorable responses. Mr. John Cochrane, House Commerce Committee chairman, and Military Affairs Committee chairman Silas Latham were both enthusiastic. In a report dated February 17, 1862, Latham waxed poetic on the matter. "We hold the ball of earth in our hand," he wrote, "and wind upon it a network of living and thinking wire, till the whole is held together and bound with the same wishes, projects and interests."[17]

The private sector meant Western Union. With several partners, Hiram W. Sibley formed the Rochester, New York-based firm in 1856, uniting the efforts and resources of various regional companies. By October 1861, wires and poles reached all the way to the Pacific coast when Overland Telegraph and Pacific Telegraph lines were joined at Salt Lake City. Three years later, Western Union gained control of this continental communication originally championed by Sibley. The Collins project would make it supercontinental.

Collins initiated correspondence with Sibley in 1861 to discuss the venture. The very month that east and west were linked by telegraph, Western Union's president replied: "The work is no more difficult than what we have already accomplished over the Rocky Mountains and plains to California. . . . [I]n my opinion, the whole thing is entirely practicable (and could be accomplished) in much less time and expense than is generally supposed by those most hopeful. No work costing so little money was ever accomplished by man that will be so important in its results."[18]

Seeking further backing and support, Collins wrote to telegraph pioneer Samuel F. B. Morse, who responded that he foresaw no difficulties regarding the wire surviving the vicissitudes of high northern latitudes. In fact, he believed it "would conduct *better* [italics mine] than in warmer ones."[19]

His informed supposition was borne out by European lines that functioned satisfactorily above 60 degrees north latitude in Russia and Sweden. The northernmost point of the Collins overland line was 66 degrees, where it crossed the Bering Strait from Russian America to northeast Siberia's Chukchi Peninsula.

Some individuals who were aware of the project might have considered it a waste of time and money with the United States embroiled in civil war. To them and other like-minded citizens, Senator Latham responded, in 1863: "Let this not be called an improper time to present this subject to congress, because we are engaged in a war for our national existence, and because we are already taxing the whole energies and resources of the nation in a time of great peril; let us rather say that the United States is not only able to suppress rebellion at home, but . . . to extend her great commercial and scientific power over the earth."[20]

During the Civil War, Russia was the only great power to be pro-Union. England, knitted to the South by King Cotton, had been angered by the seizing of its diplomats in the *Trent* affair and was massing troops in Halifax. Napolean III sent French troops to Mexico to install Maximilian. Prompted by equal parts of geopolitical calculations and loyalty to the United States government, Russia deployed Pacific and Baltic fleet squadrons to San Francisco and New York in the autumn of 1863 to signal solidarity and thwart any French or British notions of naval support for the Confederacy.

Rear Admiral Lisovski, in his flagship *Alexander Nevski*, commanded the ships that steamed into New York Harbor, among them the sleek corvette *Variag*. Navy Secretary Gideon Welles wrote the Russian minister how pleased Americans were at seeing the Russian squadron. To his diary he confided: "In sending them [ships] to this country there is something significant. What the effect will be on France or French policy we shall learn in due time. It may moderate; it may exasperate. God bless the Russians." In New York and San Francisco, ships there commanded by Admiral Popov, officers, and men were greeted warmly, welcomed, and entertained. Collins, meanwhile, was hoping the Russians would positively consider his project.[21]

Since the majority of the proposed route ran through thousands of rugged miles in Russian America and eastern Siberia, permissions regarding right of way, building and maintaining the line, and other matters such as rates would have to be obtained from the imperial government of Tsar Alexander II. Collins had appreciated this fact from the outset, of course, and in an 1862 letter to Sibley stated: "As I have always contended, our first task is with Russia."

In that same letter, the indefatigable entrepreneur suggested that he travel to St. Petersburg on a mission to secure all the necessary grants and permissions. Sibley agreed. Three years later, in March 1865, Perry M. Collins and Hiram W. Sibley signed the final agreement in St. Petersburg. Director in Chief, Department of Imperial Posts and Telegraphs, I. Tolstoy, inked the "Act of the Siberian Committee sanctioned by His Imperial Majesty" (grant no. 820) for the Russian government. What took so long? Both Collins and Sibley discovered that imperial bureaucrats were tough negotiators who weren't above manipulation in the service of national self interest.

The agreement Collins worked out with St. Petersburg officials in 1863 was worded clearly in all its sections. Most importantly, Western Union would achieve its desideratum of exclusive right of way, for thirty-three years, along the route of the line, whose course they were completely free to choose. Along it, they could build posts or stations as needed. And the Russians included a sizeable monetary inducement in Section 17, knowing the company would use it as basis for selling stock and buying materiel to begin the massive project. Satisfied, Collins returned to America.

Late in 1864, Sibley accompanied Collins back to the Russian capital to put the finishing touches on the agreement, only to learn that Section 17 had been "re-interpreted" in favor of their negotiating partners. For months they protested, in vain, to Minister Tolstoy. "Yes, yes, my friends, we understand that you have purchased ships, other telegraph components, and subscribed investors," he probably told them, "but His Imperial Majesty has given you what you wanted. Besides, your country will benefit more from the completed line than will Russia. Should you decline signing the grant, we will begin negotiations with another firm." What were Sibley and his new managing director to do, presented with this *fait accompli*? With the company committed, they were compelled to sign of course.[22]

During the 1863–65 interim, Collins wrote Sibley that he thought the best way to proceed with his project would be to construct it under Western Union's banner "for many reasons: among them . . . time and money saved incidental to the formation of a new company—the experience, faith and credit of Western Union . . . and [its] thorough knowledge of what is requisite in such an enterprise."[23]

Western Union took Collins up on the offer immediately. In March 1864, company secretary O. H. Palmer informed stockholders that "the grand enterprise of uniting Europe and America overland by way of Bering Strait has been inaugurated under the auspices of this Company" and that "Mr. Collins retains the right to one-tenth of the newly created stock for construction of the line . . . as paid up stock. . . . [H]e is to receive as compensation for eight years services and expenses, when he secured the grants, the sum of $100,000." That money came from the sale of company extension stock, all of which was purchased quickly. Managing directorship ensued.[24] The other grant, similar to that which Collins had negotiated with the Russians, minus surprises and reinterpretations, was secured by him in London and gave Western Union route of line right of way through British Columbia.

Then, in February 1866, D. I. Romanoff decided to sound off on the subject of Western Union's decision to build its line through eastern Siberia according to the route proposed by Collins. His eleventh-hour objections were published in the *St. Petersburg Gazette* and based upon his eight years' service in that territory. Citing his previously published articles, Romanoff argued for more submarine cables: across the Sea of Okhotsk to the tip of the Kamchatka Peninsula, from there under the ocean to the Aleutians, and thence to the mainland. He could not understand the company's insistence on an overland line that would run from its Nikolaevsk terminus, north through Siberia's maritime provinces to the Anadyr River, and *then* across the Bering Strait to Russian America. He warned of a "wild nature and rough climate" consisting of a "woody and morasty desert" with tundra underfoot, interspersed with subarctic taiga forests. He described a "desert and savage" coast devoid of useful ports whose littoral was icebound much of the year. Here was a land of terrible "poor-gaws" or windstorms that leveled everything and lasted weeks on end, of scarce food and "clouds of mosquitoes and other insects [which could] excite to a rage every living creature." They drove men mad and might send animals to their deaths.[25]

The Russian Cassandra's words were read and heard but not heeded. Western Union and Collins were confident their planning and resources were sufficient to meet the challenges. The enterprise, known variously as the Collins Overland Telegraph, Western Union Company's Russian

Extension, and the Russian-American Telegraph Company, was under way.

In the meantime, Congress appropriated one hundred thousand dollars to help fund it and designated the USS *Shubrick*, a fore-and-aft rigged brigantine, to serve as survey vessel.

Wiring the world was going to require a five thousand-mile-long line through terrain and weather that was very much as Romanoff had described it. In some places, hostile natives could possibly be encountered. As for materials, wire and insulators were relatively light and easily transportable. Timber for poles was readily available in British Columbia and most of Russian America, though sectors of eastern Siberia featured timberless steppes. There, poles would be brought in by ships or river steamers.

Since nature's waterways enabled the activities that evolved into the globe-girdling project, it was only fitting that the route would follow, wherever possible, riverine pathways: the 850-mile-long Fraser in British Columbia, the mighty 2,000-mile course of the Yukon in Russian America, and the 450 miles of the Anadyr in Siberia. All connected with the Amur and beyond, west to St. Petersburg and the capitals of Europe.

In addition to all these considerations was the matter of the Atlantic cable. Collins and other like-minded souls viewed it as complementary to their world wiring work. Realists within Western Union and elsewhere knew full well that, if, after four unsuccessful attempts, Cyrus Field's persevering people brought it ashore at Cape Clear, Ireland, that work on their own venture must cease.

In light of this reality and the multiple challenges they faced, Sibley, Collins, and fellow Western Union executives decided that a quasi-military organization would be required, that only such an organization could sustain the requisite discipline and efficiency needed to overcome the rigors of weather, terrain, and natural hardships. Since the expedition members would be working in British Columbia, Russian America, and Siberia, across the North Pacific, the organization had to have land and sea forces, the former to conduct explorations and surveys and to build the line, the latter to transport men and supplies.[26]

It was up to Collins to select a man to lead this telegraph force. He chose, with advice from Colonel Anson Stager, a company official then serving as superintendent of the U.S. Military Telegraph Corps, Charles S. Bulkley. Colonel Stager knew Bulkley well from his service as his assistant, and as superintendent of the U.S.M.T.C.'s Department of the Gulf. The corps itself was quasi-military, and since it provided men and expertise to Western Union, let us take a closer look at that little-known, relatively small group of brave, dedicated men.

NOTES

1. Perry MacDonough Collins, *Siberian Journey: Down the Amur to the Pacific, 1856–1857*, A new edition of *A Voyage down the Amur*, ed. with intro. Charles Vevier (Madison: University of Wisconsin Press, 1962), p. 201.

2. Benson Bobrick, *East of the Sun* (New York: Henry Holt & Co., 1992), p. 37.

3. Walter A. McDougall, *Let the Sea Make a Noise: Four Hundred Years of Cataclysm, Conquest, War, and Folly in the North Pacific* (New York: Avon Books, 1994), p. 59.

4. Collins, *Siberian Journey*, p. 15.

5. Ibid., p. 10.

6. Ray Allen Billington, *Westward Expansion: A History of the American Frontier*, 3rd ed. (New York: The Macmillan Co., 1967), p. 446.

7. Dumas Malone and Basil Rauch, *Empire for Liberty: The Genesis and Growth of the United States of America*, vol. 1 (New York: Appleton-Century Crofts, 1960), p. 394; and McDougall, *Let the Sea Make a Noise*, p. 161.

8. Collins, *Siberian Journey*, pp. 10–13.

9. McDougall, *Let the Sea Make a Noise*, p. 296, and Collins, *Siberian Journey*, p. 20.

10. Collins, *Siberian Journey*, pp. 45–46.

11. *Dictionary of American Biography*, vol. 7, ed. Dumas Malone (New York: Scribner, 1934), p. 520. Peyton article by William G. Bean. Collins, *Siberian Journey*, p. 7 and p. 177.

12. Collins, *Siberian Journey*, p. 14 and p. 289.

13. Ibid., p. 28.

14. "Origin, Organization, and Progress of the Russian-American Telegraph," Western Union Telegraph Company, Rochester, N.Y., 1866, pp. 51–52, and Collins, *Siberian Journey*, p. 28.

15. Collins, *Siberian Journey*, p. 35.

16. "Origin, Organization, and Progress of the Russian-American Telegraph," pp. 145–47. An abridged version of a December 1865 Collins speech to the New York Traveler's Club is included in the Western Union historical document.

17. "Memorial of Perry McD. Collins . . ." Documents authorized by Senate Commerce Committee Chairman Z. Chandler on the Collins Overland Telegraph project transmitted to Secretary of State William H. Seward, April 14, 1864. Latham speech excerpt, p. 44.

18. "Origin, Organization, and Progress . . . ," p. 37.

19. Ibid., p. 36.

20. "Memorial of Perry McD. Collins . . . ," pp. 50–51.

21. James D. Horan, *Mathew Brady: Historian with a Camera* (New York: Crown Publishers, 1955), pp. 48–49, and McDougall, *Noise*, pp. 303–4.

22. Translation of letter from Melnikoff, Engineer Lieutenant General, Director of Ways and Communications dated June 9, 1863, St. Petersburg, to Perry M. Collins, and "Protest against Decisions of the Russian Government regarding Remarks Added to Section 17 of Agreement signed March 1865 by Hiram Sibley and P. McD. Collins, St. Petersburg, Russia."

23. "Origin, Organization, and Progress . . . ," p. 6.

24. Ibid., pp. 7–8.

25. D. I. Romanoff, "The Russian-American Telegraph, Collins Line," *St. Petersburg Gazette*, February 1866, nos. 37, 41, and 44.

26. "Origin, Organization, and Progress . . . ," pp. 11–12.

Chapter Two

The United States Military Telegraph Corps

Western Union's Anson Stager was serving as George B. McClellan's telegraph operations superintendent, Military Department of the Ohio, when the general was ordered to Washington in November 1861 to take command of all Union forces. The establishment of a centralized telegraph bureau was an important element of McClellan's military reorganization scheme. Assistant Secretary of War Colonel Thomas Scott, recently manager of the Pennsylvania Railroad, assisted by Pittsburgh Division Superintendent Andrew Carnegie, had been brought in earlier to impose organizational discipline on government railways and telegraphs. Since the railroads demanded their full-time attention, McClellan asked Stager to be his superintendent for all military telegraphs. Colonel Stager assumed the post on November 25, 1861, at the same time retaining his Western Union position. One of his first acts was to appoint fellow company executive Thomas T. Eckert to handle day-to-day supervisory duties. The newly commissioned major was then put in charge of Department of the Potomac and Washington telegraphs. That accomplished, Colonel Stager returned to Cleveland to resume his duties as Western Union's regional manager.

Before going back to the Buckeye State, Stager drew up a telegraph department restructuring plan. With its approval by the War Department, and by McClellan, in December 1861, the United States Military Telegraph Corps was born. One of the first tangible results of the Stager plan was the January 1862 merger of American Telegraph Company and Western Union lines at McClellan's headquarters, placing him in direct contact with field commanders such as Buell in Louisville, Halleck in St. Louis, and Commodore Foote in Cairo.[1]

Not long afterwards, Stager, working with Washington-based telegraphers Homer D. Bates, Albert B. Chandler, and Charles A. Tinker, developed the first army telegraph cipher. By war's end, a dozen more were devised. For his part, newly appointed War Department Chief Edwin M. Stanton ordered that no messages containing any military information could be sent by telegraph without department approval to prevent leaks of sensitive information.[2]

At its inception, the Telegraph Corps could count only 1,137 miles of line up and working in far-flung departments, for which there were 163 operators and 106 offices. Eight hundred fifty-seven miles of that line, along with 56 offices and 80 operators, were outside the Department of the Potomac.

Stager later wrote:

> In many instances the wires followed the march of the army at the rate of 8 to 12 miles per day, there being no other lines of communication upon the routes where these lines had been placed. The capacity of the telegraph for military service has been tested, and in affording rapid communication between the War Department, the Commander-in-Chief and different divisions in the army, in directing the movement of troops and transportation of supplies, it may be safely asserted that it is an indispensable auxiliary in military operations.[3]

Approximately twelve hundred young men comprised the Telegraph Corps. In dangerous, arduous conditions they carried out assigned duties. Jimmy Nichols was a seventeen-year-old telegrapher for General Edwin V. Sumner during the 1862 Peninsular Campaign in Virginia. One day the general asked Nichols if he could get in touch with McClellan by using a nearby telegraph line. Since his portable key box had only three feet of wire for quick connections, and those required cutting main lines, which in this case would have disrupted other important communications, Nichols had another idea. Why not pile empty cracker boxes high enough so he could make the connection without cutting the line? Troops erected a box pyramid. On top of it, at night, illuminated by a lantern that made him a perfect target for Confederate sharpshooters, the young man completed the job, unharmed.

Jesse Bunnell was General Fitz-John Porter's telegrapher. When Porter's forces retreated from Mechanicsville, he was left behind without a horse. As he neared Gaines's Mill on foot, Bunnell realized a battle was imminent. On his own initiative, he tapped a field wire and established contact with McClellan's headquarters. The commander in chief ordered him to stay put and report from the scene. With fifteen mounted orderlies assigned to him, his instrument set up behind a large tree, Bunnell kept McClellan informed on battle details for several hours. Not all the orderlies survived, but young Jesse did.[4]

In John Emmet O'Brien's *Telegraphing in Battle* we read:

> Most of those who responded to the call for operators were in their teens, but they were enthusiastic, already trained to faithful performance of duty, and ready to face danger when necessary. At Great Falls, an outpost on the Maryland side of the Potomac, the pickets were one day withdrawn, and the Confederates began to shell the telegraph office. As steps, porch and roof were successively shot away, the operator, Ed Conway, reported progress to the War Department, adding that his office would now "close for repairs," and he withdrew with his instrument as the enemy crossed the river.[5]

These are but a few of numerous instances of fidelity and bravery under fire. Quartermaster General M. C. Meigs would later write Stanton that he had seen a telegraph operator, shivering with malarial ague, in his camp cot, "his ear near the instrument listening for messages which might direct or arrest the movements of mighty armies. Night and day they are at their posts . . . in exposed positions . . . favorite objects of rebel surprise."[6]

By 1862 the Corps had 3,571 miles of line in operation; by June of 1863 that had grown to 5,326. Messages averaged 3,300 per day. Some of those lines were in the Department of the Gulf, supervised by Charles S. Bulkley.[7] A native of Rye, New York, Bulkley was employed by the Washington and New Orleans Telegraph Company as an engineer. After supervising construction of their main line, he became its superintendent. During this period, he invented what fellow telegraph engineer and Edison partner Franklin L. Pope called "a marvellous triumph of ingenuity." He was referring to the automatic repeating instrument which, in effect, divided a line into ten circuits, with a repeater for each, thus allowing messages to be sent directly from New York and Washington to New Orleans.[8]

William R. Plum, author of the two-volume seminal work *The Military Telegraph during the Civil War in the United States* opens his chapter on the Department of the Gulf with this statement:

> Very little occurred in this department of noteworthy consequence, in the telegraphic point of view, until after the coming of Charles S. Bulkley, who was commissioned captain, assistant quartermaster, and superintendent of military telegraphs in January 1863. Indeed, no military or naval warfare took place here until the last of April 1862.[9]

Captain Bulkley brought with him a number of able assistants and operators, including Edward Conway and J. W. Pitfield. Their first challenge had nothing to do with telegraphy. Rather, Bulkley and his men were ordered to clear the Bayou Teche, vital waterway for a Union army-navy operation that departing Confederate forces had clogged with sunken ships and other debris. In January 1863, Bulkley's command, assisted by a black engineering regiment under Colonel Robinson, cleared the channel using twenty-five-pound and fifty-pound charges. In his report Bulkley stated:

Our conducting wires were 2000 feet in length—the electric current from this over a small platina wire fixed in a cartridge in the case containing the charge. This conducting wire is part of a lot captured in New Orleans, of Confederate manufacture, rather imperfect, and intended for exploding torpedoes in the Mississippi River. In compliance with the order of Major General [Nathaniel P.] Banks, the United States Military Telegraph Corps has furnished the necessary apparatus, material and superintendence for this work. The colored regiment, Colonel Robinson commanding, rendered the most willing and efficient aid.[10]

In this campaign, Port Hudson, Louisiana, was beseiged, and General Banks named Edward Conway manager of his headquarters telegraph operations and, later in 1863, supervisor of his lines that were beginning to extend into Texas. The subsequent Red River campaign found Bulkley's men harrassed constantly by small Confederate cavalry detachments, some of whose troopers were captured by his command. Maintaining the line to New Orleans, which was interrupted repeatedly by the enemy, became so difficult that the section between Port Hudson and Baton Rouge was moved to the west bank of the Mississippi. This interference became a matter of ultimate annoyance, then supreme anger, for General Banks. He issued an order that, whenever the wire was molested, every house within twenty miles of the damaged line should be destroyed. Thereafter, they were left untouched.

At one point in the campaign, while a telegraph party slept, the army unit it was accompanying moved on. Bushwhackers took the opportunity to fire away at the small group. When Banks was made aware of the situation, he ordered the Second New York Cavalry, through his cipher operator, Conway, to rescue the stranded telegraphers. They arrived just in time to drive off the guerrillas.[11]

In one of his last reports Bulkley noted proudly that in his department there were "soldier operators," that the "click of our instruments" has been heard and read by civilians "in the roar of cannon and the din of war." He described his force as consisting of "fifty-two white men, including operators at twenty-three stations, thirteen negroes, four horses, ten mules, two army wagons and one ambulance, with 510 miles of line now working."[12]

Towards the close of 1863, War Secretary Stanton reported to President Lincoln that "The Military Telegraph, under the general direction of Colonel Stager and Major Eckert, has been of inestimable value to the service, and no corps has surpassed, few have equalled, the telegraph operators in diligence and devotion to their duties." By August 1, 1864, members of that Corps in the Department of the Gulf had constructed 695 miles of telegraph lines, some connecting New Orleans to the mouth of the Red River, to Lake Port and Fort Pike; others linked LaFourche to Fort Butler and Baton Rouge to Port Hudson.[13]

It was at this juncture that Bulkley must have received word from Stager that he had recommended him to Collins for the top job with the North Pacific telegraph project. Bulkley requested an indefinite furlough without pay so he could make the necessary arrangements before traveling to San Francisco, where headquarters for the "telegraph army" were being established. He was going to be its engineer in chief. To assist him in the great enterprise, he brought along some of his own men from the Department of the Gulf: chief assistant Frank N. Wicker, headquarters cipherer Scott R. Chappell, the redoubtable Ed Conway, and soldier-operator J. W. Pitfield. About Chappell, Conway, and Pitfield, we know only of Conway.

More is known about chief assistant Wicker. He joined the army in 1861 as a lieutenant in the Twenty-eighth New York Regiment, then was detailed as one of the original Signal Corps officers. He served in several Virginia campaigns and participated in the battles of Winchester, Antietam, Chancellorsville, and Gettysburg. Commanding officers cited him for daring actions on a number of occasions. Subsequently, he was detailed by the War Department to instruct the Mississippi squadron in army signal code and served on Admiral Lee's flagship during the Tennessee River campaign, which ended with the defeat of Hood.[14]

Bulkley, meanwhile, informed Western Union that he would not be able to travel to San Francisco until December or early the following year. Western Union secretary O. H. Palmer wrote to Bulkley on December 16, 1864:

> I should not feel that I had done my duty as an officer of this Company if I failed to bid you God speed in the arduous enterprise upon which you are entering, and to express my gratification in hearing you so warmly commended by those with whom you have been brought into more immediate contact in fitting out the expedition. . . . I feel confident that you will find no obstacles which perseverance and a determined will cannot overcome.

Perry M. Collins added his authoritative comments:

Be it known that Colonel Charles S. Bulkley, Engineer-in-Chief for the construction of the said telegraph herein mentioned, and acting in such capacity, is entitled to all the benefits of this order.

Acting for the Company, in my capacity as Managing Director, I hereby request the local authorities to give full force and effect to the requirements of said order, No. 318, and to render Colonel Bulkley the same good offices as if I were personally present, in the achievement of said telegraph.[15]

As can be seen, Bulkley was given appropriate rank for his command position as leader of the telegraph army, a quasi-military colonecy that not only appealed to his ego, but satisfied what the government and Western Union perceived to be Russia's love of military status and unquestioned authority. They were going to be working very closely with the Russians and were willing to take reasonable steps to help ensure full cooperation.

As Bulkley prepared to establish his headquarters in San Francisco, others who would serve in the telegraph army and telegraph "navy" or Marine Service were making their own ways to the Golden Gate.

More so than Bulkley, those men—whether battle-hardened Civil War veterans volunteering to face nature's challenges or outdoorsmen, sailors, scientists, or adventurers seeking more distant horizons—would need all the perseverance and determination they could muster as they ventured across the North Pacific to the deep woods of British Columbia, the wilds of Alaska, and the wintry wastes of Siberia.

NOTES

1. Robert L. Thompson, *Wiring a Continent* (Princeton, N.J.: Princeton University Press, 1947), pp. 384–86, and Lewis Coe, *The Telegraph: A History* (Jefferson, N.C.: McFarland and Co., 1993), p. 52.
2. Thompson, *Wiring a Continent*, p. 387.
3. Ibid., p. 387.
4. Coe, *The Telegraph*, pp. 53–54.
5. John Emmet O'Brien, *Telegraphing in Battle: Reminiscences of the Civil War* (Scranton, Penn.: Raeder Press, 1910), pp. 23–24.
6. Thompson, *Wiring a Continent*, p. 393.
7. Ibid., p. 393.
8. James D. Reid, *The Telegraph in America* (New York: John Polhemus Publisher, 1886), pp. 144–45.
9. William R. Plum, *The Military Telegraph during the Civil War in the United States* (New York: Arno Press, 1974), p. 37.
10. Ibid., p. 40.
11. Ibid., pp. 45 and 46.
12. Ibid., p. 99.

13. Ibid., p. 104.

14. "Origin, Organization, and Progress of the Russian-American Telegraph," Western Union Telegraph Company, Rochester, N.Y., 1866, p. 12.

15. Ibid., p. 82 and p. 92

Chapter Three

Western Union's Telegraph Army

What man has endured, we thought, he can endure again, and as we were all young, stout, healthy and ambitious, and the enterprise one we thought worthy to chance one's life upon, we entered it resolved not to be alarmed at imaginary evils, to push forward, to accept whatever fate was in store for us, to test the powers of these polar denizens in actual encounters, and win, if possible; if not, to succumb with the best possible grace. These were the motives that actuated most of us; were the feelings with which we embarked upon the enterprise.[1]

These stirring words were written by Richard J. Bush, a young soldier-artist fresh from three years service in the Carolinas where, we are told, "he was the central figure in many hair-raising exploits." There can be no doubt that the spirit of adventure motivated many of those who volunteered for the expedition.[2]

Bush was destined to spend two years in eastern Siberia. Men of the telegraph army contingent deploying to that furthest destination were under the command of Siberian Division chief Serge Abasa. A Russian engineer and diplomat described as "bursting with good humor with an even temperament, having the resiliency of rubber and the hardness of steel," Abasa spent about ten years working for Western Union at its

Richard J. Bush. Courtesy of The Bancroft Library, University of California, Berkeley.

Rochester, New York, headquarters and spoke English fluently. Of him Colonel Bulkley wrote:

> In securing the services of Mr. Abasa I believe we are very fortunate: his knowledge of the people, language, customs, laws—his interest in the work, together with the position of his family in Russia, are all of the utmost importance.[3]

Abasa held the title of baron, and his brother, Basil, worked for Minister of Imperial Posts and Telegraphs Tolstoy. In further support of Siberian exploration, survey, and construction efforts, M. Karsackoff, then governor-general of eastern Siberia, sent his agent, Paul Anosoff, to "render all possible aid to the Honorable Telegraph Company in regards to its proceedings and communications with the local authorities and natives."[4]

Other "junior officers" listed on the official Western Union roster for the Siberian Division were: George Kennan, quartermaster and secretary; James A. Mahood, chief of explorations, Lower Siberia; Richard J. Bush,

George Kennan. Courtesy of The Bancroft Library, University of California, Berkeley.

secretary and quartermaster; Collins L. MacRae, chief of explorations, Upper Siberia; A. S. Arnold, quartermaster; Alexander Harden, interpreter.

Distant cousin of the diplomat George F., Kennan was born February 16, 1845, in Norwalk, Ohio. His father managed Western Union's office in town and young George learned telegraphy at an early age. At age eighteen he was working as an operator in Cincinnati for the U.S. Military Telegraph Corps. In 1864 a message came over the wire for him from San Francisco, asking if he would like to join the expedition.

> Led by a desire of identifying myself with so novel and important an enterprise, my natural love of travel and adventure which I had never been able to gratify, I offered my services as an explorer.[5]

James A. Mahood was a well-known civil engineer in California. C. L. MacRae had been an army engineer. Arnold was a war veteran who had been promoted to officer from the ranks. Of Harden nothing is known except his obvious language ability.[6]

Men destined for British Columbia and Russian America were assigned to what Bulkley designated the American Division. He put the redoubtable Edward Conway in charge of construction for British Columbia. His former U.S.M.T.C. colleague J. W. Pittfield was assigned to be his agent in New Westminster, British Columbia.

Franklin L. Pope was made chief of explorations there. A native of Great Barrington, Massachusetts, he gravitated towards natural philosophy, geography, and mechanical drawing. When a branch of the American Telegraph Company's line was extended into his town in 1857, he was selected by A.T.C. to become a telegraph printer operator. Pope resigned three years later, but signed up again with the company at the outbreak of the Civil War. For two years he drew maps of American's lines from Maine to Virginia. During the draft riots of 1863, Pope disguised himself as a farm laborer and reestablished communication between Boston and New York by repairing severed telegraph lines.[7]

Pope's first assistant was Dr. J. Trimble Rothrock, another of the expedition's Civil War veterans. A professional botanist, he was a member of the Scientific Corps, established under Smithsonian and Chicago Academy of Sciences auspices. Academy director Robert Kennicott was appointed to head that Corps. Through Kennicott was somewhat sickly as a child in New Orleans, then Illinois, his love of the outdoors brought him health; his activities led him to become a leading naturalist who traveled extensively in the Great Lakes region, western Canada, and Alaska before joining the expedition. His first assistant was William H. Ennis.[8]

Thanks to the efforts of Harold F. Taggart, we have access to the journal Ennis kept during his service with the Russian-American Telegraph Exploring Expedition.

After an arduous trip of five months across the plains, I found myself in the great metropolis of the Pacific coast, San Francisco, without friends or money, but by means of telegraphing and the aid of friends at home, I was the happy recipient of sufficient funds to enable me to live in ease and luxury for many long days. . . . I enjoyed the world and all its pleasures . . . for the simple reason that after suffering many privations and hardships during my trip across the plains, I came to the conclusion that I would taste the pleasures of the City life. . . . [A]fter remaining several months I heard news of a gigantic expedition . . . an undertaking of such magnitude, replete with adventure and the thought of traveling through Arctic regions, seeing the Esquimaux and making myself familiar with their mode of living, hunting and customs, induced me to apply for a position in the Company's service and . . . entered the office of the *one* whom I then supposed to be the leader. Upon my entering the room I noticed it filled with Gentlemen, some busily engaged in drafting charts, others drawing designs of shoulder straps and buttons for Company officers. . . . With the deferential air and with all the politeness an American could command, I entered the "sanctum." While scrutinizing the room and its inmates I was questioned by a sharp, quick voice as to my business. . . . [M]y questioner was a small man who spoke a great deal and required many words to say but little. After informing him as to my business, I was asked as to my ability to pack mules, make canoes with a sharp stick, and many other accomplishments. To these and many similar questions I answered according to my talent and on being informed that the pay was small, was asked if I went for pay or adventure. The salary that he offered for a man to risk his life in the Arctic was insignificant indeed, but pay to me was a secondary consideration. I replied that adventure and my love for roaming alone induced me to take the trip. Having previously served for five years as an officer in the Naval Service of the United States and my knowledge of signalling being thought of service to the Expedition, I was placed at work drawing designs for signals and to make requisitions for articles needed by the department. After fulfilling this duty I was requested to report next day at 10 a.m. Punctual to the hour I presented myself and was given charge of the recruiting office, where I was to recruit 50 men for the company's service, with instructions to take none but those I thought capable of performing the necessary duties. At this business I was engaged for four or five days, surrounded by as rough a set of men as San Francisco could produce; rejecting many, selecting but few I recruited the requisite fifty.[9]

To the deep disappointment of Ennis, after his good work for the company, he was informed by his boss that he could not go on the expedition; that he had no authority to enlist anyone. The Navy veteran smelled a rat. He realized he had not, in fact, been working for the expedition's leader. When he learned from a friend that it was Colonel Bulkley, he went to see him.

I was taken to the rooms of the Chief Engineer and found him to possess all the qualities which in my mind make a great man, and after a few hours conversation came to the conclusion that the Telegraph Expedition was one of magnitude with a "Head" who would carry through successfully the gigantic undertaking. I was kindly informed that I could consider myself engaged and could accompany any of the Exploring parties, either in British America or in the Arctic (Russian America). Preferring the latter on account of the novelties attending it, I determined to go with Major Kennicott.[10]

The reader will notice the rank given Kennicott. All the chiefs were majors in the telegraph army. Immediate juniors were captains or lieutenants. One of those lieutenants was George R. Adams of California. Having read several articles about the expedition and its purpose, as well as the dangers involved, he couldn't wait to sign up.

After obtaining letters of introduction to Col. Bulkley, I called on him at his headquarters in the Cosmopolitan Hotel, corner of Bush and Sansome streets (Western Union Hqs at Commerce & Montgomery). I was politely received by him, but was told there were no vacancies. He also said that, judging from applications received, it looked to him as if all the city's young men were anxious

Col. Charles S. Bulkley, Engineer-in-Chief, Western Union Telegraph Expedition. BC Archives Photo # B–04339. Reprinted by permission. Copyright © by BC Archives.

to risk their lives exploring the unknown. However, to get rid of me, he gave me a note to Major Kennicott. It was his party I wanted to join since it was going furthest north and promised great adventures through unknown arctic regions.

Upon calling on the major, he told me that all 12 party members had been engaged. Under no conditions would he add more. He was very friendly and I called on him for several days listening to his stories of hardships and deprivations on the Mackenzie River. His talks made me more anxious to go. To finally discourage me, he told me his men must be able to undergo any amount of pain and suffering without complaining, citing a man he'd heard of who burnt his arm with a cigar without flinching to show his willpower.

I was smoking a cigarette, and when he had concluded his remarks, I drew back my coat and shirt sleeves and placed the lit end on my bare arm and puffed away as flesh sizzled. My God, boy, the major exclaimed, jumping up and drawing my arm away from the cigarette, you might burn an artery and have blood poisoning, all sorts of dangerous complications. I said it was just a matter of making up your mind then doing it.

My impromptu, fool act impressed the major. However, he finished his remarks by saying, "Well, Adams, fools like you are the ones that do things and seem to pull out all right on the kind of trip I'm going on. If there's a vacancy, you can have it.[11]

Adams ensured a vacancy by bribing one of the expedition members who was getting cold feet, or didn't like the idea of having them frozen. A few days later, he signed on as the new member. "I found I'd been appointed 2nd LT, with the pay of $50 per month plus expenses, plus a uniform of that rank with gold lace trimmings and epaulets. I was the youngest member of our party of 13 at 20 years, 3 months old."[12]

At the top of Western Union's organizational pyramid was the Land Service. Bulkley named his former Telegraph Corps chief assistant, Frank N. Wicker, to head it. Another Department of the Gulf veteran, Scott R. Chappell, was appointed Wicker's chief quartermaster. Other veterans filled out most of his staff. Surgeon in chief was Dr. Henry P. Fisher, who had served as an acting assistant surgeon. George M. Wright was Wicker's adjutant and secretary. He had been a lieutenant of artillery. The Land Service's chief carpenter was Lawrence Conlin. His military career dated back to the Mexican War. After that, he had served seven years on the Texas frontier, then in the Civil War as lieutenant in the Third Massachusetts Cavalry. He still carried a bullet from his participation in the Battle of Hanover Junction. Rounding out the staff were chief draftsman John F. Lewis, chief interpreter Eugene K. Labonne (also spelled Laborne and Labourn in other sources), and Frederick Whymper, artist.

Interesting character, Whymper.[13] He was born in London in 1838, and with his brother, Edward, enjoyed a life of travel and adventure. Both were artists.

While Edward went off to climb mountains in France and South America, Frederick sailed for California in 1862. He arrived in San Francisco, later noting his impressions in his book, *Travel and Adventure in the Territory of Alaska*:

There are few who know California who do not become warmly attached to it. They may leave, but they soon return to their "first love," finding no other like it.

Though at present gold, silver, mercury and coal yield abundant returns, they are eclipsed by cultivation of the soil. Wine manufacturing has become a leading industry. California now produces 3,000,000 gallons annually. [This was in 1866.]

The writer has noted rapid changes on each of his visits. From a village of shanties and tents, San Francisco is now an orderly city of 140,000 souls. Its best streets are almost Parisian, with public buildings a credit to the city.

San Francisco is as much the center of American interests on the Pacific as New York is on the Atlantic.

The menu at first-class hotels contains in one harmonious whole the delicacies of London, Paris and New Orleans.

Society in the Bay City is much jollier, healthier, a more sincere thing than anywhere else.

Though there is a dash of "fastness" on the surface, ladies, refined, educated and virtuous are as abundant here as elsewhere, and the girls born in California will bear the palm in a country famous for its pretty girls.[14]

Whymper truly loved the state, sketching and painting scenes and landscapes for two decades. He also enjoyed the rugged beauty of the Pacific Northwest and happened to be visiting Victoria, British Columbia, when Bulkley first traveled there in early 1865. "I met the colonel and immediately volunteered to serve in the expedition. He expressed gratification with the idea of an artist accompanying him." Whymper heard Bulkley say that "no old man or woman should serve on the expedition," observing wryly that, "Doubtless Col. Bulkley's preference for youth and activity is that of Americans generally. In England I've sometimes thought that youth was considered more of a crime than a recommendation; that you were nowhere until you had, like old port, acquired body and age!"[15]

Bulkley had sailed from New York in December 1864, arriving in San Francisco January 1865, establishing his headquarters in the Customs Building at Commerce and Montgomery Streets. As we know from George Adams, his recruiting offices were located in the Cosmopolitan Hotel.

Edward Conway and other expedition personnel had preceded Bulkley to California. Acting on orders from Western Union, Conway traveled to New Westminster, British Columbia, in November 1864 to meet with Governor Seymour about the project. J. W. Pittfield arrived the following February as Bulkley's agent; he and Conway set up temporary offices in the Columbia Hotel. The small city became intensely aware of the magnitude of the project. *The British Columbian* editorialized: "an infant city established only 6 years before amid towering trees that seemed to smile on man's puny efforts . . . was about to be linked with the electric systems of Asia, Europe and North Africa."[16] Back in San Francisco, Bulkley was immersed in devising the organization for his telegraph army. In that work he was aided by William B. Hyde, "a civil engineer I have chosen as my first assistant." He does not appear on the official roster, but appears to have been Bulkley's right-hand man. "He will be thoroughly conversant with my plans and the general direction of the enterprise," Bulkley wrote. Bulkley then put Hyde in charge of the "land parties destined for the Bering Strait region."[17]

Since the organization was quasi-military, Bulkley drew up General Rules of Organization and Government for the expedition. Instead of battalions, companies, and platoons, Bulkley established working divisions, parties of construction, and working squads, headed by superintendents and foremen. The chief foremen of construction parties had the power to fire anyone for violations of company rules and report his action to his division superintendent.

General supply depots were to be set up at convenient points. "Camp guards," the rules stated, "will be kept on duty at night, and, when necessary, will be responsible for all property stolen from the camp. Working and exploring parties will be properly picketed to prevent surprise.... The strictest discipline must be enforced. Foremen and others in authority will conduct themselves so as to ensure the respect and obedience of their subordinates."

Bulkley insisted that natives, whether Indians, Aleuts, or Koraks in Siberia, be treated "with the utmost kindness and consideration, and, as far as practicable [be] employed in the work.... Their interest in the work," he reasoned, "will be best secured by understanding that the success, condition and permanency of the line will result in continued profit to them."

Trading with natives was expressly forbidden. This restriction helped ensure continued support from the Hudson Bay Company and the Russian American Company, still operating in their respective imperial outposts.[18]

Captain L. Gavrischeff was the governor of Russian America. In August 1865 he signified his willingness to assist Bulkley by responding to the colonel's request for native interpreter-guides:

> In compliance with your request I shall send today [to be] at your disposal one Kodiak Aleutian, and the Finlander Granberg, for the Kvitchpack exploring party.... I send you a native of Kodiak, for only the natives from that island may answer the purpose; others speak quite a different language.... If you like, I can furnish you from here [New Archangel, Sitka] with an Aleutian skin boat.[19]

Kennicott's previous working relationship with the Hudson's Bay Company facilitated matters when Western Union sought assistance from that quarter and HBC's governor, Sir Edmund Head. Their concerns about maintaining control of their strategically located posts were easily met and their help secured.

Finally, regarding expedition members and contact with indigenous peoples, Bulkley's General Rule Number 10 stated that "spiritous and intoxicating liquors will not be allowed in camp, nor, under any circumstances, furnished to the natives."

When sailing from San Francisco to New Westminster, British Columbia, the traveler moves through 10 degrees of latitude, north past Marin, Sonoma, Mendocino, Humboldt, and Marin Counties, past Fort Ross, California, where the Russians established an outpost in 1812, past Cape Foulweather, Oregon, so named by Captain Cook in 1778, then on past the mouth of the Columbia River, discovered by Boston-based Captain Robert Gray in 1792 and named after his ship. The traveler is now north of 48 degrees latitude and the ship must maneuver east around another Captain Cook-named coastal feature, Cape Flattery, and into the Strait of Juan de Fuca, then northeast and north of the San Juan Archipelago and into the Strait of Georgia. Noted British explorer-navigator George Vancouver, after whom the offshore island is named, thus honored King George III in 1792. New Westminster is located just south and east from where the mighty river named after Simon Fraser finishes its magnificent 850-mile run to the sea.

Colonel Bulkley made his first official visit outside the United States to the small town of New Westminster in March 1865, arriving on St. Patrick's Day aboard the USS *Shubrick*. He stayed only one day before hurrying on to Sitka, long enough to unload the cable needed to span the Fraser, the only underwater section for the British Columbia route.[20]

Ed Conway had already made arrangements to use British Columbia Governor Seymour's steam yacht, *Leviathan*, to install the cable. Seymour was very interested in the project, having already presided over the laying of its first mile in his territory, a line that linked Government House with the city proper. Stormy weather foiled the first attempt; however, on March 21 it succeeded, with Governor Seymour himself at the helm of *Leviathan*, a small craft for so big a name.

The governor, a savvy politician, was fully aware of the importance, the international nature, of the event. So with Old Glory at the top of the masthead, he sent the first message:

Opposite New Westminster
March 21, 1865, 11:45 a.m.

To The Editor, *British Columbian*
We have to announce that the Cable is laid and working.
It was laid in seven (7) minutes.

It must be mentioned here that the telegraph path into British Columbia had already been blazed for Western Union by Horace W. Carpentier's California State Telegraph Company. Its crews had completed a line from San Francisco to Portland, Oregon, with plans to push further northward.

Carpentier visited the colony in early 1864, and on March 1 he petitioned the Legislative Council for permission to extend his line to New

Westminster. A favorable response came ten days later, and Governor Seymour approved what became known as the First Telegraph Act that year. Building and operating rights were granted for twenty-five years. The deal Collins made with the British trumped all this, and Western Union assumed all former California State Telegraph Company's rights and absorbed it.[21]

Captain Charles M. Scammon ordered steam up aboard the *Shubrick*. Soon, her 284-horsepower engine brought the big, portside paddlewheel to life as the veteran mariner plotted a course for Sitka. Bulkley was in a hurry. Once the ship had rounded Vancouver Island, stormy weather impeded the brigantine's headway. Ice began forming on the rigging as she fought her way into the Gulf of Alaska. Scammon was forced to seek shelter at Fort Rupert (Prince Rupert today), east of the Dixon Entrance and opposite the northern end of Queen Charlotte Island. Captain, crew, and passengers then waited out a sea-churning gale in Port Conclusion, which was only a few more miles up the Inside Passage.

Sitka, what the Russians called New Archangel, is situated on the northwest coast of Baranof Island, in the Alexander Archipelago, at 57 degrees latitude. All hands were relieved to have finally reached their destination. Scammon later reported:

> On arrival there we were visited by the then Russian Governor—Prince Maksutoff who informed us that the *Shubrick* was the first United States Government vessel to visit Sitka.

Bulkley and Scammon saw to it that every one of their men was properly attired in their uniforms to meet their Russian hosts. Unlike the quick stop at New Westminster, this visit lasted several days while Bulkley discussed expedition matters with officials. Among other things, he informed them that Kennicott and his telegraph army contingent would be their next visitors.

For his part, Scammon tended to his ship and crew, noting in his log:

> We remained at Sitka but a few days; meanwhile obtaining a small supply of coal. . . . Col. Bulkley, having concluded his conference with the governor, we departed upon our return passage to San Francisco, taking the same general inland route by which we came.[22]

To the relief of everyone, the return trip was made in fine weather, and the *Shubrick* tied up at Mare Island Navy Yard in late April. Thus ended the first voyage by Captain Scammon in support of Western Union's North Pacific telegraph project. This was his first acquaintance with Charles S. Bulkley, accomplished within the context of temporary duty. All of that was about to change. Scammon was about to become the commodore of Western Union's "navy."

NOTES

1. Richard J. Bush, *Reindeer, Dogs, and Snowshoes: A Journal of Siberian Travel and Explorations* (New York: Harper and Brothers, 1871), p. 1.
2. Vilhjalmur Stefannson, *Northwest to Fortune* (New York: Duell, Sloan & Pearce, 1958), p. 255.
3. "Origin, Organization, and Progress of the Russian-American Telegraph," Western Union Telegraph Company, Rochester, N.Y., 1866, p. 118.
4. Ibid., p. 128 and p. 105.
5. *The Firelands Pioneer*, n.s. 23, The Firelands Historical Society, Norwalk, Ohio, April 1925, p. 502, and George Kennan, *Tent Life in Siberia* (New York: G.P. Putnam's Sons, 1893), p. 3.
6. "Origin, Organization and Progress . . . ," p. 11.
7. *Dictionary of American Biography*, vol. 7, ed. Dumas Malone (New York: Scribner, 1934), p. 75.
8. Donald Culross Peattie, "Robert Kennicott, 1835–1866," 1935 article from the Smithsonian's Biographical Information File, Record Unit 7098, pp. 71–72.
9. "Journal of William H. Ennis, Member, Russian-American Telegraph Exploring Expedition," transcribed, with intro. and notes by Harold F. Taggart, *California Historical Society Quarterly* 33 (March 1954): p. 4.
10. Ibid., p. 5.
11. George R. Adams, *Life on the Yukon, 1865–1867* (Ontario, Canada: The Limestone Press, 1982), pp. 20–21.
12. Ibid., p. 21.
13. "Origin, Organization, and Progress . . . ," pp. 11–12.
14. Frederick Whymper, *Travel and Adventure in the Territory of Alaska* (Ann Arbor: University of Michigan Microfilms, 1966), pp. 269–85.
15. Ibid., p. 69 and p. 71.
16. Corday Mackay, "The Collins Overland Telegraph," *British Columbia Historical Quarterly* 10 (1946): p. 200.
17. "Origin, Organization, and Progress . . . ," p. 118.
18. Ibid., pp. 78–79.
19. Ibid., p. 95.
20. Mackay, "The Collins Overland Telegraph," p. 201.
21. Ibid., pp. 202–203.
22. Lyndall Baker Landauer, *Scammon: Beyond the Lagoon, A Biography of Charles Melville Scammon* (San Francisco, J. Porter Shaw Library Associates, 1986), Pacific Maritime History Series, no. 1, p. 85.

CHAPTER FOUR

WESTERN UNION'S NAVY

With the ratification of the United States Constitution, Treasury Secretary Alexander Hamilton, wanting to safeguard merchant ships, their cargoes, and the revenues they produced, requested establishment of a lighthouse service and ships to protect the new nation's coasts. Ten small, fast, agile cutters manned by fifty officers became the first coast guard, whose duties consisted of preventing smuggling, aiding ships in distress, and keeping East Coast trade routes open. The Revenue Marine, or Revenue Cutter Service, was born.[1]

Pittston, Maine, native Charles Melville Scammon, son of lawyer, financier, and civic leader Jonathan Scammon, went to California in 1850 where, before long, he became a highly successful whaling captain. He joined the Revenue Marine in May 1861 at its San Francisco homeport. With the Civil War under way, the service became a component of the U.S. Navy and was kept busy trying to stop or slow down Confederate privateers and blockade runners. It was not equipped adequately for these missions at the outset, having only two steam cutters, the *Harriet Lane* and the *Shubrick*, on the East and West Coasts, plus twelve sailing cutters—two-masted vessels, eighty or ninety feet long, usually schooners or brigantines.

The *Shubrick* was a 140-foot long, 350-ton ship built in 1857. She

Figure 4.1. Captain Charles M. Scammon, Chief of Marine, Western Union Telegraph Expedition, drawing by J. B. Dwyer; adapted from photo in Lyndall B. Landauer's book, *Scammon: Beyond the Lagoon*, J. Porter Shaw Library, San Francisco, 1986.

mounted a cannon, a 24-pounder, in the bow, and two twelves in her stern. Her bright red portside paddlewheel, powered by a 284-horsepower steam engine, could propel the ship at eight knots.[2]

In April 1863, following tours aboard the cutters *Murey* and *William C. Nye*, thirty-eight-year-old acting lieutenant Charles M. Scammon was ordered to take command of the *Shubrick* at Port Angeles, Washington Territory. The "square rig sailor" adapted quickly to handling this new, steam-powered vessel. On the way back to San Francisco, he learned that her sails, including a flying jib and foretop-gallant, supplied speed equal to that generated by the paddlewheel.

Upon returning to port, Scammon's ship, the only Revenue Marine vessel stationed in the Bay Area during the Civil War, was given three missions: enforce customs laws, maintain navigational aids, and rescue ships in distress in and out of the Bay. Scammon was well aware of the navigational difficulties of those waters:

> The entrance to San Francisco harbor is fronted by a bar which is frequently very rough and at times in the winter season, extremely dangerous. So much so that pilots often wait outside with the largest class of ships, awaiting a favorable opportunity to cross. Northwest winds prevail during the year . . . and in summer they are seldom interrupted.[3]

Eighteen sixty-three was an important year for the big, bearded Revenue Marine officer. Scammon and his crew rescued no fewer than six ships in various stages of distress. One of those rescues held important future implications. One of the Russian Pacific Fleet ships under Admiral Popov that sailed into San Francisco as part of the tsar's 1863 "friendship tour" was the *Novick.* During its approach to San Francisco's north coast, the steam-powered vessel ran aground at Point Reyes, about twenty-five miles from the city. The *Shubrick* managed to arrive quickly enough to rescue all hands, 160 officers and men, with the cutter's small boats. Personal effects, ship's papers, and other valuables were also taken off the doomed *Novick.* No one was more thankful than Edouard de Stoeckl, Russian minister to the United States, one of the passengers, who was later instrumental in the sale of Alaska. The minister sent Scammon a personal letter of thanks for his rescue; the entire incident became a national news story. So on October 13, with the entire Russian squadron anchored in San Francisco Bay, it fell to the *Shubrick* to exchange official gun salutes with Popov's flagship, *Bogatyre.* Scammon fired his twenty-four-pounder fifteen times.[4]

There can be no doubt that, two years hence, when men were being considered for the post of Western Union's chief of marine, this incident resonated with the Russians. "Major Collins, we would like it to be Captain Scammon," they no doubt informed him. Well aware of the obvious benefits that this bond entailed in terms of mutual cooperation, Collins okayed Scammon's appointment. There would be more rescues and a tour in Puget Sound for Scammon before he was promoted to captain in July 1864. He had married and settled down in the Bay Area when those projected overland lines reached into his life the following year.

Western Union had begun tending to maritime support of its North Pacific expedition in 1864 with the shipping of insulators, brackets, instruments, tools, carts, wagons, other needed items, and twelve hundred miles of wire from England and New York to the West Coast aboard such ships as the *Royal Tar*, *Edgmont*, and *Mohawk*.[5] By act of Congress, the secretary of the navy detailed the USS *Saginaw*, a steamer assigned to the Pacific Squadron, to assist in company fleet operations.[6]

In San Francisco, Bulkley had been authorized to buy such ships as he deemed necessary to transport men, materials, and supplies. Among his first purchases were the schooner *Milton Badger* and the whaling bark

Clara Bell. The acquisition of barks *Palmetto* and *Golden Gate*, along with another steamer, the *George S. Wright*, followed. Bulkley realized he needed someone to command this growing fleet of Western Union ships, a post he designated as chief of marine.[7]

About a month after Scammon returned from Sitka, his then-temporary Western Union assignment became permanent. In June 1865 he received a telegram from his boss, the collector of the port of San Francisco, granting him leave of absence from the Revenue Marine, without pay, to join the expedition. Bulkley had initiated the request. After arriving in Frisco, he must have heard about Scammon, his notable career, and his whaling background. A check with Collins would have probably led to vigorous approval by his Russian counterparts.

Bulkley and Scammon had already met during the Sitka voyage, which resulted in the former seriously considering the latter for his chief of marine. Bulkley had previously received a report from Scammon on *Shubrick*'s fitness as an expedition support ship. In it, the veteran mariner told him she wasn't suitable, and why. To emphasize his sound judgement, he reminded Bulkley of his experience, specifically of his years of sailing in northern latitudes.

In replying to Bulkley's invitation to join his expedition, Scammon made it absolutely clear that if he took the job, he would have final say in all marine matters and that he wanted suitable ships under his overall command.

Much depends on having the expedition by sea start with suitable vessels, and unless a vessel that is able to stand heavy weather, without sustaining damage from every gale of wind that is met, I must respectfully decline my services unless preemptorily ordered by the department.[8]

In a follow-up letter, Scammon let it be known that he wanted a chain of command through which masters of company vessels would receive orders from him via Bulkley, that he be subordinate only to Bulkley. And he urged haste in assembling and fitting out expedition ships so as not to waste the summer season. Scammon also desired a flagship capable of North Pacific passages.

On June 7, 1865, Bulkley issued the following order:

Headquarters, Overland Telegraph Co., General Order Number 3:

1st—Captain Charles M. Scammon of the U.S. Revenue Service is hereby assigned to duty as Chief in command of the Marine Service of this expedition with the title of Chief of Marine. He will be obeyed and respected accordingly.

2nd—Captain Scammon will at once take command of all Naval forces connected with the expedition and will obey no orders except those emanating from these headquarters.[9]

Barks combined features of square-rigged ships and schooners, most of them having three masts, with foremast and mainmast square-rigged; the mizzen—third mast—was fore-and-aft rigged. These were the blue-water workhorses of the nineteenth century. Most whaling ships operating from Nantucket or San Francisco were barks.

Two weeks after Captain Scammon was named chief of marine, he went aboard his new flagship, a 450-ton bark named, appropriately, the *Golden Gate*. Navy veteran William Ennis describes his excitement at seeing all the ships being readied for the expedition:

About the middle of June I visited the Company's ship called the *Golden Gate*, undergoing repairs and being altered to be capable of carrying all the Officers of the Expedition to their different destinations. At another wharf the steamer *Geo. Wright* was undergoing similar alterations. A hired brig called the *Olga* was getting ready for sea to carry Major Abasa, LTs Bush, Kennan and Mahood to the Asiatic coast. . . . [O]ne vessel, the *Palmetto*, started to the North with coal, while the bark *Clara Bell*, which was to be in Sitka in June, [was] loaded with everything from a needle to a small river steamer, the *Lizzie Homer*, to be run up the Yukon River in Russian America. Seeing all these preparations, I was eager as a schoolboy for vacation [and] thought the time would never arrive.[10]

The *Olga* was one of Russia's contributions to Western Union's fleet. Like others of her class, she was a two-masted, square-rigged ship with fore-and-aft sails set in her mainmast. Russia also provided a river steamer and the screw corvette *Variag*, member of Admiral Lisovski's squadron that visited New York in 1863. It was 2,156 tons, had 365-horsepower engines, a crew of 306, and seventeen guns. Western Union had requested a ship, and its expeditionary partner was more than willing to provide one, as Minister Tolstoy informed Collins in November 1865:

My Dear Sir—The request of your Company soliciting as a new grant the co-operation of one of the vessels of the Imperial navy in the surveys to be done along the Russian territories, addressed to His Imperial Highness, the Grand Duke Constantine, was forwarded for my approval; and desiring to assist your Company by all the means in my power, I gave my immediate consent. [Grand Duke Constantine was the tsar's brother and chief of Russian's navy.] I have now the pleasure to inform you that his Imperial Majesty the Emperor, has been graciously pleased to give the order appointing one of the ships now on the Pacific station, the *Variag*, to assist your Company in the construction of the telegraph line that is to unite America with Europe.[11]

Captain W. H. Marston commanded the *George S. Wright*, Captain John R. Sands, the *Clara Bell*. Other ships acquired by Western Union were the barks *Onward* and *H. L. Rutgers* and the schooner *Milton Badger*. This class of sailing vessel featured two or more masts, all fore-and-aft rigged.

Schooners could be handled by small crews. Only a captain, mate, cook, and four men were required for a three-masted one.[12]

By 1866 Captain Scammon commanded a fleet of some twenty-five vessels, from small river steamers to a clipper ship. That same year the *Golden Gate,* Lieutenant Davidson commanding, sailed to the mouth of the Anadyr River with provisions for the Siberian detachment. Winter closed in and the ship fell victim to the crushing embrace of ice that had formed quickly in the anchorage. Nevertheless, Davidson and his crew, assisted by construction personnel, managed to get away and salvage the cargo. Western Union designated the *Nightingale,* a recently acquired clipper, as its new flagship, one with quite a history.[13]

Perhaps no other ship embodies the maritime mystique of the age of sail than the clipper. "Skyscrapers" and "moonrakers" were some of the nicknames given these tall-masted beauties that roamed nineteenth-century seas. What could have been more inspirational than a clipper, bound for China or the goldfields of Australia, knifelike prow slicing through Pacific sealanes, under a cloud of sail? The prototype for this class, though not designated "clipper," was designed by well-known sailor-navigator Captain Nathaniel Palmer, who had recently worked for Edward Knight Collins in New Orleans, where the expedition's originator was once employed. The *Rainbow,* built by Smith and Dimon of New York and designed by John Wills Griffiths in 1845, is generally regarded as the first of the clipper ship class.[14]

These "greyhounds of the seas" were designed and built for speed. The clipper *James Baines* once averaged twenty-one knots during a voyage to Australia.[15] The *Nightingale,* named after "Swedish nightingale" Jenny Lind, was designed and built by Samuel Hanscomb Jr. at Portsmouth, New Hampshire, as an extreme clipper. He intended to surpass in speed, beauty, and class anything afloat. She was 185 feet long on deck with a 19-foot beam. Her ends were sharp as was her bottom. Her mainmast rose 77 feet, and with foremast and mizzenmast was raked—slanted aft. *Nightingale*'s bow featured a bust figurehead of Jenny Lind, at her stern, a reclining Jenny, nightingale perched on her finger. These specifications, plus a lavish interior design, qualified *Nightingale* for her builder's purpose: an exhibit for the London International Exposition. But her owners suffered financial difficulties and, four months after her June 1851 launching, the *Nightingale* was bound for "Oceania and China," under the command of veteran navigator John H. Fiske. For her new owners, Sampson and Tappan of Boston, she became one of the pioneers of trade between Atlantic ports and Australia. Swifter travel was made possible by Lieutenant Matthew F. Maury, founder of the Naval Observatory and Hydrographic Office, who organized existing data on winds and currents, bringing navigational charts up to date. His studies revealed that if a ship continued sailing south, then west, of

Capetown, it would find strong, steady tradewinds. Further south, below the Cape of Good Hope at about 48 degrees south latitude, ships would pick up even stronger westerlies that would fill their sails all the way to Australia, where gold had been discovered.[16] Though her maiden voyage from Boston to Sydney took a disappointing 90 days, the *Nightingale* did manage to log 263 miles in one twenty-four-hour period.

Then it was on to Canton and Shanghai, there to take on Britishers' favorite beverage, tea. Upon her return home her owners, knowing she hadn't shown expected speed, were undeterred, and offered a purse of ten thousand pounds to any ship that could beat *Nightingale* to China and back. Sampson and Tappan had no takers. After thousands of more miles logged sailing back and forth from New York, London, Australia, and China, *Nightingale* came to be owned by the notorious Francis Bowen, "Prince of Slavers." For eight months, from 1860 to 1861, the clipper was used to transport slaves until seized by the U.S. sloop of war USS *Saratoga* under Commander Alfred Taylor. The case was adjudicated in U.S. district court, and *Nightingale* became property of the government, which paid thirteen thousand dollars for her.

Fitted with four thirty-two pound guns, the clipper was ordered to Key West, Florida, headquarters, Gulf Blockading Squadron. She served through 1864, when yellow fever onboard caused her to be removed from the squadron. On February 11, 1865, *Nightingale* was sold at auction for $11,000 to D. E. Mayo of Boston, and became once again a merchant vessel. Captain Mayo sailed the ship to San Francisco in March 1866 with twenty-one thousand dollars worth of cargo. Soon afterwards, the extreme clipper was purchased by Western Union for $23,381. Captain Scammon transferred his flag on March 27 after *Nightingale* had been refitted to carry more officers and passengers. She would now have to navigate the westerlies, northeast trades, storms, and gales of the North Pacific in Arctic Circle latitudes. So would the other ships of Western Union's navy.[17]

NOTES

1. Lyndall Baker Landauer, *Scammon: Beyond the Lagoon, A Biography of Charles Melville Scammon* (San Francisco: J. Porter Shaw Library Associates, 1986), Pacific Maritime History Series, no. 1, p. 1.
2. Ibid., p. 70.
3. Ibid., p. 75.
4. Ibid., pp. 75–76.
5. "Origin, Organization, and Progress of the Russian-American Telegraph," Western Union Telegraph Company, Rochester, N.Y., 1866, p. 14.
6. Ibid., p. 14.
7. Ibid., p. 13.

8. Landauer, *Scammon*, p. 86.

9. Ibid., p. 87.

10. "Journal of William H. Ennis, Member, Russian-American Telegraph Exploring Expedition," transcribed, with intro. and notes by Harold F. Taggart, *California Historical Society Quarterly* vol. 33 (March 1954): pp. 5–6.

11. "Origin, Organization, and Progress . . . ," p. 89.

12. Ibid., p. 13.

13. Richard J. Bush, *Reindeer, Dogs, and Snowshoes: A Journal of Siberian Travel and Explorations* (New York: Harper and Brothers, 1871), p. 466, and Landauer, *Scammon*, p. 96.

14. John Jennings, *Clipper Ship Days: The Golden Age of American Sailing Ships* (New York: Random House, 1952), pp. 6–7.

15. John and Alice Durant, *Pictorial History of American Ships* (New York: A. S. Barnes and Company, 1953), p. 75.

16. Octavius T. Howe and Frederick C. Matthews, *American Clipper Ships* (Salem: Mass.: Marine Research Society, 1927), pp. 427–29, and Jennings, *Clipper Ship Days*, pp. 137–38.

17. Howe and Matthews, *American Clipper Ships*, pp. 430–37.

CHAPTER FIVE

ADVENTURES IN BRITISH COLUMBIA

When Edward Conway arrived at New Westminster to initiate survey work for Western Union in the fall of 1864, British Columbia had only been a crown colony for six years. Queen Victoria's parliament had so proclaimed it following the discovery of gold along the Fraser River in 1858.[1] The men who rushed there were but the latest in a long line of seekers and searchers who probed and charted its maritime perimeter, Spaniards and Englishmen who claimed the new land for their sovereigns until the matter was settled in 1790, navigators looking for the fabled Northwest Passage (whose existence was disproved forever by Captain George Vancouver in 1792), and men like Simon Fraser, who penetrated its interior to expand fur trapping and trading opportunities.

British Columbia is wedged into the North Pacific's eastern flank between 49 degrees and 60 degrees north latitude. Its labyrinthine islanded and inleted coast is shielded by mountains that give way to plains and plateaus bejeweled by a blue maze of lakes and rivers. Among the fauna roaming its rich environment were numerous fur-bearing animals with their highly prized peltries.

And so it was that in 1793 Alexander Mackenzie of the mighty Northwest Company journeyed across western Canada, beyond Hudson's Bay Company's Rocky Mountain boundary, to Elcho Harbor near Vancouver

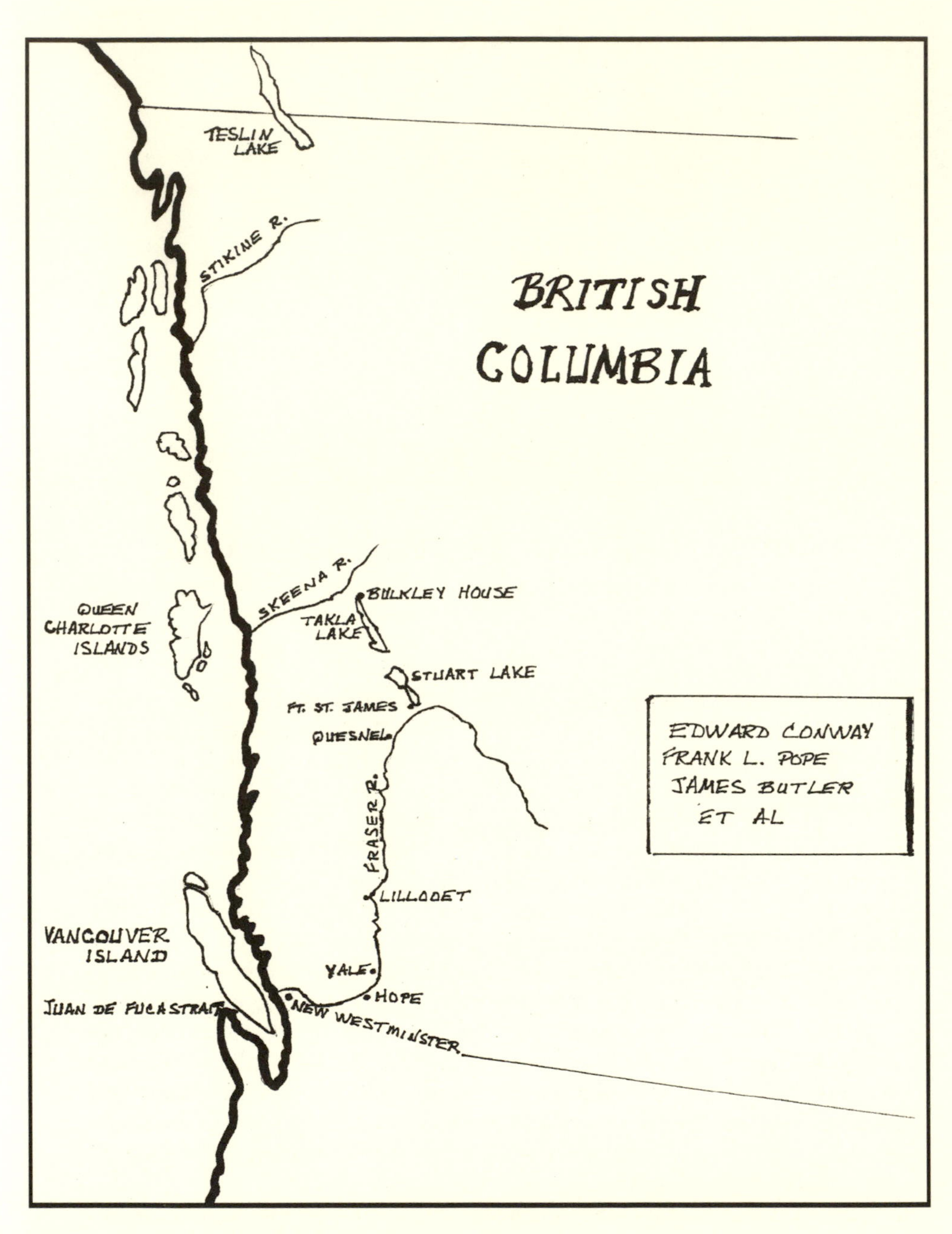

Map 5.1. British Columbia, drawing by J. B. Dwyer.

Some British Columbia expeditioners, 1865. James Butler, far left. Edward Conway in middle. BC Archives Photo # F–02960. Reprinted by permission. Copyright © by BC Archives.

to open up the new territory. It took twelve years for the Northwest Company to follow through on his explorations.

In 1805 its partners selected a man known more for his courage and perseverance than his scientific knowledge, Simon Fraser. Armed with these attributes and aided by information from the Thompson and Finlay expeditions, Fraser set his face westward.

One of his early accomplishments was establishing the first post west of the Rockies. With the help of James McDougall, he built Fort McLeod. That autumn he founded Rocky Mountain Portage at the lower end of Peace River Canyon. The following year, with John Stuart, he established Fort St. James on Stuart Lake. Its strategic location made it the future center of a fur-trading district Fraser called New Caledonia. In 1807 Fraser built Fort George at the junction of the Fraser and Nechako Rivers. He first entered the river that would bear his name in May 1808. Four canoes carried him, John Stuart, Jules Maurice Quesnel, nineteen *voyageurs,* and two Indian guides as they descended its wild, sometimes dangerous, waters. By the time they reached Hell's Gate, Fraser was moved to write:

An expedition camp scene "somewhere in British Columbia," 1865. James Butler seated at left. BC Archives Photo # F–02961. Reprinted by permission. Copyright © by BC Archives.

> I have been for a long period among the Rocky Mountains, but have never seen anything like this country. It is so wild that I cannot find words to describe our situation at times. We had to pass where no human being should venture; yet in those places there is a regular footpath impressed, or rather indented, upon the very rocks by frequent travelling.

There was also a suspension ladder constructed of poles and twigs about which Fraser commented:

> [It] furnished a safe and convenient passage to the Natives; but we, who had not the advantage of their education and experience, were often in imminent danger when obliged to follow their example.

After navigating that initial stretch, which required as much portaging as canoeing, they now boated downstream until the water's salinity told them they had reached a point where the Pacific commingled with this river's terminus. On July 2, 1808, the party halted a few miles from the ocean with Vancouver Island's mountains in sight. Fraser had time to determine the latitude. It was "nearly 49 degrees," he wrote in his journal. "The entrance to the Columbia is 46 degrees, 20 minutes. This river is therefore not the Columbia!" David Thompson named the new waterway after Simon Fraser, who, faced with hostile Indians, retreated inland, called a halt to the expedition, and never reached the Pacific. But he had established his company's presence in New Caledonia, opened up the new territory, and explored one of British Columbia's most important rivers.[2]

In 1821 the Nor'westers merged with Hudson's Bay Company, whose commercial realm now reached the Pacific. Thirty-seven years later, prospectors discovered gold in the Cariboo country around Quesnel, prompting improved overland access to the interior.

The "gold colony's" first governor, James Douglas, had already improved the road from Harrison to Lillooet, which paralleled the Fraser for its first eighty northward miles. He followed that up in October 1861 by ordering the company of Royal Engineers stationed at New Westminster to survey a route from Yale to Boston Bar, and contracted with a civilian firm to construct a wagon road from Boston Bar north to Lytton, and from there all the way up to Soda Creek, three hundred miles above Yale.

To call the country that had to be traversed rugged was an understatement. Listen to how Royal Engineer Lieutenant Palmer described it:

> It is difficult to find language to express in adequate terms the utter vileness of the trails of Cariboo, dreaded alike by all classes of travelers; slippery, precipitous ascents and descents, fallen logs, overhanging branches, roots, rocks, swamps, turbid pools and miles of deep mud. . . . The only good parts are on the . . . summits of bald hills; even the upper portions of slopes are in many places green, spongy swamps . . . and directly the forest is entered [and] the more serious evils begin.

Lieutenant Palmer's company built the first six miles of the Cariboo Road to Yale in the spring of 1862. Then the civilians took over, advancing in a three-stage process. First came the pioneers, or choppers, who cut down trees and spanned ravines with log cribbing, building log bridges over mountain streams emptying into the Fraser. Next came the graders, who dug up tree stumps, filled the cribbing with rock, and leveled the roadbed with crude, mule-drawn, wooden blades. Blasters were utilized in treeless canyon areas to create roadbeds in the sides of cliffs or overhanging rock. Upon completion of the Cariboo Road in 1864, some who traveled its 373 miles called it the eighth wonder of the world, one that could not have been completed without the support provided by river steamers.

Sternwheelers such as the *Umatilla* were part of a flotilla of a dozen or so American- and British-owned vessels that transported laborers, equipment, and supplies, plus oxen, mules, and hardware upriver. On each trip they also deposited five hundred prospectors that much closer to the goldfields.[3]

The year the Cariboo Road was completed saw the arrival of Edward Conway at New Westminster. As we have seen, he encountered colonial officials who actively supported Western Union's telegraph project, no doubt the result of British Columbia having passed its First Telegraph Act in 1864. Actually, the Hudson's Bay Company (HBC) itself initiated a proposal in 1862 that a telegraph be built across British North America to "the British colonies on the Pacific."[4] Western Union and Perry M. Collins were surely aware of this when they sought HBC authorization for their work in its backyard. They were specifically interested in securing the assistance of HBC employees situated in the Yukon Territory lying between Russian America and northern British Columbia. In its southern reaches, Conway was pushing ahead.

Bulkley's Civil War compatriot was well aware that spring rains would render work along the Fraser impossible, and he could not wait for Frank Pope's pending arrival to reconnoiter the way ahead. So he started without him after surveying the route east then north to Yale. Finding no insurmountable difficulties, he ordered his construction parties to begin work, utilizing an efficient method modeled on the one he employed during the war. Poles twenty-two feet high, eight inches wide at the base, and no less than four inches at the top were cut. Work parties of surveyors, markers, axemen, trimmers, peelers, hole diggers (twelve feet diameter, five feet deep), and erector teams planted poles spaced thirty to the mile. Then up went men to attach brackets and insulators. Last came the linemen, stringing the wire. (At least Conway didn't have to worry about a problem that confronted men building a line across America's plains, where herds of buffalo loved to rub themselves against poles, knocking them down in great numbers.)

In May Conway's men had two thousand poles ready for planting and had prepared the route all the way up through the Fraser Canyon. In that precipitous section, Conway had the line fastened right onto the rock with iron brackets. But now, he and his crews became too efficient. They were outrunning Bulkley's ability to supply them with sufficient material. Conway wrote his boss numerous letters urging resupply. "Where," he pleaded, "was the *Milton Badger*?" That ship finally arrived at New Westminster on June 17 with two hundred tons of what Conway needed. By September 1865, what had once been a dream envisioned by Perry M. Collins now stretched four hundred fifty miles towards fulfillment to a town called Quesnel.[5] Frank Pope passed it on his way north to the upper reaches of British Columbia.

On the morning of May 25, 1865, we awoke to find the steamer *Sierra Nevada,* in which we had made our trip from San Francisco, moored alongside the wharf in the harbor of Esquimalt, Vancouver Island.

So begins Frank Pope's narrative of his explorations, which he titled "From Victoria and Vancouver to the Stekine River."[6] (Today's maps spell the latter waterway Stikine and so will I.)

Pope found Victoria, then capital of the colony, well situated, offering visitors beautiful views of the harbor, the Juan de Fuca Strait, and beyond, the snow-capped summits of the Olympian Range. We find a more detailed look at Victoria in Whymper's book *Travel and Adventures in the Territory of Alaska.* Before signing on with the telegraph army, the artist-adventurer had spent three winters there. He tells us first, however, about the oddly named waterway.

Juan de Fuca, a Greek sailor whose real name was Apostolus Valerianos, spent forty years in service to Spain. In 1592 the viceroy of Mexico sent him on a voyage of exploration that took the veteran navigator to "the latitude of forty-seven degrees." There, Valerianos found "the land trending north and north-east, with a broad Inlet of Sea, between 47 and 48 degrees of Latitude: he entered there . . . sayling therein more than twentie dayes."

This account, recorded by Whymper and others, comes to us from a work titled *Purchas his Pilgrimes* by Michael Lok the elder. It narrates Lok's travels, which in 1596 took him to Venice, where he met old Valerianos, who told him his story. Upon his return to Mexico, he told Lok, the viceroy had met him with empty compliments, recommending that he go to Spain and tell the king about his discoveries. All he got there were more fulsome compliments. Abandoning all hope of reward, he went to Italy, where he met Lok. It was left to George Vancouver to immortalize the little-known navigator by naming the straits he found in 1792 after him.

Whymper found Victoria to have had a "forced and unhealthy career." Though it had much to recommend it by way of climate, abundant and inexpensive provisions, and communications, "it has dwindled to a very low ebb indeed." Why? Because those who made their fortunes there did not remain to settle the country. He cites California and Australia as examples of places where abundant and available land kept wealthy people, attached them to the soil, and made them contented residents. He found none of those in Victoria.[7]

Pope discovered that the Hudson's Bay Company store there had most of what he and his men needed for their expedition. After traversing the seventy-five miles across Georgia Strait aboard the steamer *Enterprise,* enjoying distant mountainous vistas, with Mt. Rainier dominating the western horizon, they arrived at New Westminster, situated fifteen miles up the Fraser, three hundred feet above its north bank. This lower stretch of the river, running about seventy five miles southeast then northeast to Hope, contains fast, tricky currents that challenged all vessels making their way upstream. The sternwheel steamer *Lillooet*, carrying Pope and his party, chugged along, passing prairies and cattle ranches. Suddenly, the sturdy steamer was bested by a fast current. Her machinery failed. As she bumped into the shore, crewmen aided by passengers made her fast with a hawser tied to a large tree. As Pope tells it, "a bellows and an anvil were produced, a blacksmith shop extemporized, and repairs were completed in four hours." By the time the *Lillooet* reached Hope, her boilers and engines had been strained to the bursting point, just making headway up the snowmelt-swollen Fraser.

Pope wrote that, next to New Westminster, Hope was the "prettiest town in B.C. Directly behind it rises a 5,000' mountain. Here the Fraser makes a graceful sweep around Hope. . . . [A] clear mountain stream joins the Fraser just above the town." That graceful sweep turned north. The fifteen-mile stretch up to the head of navigation at Yale was its most dangerous, featuring rocks, rapids, the usual strong currents, and, most daunting of all, Hell's Gate, where the wild Fraser's rushing waters are forced through a one hundred-foot-wide chute. The doughty sternwheeler just made it, her captain having to order passengers to move to her bow at times to facilitate maneuvering.

All ashore went the exploring party, landlubbers again. They traveled the fifty-seven miles to Lytton on the Cariboo Road with a thirty-mule pack train, through country "of overpowering and terrible grandeur beyond description," on past Boston Bar and sparsely timbered land, across the face of one-thousand-foot-high Jackson Mountain to the junction of the Fraser and Thompson Rivers and Lytton. Beyond that "windy, dusty, disagreeable town" the road diverged to the Thompson's south bank, then crossed it on a long, wooden bridge before striking north cross country to Clinton, "a cluster of a dozen buildings surrounded by fine farming country." Fifty miles north-northeast of there, at the lower end of the San Jose River Valley, Pope came upon beautiful Lake La Hache (now site of a provincial park), on whose shores he met Mr. McKinley, enterprising former Hudson's Bay Company officer, who raised cattle to supply meat and pemmican, a cake composed of pounded meat and berries, to miners and travelers.

After several steep ascents and descents through the northwest-trending San Jose River Valley, the Cariboo Road rejoined the Fraser's course, reaching its terminus at Soda Creek, where passengers and equipment were transferred to the one-hundred-foot-long river steamer *Enterprise*, more on which follows shortly.

The exploring party's equipment and clothing is described by Pope in his account in some detail because he believed the information would be useful to those who followed. First and foremost, proper snowshoes must be obtained. He recommended the four-foot long, one-foot wide size, laced securely to the feet. Loosely tied snowshoes led to a condition the *voyageurs* called *mal de raquet*, literally "snowshoe evil," or very painful feet. Pope admonishes those venturing forth with snowshoes, or without, to take good care of their feet. They should be covered with cotton stockings, square pieces of wool, then well-made, snug-fitting moccasins. For repairing the latter, he found that patching material and thread made from deer or caribou sinew served best. And, in words every infantryman has heard, Pope advised that extra pairs of dry foot coverings be stowed in packs. For the rest: woolen leggings, thumb and forefinger mittens, and the light, comfortable, hooded HBC *capote*, or long jacket. Pemmican constituted the standard ration. It was a combination of lean, dried strips of meat, pounded into paste, mixed with fat and berries, then pressed into small cakes. A reader of Pope's account can imagine his mouth watering as he describes this most excellent ration, "fully equal to 8 partridges, 3 rabbits or 4 dried salmon," that, when cooked with flour and dried vegetables, provided outdoorsmen a veritable Lucullan feast.

Pope duly acknowledges the estimable George Blenkinsop, expedition member and "pemmican master." The HBC veteran had stayed behind at Lake La Hache to supervise the preparation of Pope's favorite ration, rejoining the party at Alexandria, north of Soda Creek. During the course of explorations, Blenkinsop built boats, oversaw construction of "Bulkley House," and managed the dogsleds.

Though Yale marked the head of navigation on the Fraser, the river was found to be navigable by small vessel along the eighty-mile stretch between Soda Creek and the Grand Rapids. So entrepreneurial Gustavus Wright had machinery and boilers shipped overland and, using locally felled timber, built the one-hundred-foot steamer *Enterprise* at Alexandria. Pope and company disembarked *Enterprise* at Quesnel, which he described as the "northern limit of civilization in British Columbia consisting of 30 log buildings fronting the river."

Ahead lay a choice of destinations: Fort St. James or Fort Fraser, the latter about one hundred miles to the north-northwest, the former some thirty miles north of the latter. Upon learning of the existence of an old trail to Fort Fraser, the exploring party, guided by Indians familiar with the route, left Quesnel on July 5. Carrying their thirty-five-pound packs, they walked through plains, meadows, and river valleys, experiencing frost for the first time and a pestilential mosquito swarm that deprived them of sleep. July 22 found them at a lake whose Indian name Pope rendered as El-kah-taze-lah. From its northeastern shore rose a six-hundred-foot mountain that he climbed with others of his party.

From its summit we had a most beautiful view of the country for 50 miles in every direction, with its mountains, valleys, lakes and forests. The terrain appeared to be mostly level and gently rolling with a considerable number of lakes of different sizes and patches of prairie land here and there. Two conical, isolated peaks were visible in the north. One turned out to be on the northeast shore of Lake Nakosla.

Several days later they encountered their first Indian encampment on the shores of one of the lakes seen from the mountaintop. Initial tensions gave way to a palaver and some trading, especially for tobacco. Canoes had to be obtained from the Indians to transport men and supplies across the one-hundred-and-fifty-foot-wide Nechako River. Heavier baggage was taken to the far shore on a hastily constructed raft. Pack animals swam across.

At this juncture, Pope tells us about meeting a remarkable Indian woman named Too-gun-a-hen, who possessed an encyclopedic knowledge of the surrounding countryside. The expedition leader was most interested in the territory lying between Fraser Lake and the Pacific coast. Given pencil and paper, Too-gun-a-hen drew a detailed map of it that proved to be more accurate than those Pope brought with him. For instance, Pope's maps depicted mountain ranges all the way westward. Hers showed mountains only along the Pacific coast. Through an interpreter she told Pope that the route there, though difficult in places, was passable, and that, to her knowledge, no white man had ever traveled it.

Explorations there would be conducted in due course. Fort Fraser lay ahead up the Nechako. It consisted of three log buildings arranged around a square. The caretaker, "a not very intelligent Scotch youth," welcomed the wholly unexpected guests with strawberries and fresh milk. After a brief stay the men continued on towards Fort St. James, passing Lake Nakosla, looking "lonely and cheerless as we stood upon the beach watching the great waves as they successively rolled up from the far off horizon."

Several days later, by foot and canoes, weary from rugged terrain, they arrived at the fort. Built on a small plateau with sturdy buildings forming the letter "H," it was commanded by Peter Ogden, descendant of one of the original Nor'westers. Here, Pope decided to send a small party under Blenkinsop ahead to build a house for their winter quarters while he and the others returned to Alexandria to bring up necessary food and supplies. The boats that took them over the lakes and back down the Fraser were clinker built (with overlapping planks), thirty-five-foot long, four-foot deep, with a seven-foot beam able to transport six thousand pounds of freight.

On August 1, 1865, Pope and his men, along with Ogden, his brigade, and a load of furs, began their southern voyage. Three days and three hundred miles later, they reached Alexandria. By August 8 the boats were loaded again and ready for the return trip, which would include quartermaster James Butler. "The journey up the river with loaded boats was toilsome and arduous," Pope wrote, "occupying eighteen days . . . the work consisting of tracking and poling; the former hauling them by lines attached to the bows by men walking along the shore, the latter, propelling them through shallower water."

Once back at Fort St. James, Pope sent Butler once again to Alexandria for more supplies while he and the others proceeded north-northwest up the chain of lakes, canoeing and portaging across Tache, Babine, and Tatla. There, a night crossing:

> A gentle breeze sprang up, blowing from the south so we hoisted our sail and bore away to the north. During the night the wind increased to a gale but our little craft rode over the white-crested waves like a duck. On the north shore, close to the water's edge, appeared a thin line of smoke rising above the trees, and as we came nearer, the white gleam of tents.

This was Blenkinsop's encampment, where he and his men had almost completed construction of what they decided to name "Bulkley House," winter quarters for the British Columbia exploring expedition, 135 miles northwest of Fort St. James. At the upper end of the lake, not far from Bulkley House, was a river. Employing the prerogative of explorers to add names to blank spaces on maps, Pope and company called it the Driftwood, a waterway that constituted a canoe route to Lake Connoly, sixty miles to the north. The surrounding country was heavily timbered with silver pine, and thick undergrowth challenged the travelers. Variable weather produced the first heavy snowfall on September 5. The next day found HBC employee Mr. Alexander, four Indians, and two canoes arriving at Bulkley House from their post on Lake Connoly. They were on their way down to Fort St. James to stock up on winter supplies. Pope decided to go with them, and on the twelfth, was back at the fort. This time, he took the opportunity to climb Mount Nakosla, rising from the northern shore of its toponymic lake. The seven-hour ascent was rewarded. Pope spent the night at its summit:

> When I awoke the gray dawn was just breaking over far off snowy summits, the morning star shining with unwonted brilliance in the eastern sky. All around was a vast lake of mist with mountain islands breaking through the surface here and there. I arose and climbed to the top of a rocky pinnacle nearby to witness a sunrise such as one seldom sees in a lifetime. From behind the snow-crested ranges the sun shot its level rays across the intervening sea of mist, touching with a crimson glow the sharp mountain summits to the north. Looking south, the eye could trace by the winding, silvery lines of mist lying above them, the

courses of the Nechako and Nakosla rivers all the way to their confluence with the Fraser at Ft. St. George.

Descending the mountain back to reality, Pope found Butler at the fort with news requiring more plans and more trips. Ed Conway was on his way with a small mule train, bound for Babine Lake. But on learning after his October 3rd arrival about the rugged country up there, he decided instead to accompany Pope on his return to Bulkley House. Butler was dispatched to the aforementioned lake to purchase dried salmon from the Indians there.

Pope and Conway were greeted by huge flocks of wild ducks and geese flying south as they approached Bulkley House on October 13. The next day they decided to mount an expedition to explore the country towards the Stikine River which, on their maps, was about two hundred miles away to the northwest. Perhaps they should have taken more time to consider the time of year and the fact that they were nearly 55 degrees north latitude. Outbound some sixty miles, with winter setting in among the mountains, they abandoned the expedition. Back at their quarters on November 3 they found Butler, returned from Babine country with quantities of dried salmon. While at the lake he had been told by the Indians that a steamer had ascended the Skeena River and landed a man, with provisions, at a place called Aguilgit.[8]

That steamer was the *Union*, commanded by Captain Horace "Tom" Coffin, who in 1864 had taken her on a northwest coast trading cruise and pioneered steam navigation on the Skeena. Conway employed him for river explorations as he reported to Bulkley:

> In compliance with your instructions of July 22, 1865 to have the northern rivers explored and supplies taken to our interior line of exploration, I have started the steamer *Union*, in command of Capt. Horace Coffin, to make the necessary explorations. He left New Westminster August 30th, entered the mouth of the Skeena September 15th and ascended 90 miles. Here, two canoes were loaded with supplies and made it as far as Aguilgit on September 28th, 216 miles from the river's mouth. I enclose a list of supplies, stored at this village, that will probably be consumed by Major Pope's party, as the village is within 4 days travel of Babine Lake.
>
> The steamer entered the mouth of the Nasse river October 9th and ascended 43 miles. The party succeeded in ascending 40 miles further in canoes, total distance, 83 miles.

Captain Coffin returned to New Westminster on November 3. No wonder then that this adventurous steamboater would later be given command of the company ship *Mumford*.[9] Butler wanted to communicate with the man but was told that warring tribes in the area refused to allow delivery of letters.

On November 8 Conway took one of the large boats and all but eight of the men for his return to Quesnel. The octet and Pope settled in for the long winter. While snow and temperatures fell, spirits and morale were sustained by deployment of hunting parties and by festive observances of Christmas and New Year's, attended by Indians encamped nearby, so-called pemmican parties, during which the ration was prepared. Some of the provisions were stored outside, and the wintering party discovered what Indians had known for so long—that foraging marmots will defeat all attempts to keep provisions out of their reach. Their ingenuity was the stuff of legend. What other animal could steal the bait from marten traps?

February 1 brought a delegation of Indians from Aguilgit to Bulkley House. Their war was over, they assured Pope, and handed him dispatches from Captain Coffin, commander of the steamer that had ascended the Skeena. His information, plus that gathered from Indians by the winterers, led to a discussion of continuing explorations. It was decided to send out three groups: Pope and Blenkinsop would "penetrate the unknown regions to the north of Lake Connoly, reach the Stikine River, then descend it to the coast, from thence to Victoria by water. . . . James Butler and a half-breed named Harry McNeil were to proceed to Ft. St, James, thence across Babine Lake to its outlet, thence to Aguilgit and Ft. Simpson on the coast, making detailed reconnaissances of the Skeena and Nasse rivers." Pope's chief officer, Dr. J. T. Rothrock, and a Canadian, Vital Lafour, were assigned the territory "lying north and west of Lake Connoly to ascertain the source of the Stikine river."

Pope convinced an Indian of the Siccany tribe and his eighteen-year-old son to accompany his exploring party as guides and interpreters. Supplies were loaded on a six-foot-long sledge, or "tabogan" as Pope called it, pulled by four dogs. "On February 19th we bade adieu to our winter home and set out on our toilsome and adventurous journey." They reached Fort Connoly on the twenty-fifth. The high point, visually and literally, of that leg of the journey was nature's magnificent light display, the aurora borealis. "It exceeded in brilliance anything I have ever witnessed," Pope tells us, adding in a note that it was seen as far away as the Atlantic states. The fort was deserted. From the looks of things, it was determined that the only recent inhabitants had been wolverines.

Nine days later, armed with information provided by an Indian woman who knew the Stikine country from her younger days, the explorers, wearing snowshoes and carrying thirty-five-pound packs, walked on. Following a canyon, then a frozen river, the men trudged, deepening snow making the going almost impossible at times. Sometimes it was so deep only the heads and shoulders of the dogs could be seen; sometimes the men had to pull the sledge themselves; sometimes they traveled over the frozen surface of rivers on ice three feet thick. At length they came to an elevated, treeless prairie, twenty miles long and four miles wide, whose southern side presented a magnificent view of the Skeena Valley. Halfway across that prairie, in four feet of snow, they camped for a night. March 23 found them at the end of the prairie becoming hungrier by the hour. "We had to kill one of the dogs in order to supply food for the men who were becoming greatly reduced from hard labor and short rations." From this camp Pope conducted a reconnaissance of an elevated pass cutting through the mountains to the northwest. "Following up the ravine to the summit, about eight miles distant, I found it leading nearly west, apparently joining the valley of the Stikine thirty or forty miles away."

Back at camp, the "100 mile decision" was made. It was either follow the mountain pass route or follow the adjoining valley through which a tributary of the Skeena flowed. They chose the latter, learning afterwards that, had they taken what the Indians called the Klopada Pass, their journey would have been shortened by a hundred miles.

Twenty-five miles into the valley Pope was struck by another display of natural beauty:

> The scenery along the river became magnificent almost beyond description. Precipitous mountain ranges four or five thousand feet high closed in upon the valley on each side.

Cruel beauty perhaps, because the valley itself, taking them slowly upwards, was a difficult passage. Then, fifty miles from the top of the divide, they noticed an abrupt change in the terrain:

> A perpendicular range of basalt extends across the valley in a northeasterly direction, and the river, on reaching the foot of this range, turns sharply right and follows its base in the same direction for some twenty miles, subsequently bending around to the left until it flows nearly west.

The men must have experienced a great sense of relief as they walked through April 1 with no snow impeding their progress. The following day they encountered some Indians of the Nahannic tribe, who, after a long deliberation, invited them to their lodge a quarter of a mile away. Pope tells us these were the first human beings they had seen for two hundred miles. That evening the chief Nahannic hunter, whose name Pope rendered as Tchoo-a-ge-tah, told the explorers he was glad to see them, that he had heard of white men, and they were the first he had seen.

A companionable suppertime was seasoned with more information about the Stikine country, the men's pemmican meal augmented with some of the abundant rabbit killed by Tchoo-a-ge-tah's arrows. Refreshed after three days at the lodge, the men departed, leaving the Nahannics some of their powder shot and ball ammunition.

More friendly Indians were encountered a day later. Over a meal of caribou meat, they told the men that two whites had wintered at a camp further downriver but were now gone. Pope surmised they had been sent there to await his party's arrival. Their packs heavier with meat purchased from the Indians, the exploring party ventured into the fertile Stikine Valley, staying on the south side of the river.

By April 13 the dogs, having persevered and given their all, perished. What rations the men had left, plus equipment, was divided and stowed in packs. Following an evening conference, the group decided that Pope should strike out on his own, going as quickly as possible, and attempt to locate the two men the Indians had told them about, hoping they were still somewhere in the area. Any speed Pope might have achieved became a dream just one day into his journey when he was forced to put his snowshoes back on. There were no men, no rendezvous. There was only mile after mile of strenuous, or as Pope would call it, toilsome, plodding. He did come upon an old miner's camp with an empty cask and few bottles scattered about. On a stump nearby were inscribed the words "Dead Broke Bar."

Based on information at hand, he knew that there was a place called Shakesville about forty miles away, and he decided to follow the river's icebound path to it. He made his first camp inside a canyon:

> Trimming a small spruce tree which grew in a cleft in the rocks with my pocket knife, I procured enough boughs to cover a spot upon the narrow shelf of ice between the rocky wall and the roaring torrent beneath. After some difficulty I succeeded in collecting enough driftwood to make a fire and cook some pemmican, my first meal that day. Then, utterly fatigued by my 25 mile walk over difficult terrain, I willed myself into my blanket and slept.

When Pope resumed his journey on April 17, his mind was alternating between hope and fear. The ice on the river was melting. He had rations for only six more days. Then, after a few miles' travel, "to my great joy I discovered fresh moccasin tracks on the soft ice and observed the smoke of a campfire on the north side of the river." His shouts brought several Indians into view who immediately took him to their lodge and fed him a meal of boiled salmon. They were a coastal tribe who journeyed inland every year to trade with the Nahannics. As soon as the ice melted, they were going to load their two large canoes and return. It took three days for Pope to fully recover from total exhaustion. He couldn't thank the Indians enough for their great kindness, the women for repairing his torn clothes and moccasins, and for the generous supply of dried salmon they gave him.

On April 24 Pope was reunited with Blenkinsop, who had traveled virtually the same route and was the worse for wear. Rested, fed, and restored, he and Pope proceeded along the river. At a place called Buck's Bar, they were surprised to encounter Edward H. Scoville and his exploring companion, Mr. Barrett, who told them they had arrived the previous day. Western Union had sent them to survey the route of the line between the Stikine River and Babine Lake. They were now very low on provisions, so Pope and Blenkinsop gave them their remaining pemmican and a pair of snowshoes and saw them off.

At a makeshift camp the pair next came upon some miners who had been prospecting the Stikine since 1865 and were preparing to head upriver where better diggings were to be had. Twice a year they descended the river to buy provisions from the HBC trading steamer. The Stikine was now practically free of ice, so why, Pope and Blenkinsop asked themselves, shouldn't they take a cue from the miners? They saw some abandoned sluice boxes and used wood from the boxes to build a boat.

Several days later Captain Lewis of the Hudson's Bay Company steamer *Otter* looked across the broad reach of the Stikine and observed two men paddling an ugly-looking boat towards his ship. After they were brought aboard he was introduced to Messrs. Pope and Blenkinsop. "Ah," he might have said, "two more Western Union explorers," for he had landed Mr. Scoville and Mr. Barrett on March 25. These most recent company men were made comfortable onboard; the next day they were 180 miles downcoast at Fort Simpson (today Port Simpson), where they remained for several days before returning to New Westminster.[10]

There was no steamer voyage for James Butler. The expedition's quartermaster had canoed down the Nasse River to Fort Simpson and waited, per instructions, for the rendezvous with Pope scheduled for March 25. When he didn't arrive, "I engaged a canoe for $20 for my return to New Westminster, a most toilsome passage, having to paddle down the coast in heavy rains." Butler and McNeil had traveled to Babine Lake and back to the coast through heavy snows, over mountain passes, sometimes in canoes, sometimes portaging, sometimes helped by Indians, until reaching the Nasse on March 4.[11]

Rothrock and Lafour managed to journey northwest towards the source of the Stikine River, though Rothrock would explain in his report that "no one knew where any of the small streams went other than East or West. I had no means of fixing my position astronomically." He guessed, however, that his party had come within seventy miles of Dease Lake, near the Stikine's source.[12]

That effort brought route of the line exploration to within one hundred twenty miles of Yukon Territory. It was pushed up to and beyond that border by Michael Byrnes, a veteran miner from the Cariboo country who hired on with Western Union. Though motivated more by hopes of discovering gold than exploring telegraph routes, the persevering Byrnes, over the course of several seasons, journeyed north above 60 degrees latitude to Lake Teslin.[13] No nuggets glinted wet with river water; no signs of gold did he find. Western Union Russian America explorer and scientist William Dall tells us that "Mr. Byrnes returned, silent and morose, refusing to converse on the subject. It is said he has returned to the wilderness still in search of gold."[14]

Readers may recall that Ed Conway returned to Quesnel in November 1865. He and his construction crews had extended the line over three hundred miles from that town on the Fraser up to the Skeena River. Along the way they had felled trees for 9,246 poles, built fifteen log station houses, erected numerous bridges, filled in swamps, graded hillsides, and built a road along the route for supplies. It was twenty feet wide through standing timber and twelve feet through fallen timber.

Conway, of course, was reading the reports submitted by the various exploration parties with their suggested routes through northern British Columbia, but as chief engineer, his was the final word. Of the line completed to the Skeena, he wrote Bulkley:

> I can assure you that we constructed, in every respect, a first class line, omitting nothing that would help in making it a good working and durable line. It runs through an extremely favorable country, and is constructed in such a manner that it can be kept in repair with but little difficulty and at not a very great expense.[15]

To support line construction north from the Skeena, he requested a company river steamer be built that could ascend that waterway, or the Stikine, and provided his specifications for the vessel. The result was the *Mumford*, named after Western Union executive George H. Mumford, built at Puget Sound according to company specifications. Conway put James Butler in charge of the crew that would ride aboard her for the voyage north.

All hands soon discovered that *Mumford* was no match for the Skeena's currents, and after making but little headway, her skipper, Captain Coffin, had to put her against the shore. He and Butler hired a fleet of canoes, crewed by local Indians, to transport telegraph material and provisions upriver. They quit after one trip, so Butler, seeking more willing workers, decided to travel to a mission encountered during his previous explorations. Founded by the Reverend Mr. Doolan, it ministered to the coastal tribes who fished the Skeena, Stikine, and Nasse Rivers. They had treated him well and were skilled canoeists. Tribal representatives agreed to provide twenty-five canoes and crews, who transported the rest of *Mumford*'s cargo upriver. Butler and his men brought it the rest of the way inland to the new depot north of the Skeena. This was Fort

Stager, built by Conway's men, and named after Bulkley's old Civil War commander, now repository for 240 miles of wire, brackets, insulators, and twelve thousand daily food rations.

That assignment completed, Butler's work party returned to the *Mumford,* which took them back to Victoria, where a new load of supplies was brought aboard. This time the destination was Wrangell, Russian America, near the mouth of the Stikine. At a depot there, once used by the Hudson's Bay Company, they stored more telegraph material.

Between April and October of 1866, Conway continued to deploy exploring parties, wanting to ensure that the route of the line up to the Yukon Territory would be the same quality as that which connected New Westminster with Fort Stager—first class, good working, and durable. Of those parties he wrote to Bulkley:

> Too much cannot be said in praise of these men, the hardships they had to encounter were fearful; being compelled to pack their blankets and supplies on their backs through country covered with underbrush, fallen timber, swollen rivers and numerous other obstacles.[16]

Winter was setting in, the construction season coming to a close. Down in Victoria, up in Wrangell, and over in Fort Stager, men of the telegraph army settled in, waiting for spring and recommencement of their work to help wire the world.

NOTES

1. Margaret A. Ormsby, *British Columbia: A History* (Vancouver, British Columbia: The Macmillan Co. of Canada, 1959), p. 151.
2. Ibid., pp. 34–37.
3. Marian T. Place, *Cariboo Gold: The Story of the British Columbia Gold Rush* (New York: Holt, Rinehart and Winston, 1970), pp. 144–46.
4. Douglas MacKay, *The Honourable Company: A History of the Hudson's Bay Company* (New York: Bobbs-Merrill Co., 1936), p. 246.
5. Rosemary Neering, *Continental Dash: The Russian-American Telegraph* (Ganges, British Columbia: Horsdal & Schubart Publishers, 1989), pp. 45–48.
6. Frank L. Pope, "Report on Exploration of British Columbia from Victoria and Vancouver to the Stekine River," undated, p. 1. In the "Wemple Papers relating to the Russian-American Telegraph Project, 1865–1867," Special Collections, University Libraries, University of Washington, Seattle.
7. Frederick Whymper, *Travel and Adventure in the Territory of Alaska* (Ann Arbor: University of Michigan Microfilms, 1966), pp. 9–13.
8. Pope, "Report on Exploration of British Columbia . . . ," pp. 1–53.
9. Corday Mackay, "The Collins Overland Telegraph," *British Columbia Historical Quarterly* 10 (1946): p. 204.
10. Pope, "Report on Exploration of British Columbia . . . ," pp. 54–91.

11. "Report of James L. Butler to Majors E. Conway and F. L. Pope on British Columbia Explorations," May 1, 1866, pp. 14–15.

12. Neering, *Continental Dash*, p. 129.

13. Vilhjalmur Stefansson, *Northwest to Fortune* (New York: Duell, Sloan & Pearce, 1958), p. 279.

14. William H. Dall, *Alaska and Its Resources* (Boston: Lee & Shepard, 1870), p. 507.

15. Neering, *Continental Dash*, p. 130.

16. Ibid., pp. 134–35.

CHAPTER SIX

ACROSS THE NORTH PACIFIC

The bark *Golden Gate*, flagship of Western Union's telegraph navy, lay at anchor in San Francisco harbor, preparing to get under way for her voyage across the North Pacific, one that would involve sailing and tacking and wearing ship through 26 degrees of latitude and 52 degrees of longitude, sometimes in high seas with gale-force winds, from New Archangel and Plover Bay to the Kamchatka Peninsula.

After his tour aboard the steam-powered *Shubrick*, Captain Scammon must have felt more at home on the quarterdeck of this square-rigged ship, not unlike the whaling vessels he sailed for so many years. He was being kept very busy that June of 1865, supervising repairs, alterations, and improvements on his flagship, the exploring steamer *George S. Wright*, and the barks *Clara Bell* and *Palmetto*, all making ready for their voyages. The *Wright* proved to be one of the company's most useful vessels. Her two-bladed propeller allowed her to navigate practically anywhere her draft would allow; with schooner rigging she could operate under sail. As part-time consort to the flagship, the *Wright* served as her private tug whenever a tow was required.

Through the latter part of June 1865 preparations proceeded. By July 10, when Land Force personnel and Colonel Bulkley and his staff came aboard, all was in readiness. Orders were given, but Mother Nature wasn't on the company's payroll. Strong headwinds came up as the *Wright* towed *Golden Gate* down the bay, forcing them to heave to. The next day strengthening winds obliged Scammon to drop anchor off the Presidio. And now human error intervened. After the *Wright* parted company with the *Golden Gate,* she managed to foul her hawser in her propeller. Assisted by the tug *Merrimac,* the *Wright*'s crew cleared the propeller at Sausalito beach. By the afternoon of the twelfth she was under way again.

Continuing strong headwinds, accompanied by heavy seas, greeted the ships off Point Reyes, so Captain Scammon gave the order to bear up for Drake's Bay, anchoring there the morning of the thirteenth. When the *Wright* came alongside, her skipper, Captain Marston, came aboard the flagship for a conference with Bulkley and Scammon. It was decided that *Wright,* with Bulkley, Chief Quartermaster Chappell, and Chief Draftsman J. R. Lewis, would proceed directly to Victoria, then join the *Golden Gate* at her destination, Sitka.

Bulkley and the others transferred to the *Wright,* departing the place where Sir Francis Drake landed in 1579 after towing the flagship into the stream so she could set sail. No doubt all hands and passengers emitted a silent, heartfelt "finally!"

Twenty-five days outbound from San Francisco, the *Golden Gate* dropped her hook in Sitka harbor. The voyage had featured mostly thick and heavy weather, some whale sightings, and shipboard routine that included the piping of all hands on Sundays for the reading of company Rules and Regulations.[1] And, as veteran sailor and expedition member William Ennis recalled:

> On the passage from Drake's Bay to Sitka the officers amused themselves reading, smoking and card playing. Hyde, our commander, amused himself by issuing orders. . . . [He] ordered that guards be posted with Sergeants of the Guard and Officers of the Day; the writer had the honor of being appointed Officer of the Day, my duties not being very fatiguing . . . I amused myself sleeping, eating and card playing. Supposing that the officers were becoming indolent, Hyde issued another flaming order that all officers should drill the Sword Exercise and Bayonet Drill, which we did from 10 to 11 a.m.
>
> Our eating was passably good, having hash three times a day and on Sunday, a kind of pudding called "Duff." Butter, which had a tendency to perform maneuvers over the table, was served in profusion, and raw onions formed a delectable lunch around midnight.[2]

Duff or plum duff was a staple in the British navy for centuries, being a stiff flour pudding boiled in a cloth bag or steamed. Food and drink were accompanied at times by song. A quartet consisting of Joseph Dyer, Thomas Denison, Frederick Smith, and George Adams regaled Ennis and his friends with old favorites, some songs causing pangs of homesickness. But there was little time to dwell on that. The North Pacific imposed itself on all aboard, inspiring fear and awe, as Adams recalled:

One day while I was standing on the main deck talking to the first officer, on watch during a heavy gale, with high seas running, but the sun was shining and it was comfortable on deck sheltered by the high bulwarks from the wind, when suddenly the bow of the ship went down into a trough between two waves and before it could rise, the advancing wave, high above its bulwarks, swept over them, flooding the deck, sweeping aft two or three feet in depth to where the first officer and I were standing. At the same time, the vessel gave a huge roll to starboard, the water sweeping us off our feet. Down we went into the lee scuppers and several feet of water that might have swept us overboard if it had not been for the five foot high bulwarks.[3]

Ennis recounts that Mr. Quartermaster Arnold's birthday, July 30, was celebrated in grand style with vast quantities of champagne and liquors imbibed. Having caroused with his compatriots, much to the chagrin of the martinet Hyde, Ennis was surprised to receive an invitation to dine with him and Captain Scammon. We learn from Ennis that dining with superior officers has its drawbacks:

Of all the ills subordinates are beset with, the greatest is to dine with your superior. You are necessitated to be over polite, to refuse handing over your plate for a second helping of pie, when you could eat five whole ones, and to laugh and smile at all the incipient jokes that he may condescend to offer for your amusement.[4]

On Wednesday, August 9, the weather was hazy, with intervals of rain. As had been the case for the previous five days, the sea's surface was full of kelp and seaweed. At seven o'clock that evening Scammon ordered the signal gun fired to bring out a pilot to guide the *Golden Gate* into Sitka harbor.[5]

Here was the place Alexander Baranov landed in 1799 in search of a more southern capital for Russian America. His small colony was massacred by fierce Tlingits in 1802, but two years later the warship *Neva* recaptured Sitka, on the northwestern coast of the island named for Baranov, and secured it. Russians immediately got to work building their new fort, Novo Arkhangel'sk.[6]

Golden Gate's deep sea line showed thirty-five fathoms as she headed northeast by north into Sitka harbor, Mount Edgecumbe rising to the northwest. Observing maritime and diplomatic etiquette, Captain Scammon ordered a twenty-one-gun salute fired as he approached the imperial outpost; the Russian shore battery boomed its reply. The *Wright* was already there. Bulkley and Captain Marston came aboard the flagship for a discussion with Scammon, during the course of which he learned that the *Clara Bell* had been waiting patiently for them at Sitka these past two months. The first order of business, calling on Governor Gavrischeff, was conducted on August 10. He promised full support for the expedition, telling Scammon in an official letter that he had ordered all "Officers in command of the Settlements in our colonies to provide any goods, stores or materials which can be spared to ships of the Telegraph Company."

His governor general, Prince Maksutoff, invited Scammon, Bulkley, and their officers to dine at his residence. Ennis was there:

> I had the honor of being introduced to Madame the Princess Maksutoff and had the pleasure of her company for the Lancers. She speaks English and is a most beautiful as well as highly entertaining lady. She had given birth to a daughter on the 4th of July named Clara Bell, in honor of which, the *Clara Bell* fired a salute.[7]

Ennis and the others stayed busy seeing the sights in New Archangel and helping to gather wood and water for their ship. At anchor, *Golden Gate* was practically beseiged by flotillas of native canoes, or *bidarkas*, to the extent that her first lieutenant ordered a stream of water be sprayed to drive them off. The ensuing ill will needed to be dealt with, so Bulkley called for a meeting of all local chiefs. The powwow, held aboard the flagship, included Scammon, Bulkley, Captains Marston and Sands of the faithful bark *Clara Bell*, and Robert Kennicott. It was a success. The Indians pledged full support for the expedition. Speeches over, they received gifts of blankets, tobacco, and powder and were given a tour of the ship.

On August 13 Captain Harding sailed the *Milton Badger* through persistently foggy, drizzly weather into Sitka harbor. After reporting to Scammon, his schooner came alongside *Golden Gate* to take on equipment for her voyage to the Chukchi Peninsula. Now came a flurry of personnel transfers: Alex Harder, master's mate of *Golden Gate* to the *Milton Badger*, transporting the Anadyr River party; Mr. Norton, Land Forces, to the flagship as master's mate; Charles Cotter to the *Clara Bell* as seaman; *Milton Badger* mate Aaron Luce to the *Clara Bell* as passenger; James McCaulley from the *Wright* to the *Clara Bell*. Also transferred to the *Golden Gate* at this time was artist Frederick Whymper, bound for Russian America.

Reporting aboard *Golden Gate* on August 18 was expedition surgeon Dr. Henry Fisher. He had traveled to Sitka that May to gather all possible pertinent information that might "further the object of the expedition" to include barometric pressure recordings and to learn of the country and its customs. Dr. Fisher held definite views about the men's welfare as regards their dietary regimen, and he informed Bulkley and Scammon that they be fed "judicious amounts" of beef, mutton, clams, peas, beans, and tomatoes.

With sailing orders having been transmitted to the other company ships, the *Golden Gate*, with an Aleut pilot onboard, prepared to depart Sitka. Gun salutes were exchanged. But as the flagship passed the Rocky Islands, she was met by a strong southwesterly swell and a southeasterly wind that hauled ahead, forcing Scammon to take in all sail. Once again the *Wright* took her in tow. The following day Scammon was able to signal *Wright* "let go hawser" as he ordered that all sail be made in a freshening south-southeast breeze.

Scammon's private journal entry, August 26:

> This morning a sea bottle was thrown overboard containing the names of flagship and the Exploring Steamer, together with the names of the Engineer-in-Chief and Chief of Marine of Western Union Telegraph Company, and giving latitude and longitude (55deg. 08, 148deg. 36).

A westerly course was set as the *Golden Gate* sailed towards the Aleutians and Unga Island, with Unimak Pass, entryway to the Bering Sea, lying to the west-southwest.

The bark had been under full sail, close hauled to the wind, before her lookout sighted Unga Island. Under its lee she had to be taken under tow by the *Wright*. Bulkley ordered soundings to be taken as the ship entered the harbor, where her anchor was dropped in eight fathoms. Most expedition members then went ashore to explore and make scientific observations and collections. Two boatloads of crewmen rowed into the harbor to make a survey and more detailed soundings. Others fished, hauling in great quantities of good-sized rock cod. Before departing, Bulkley left a message for Prince Maksutoff. In red chalk writing on a board nailed to the island's only structure, he stated that the exploring party had visited, that they were leaving for Fort St. Michael on August 31, and that he hoped to see the prince there.

On September 1 the *Golden Gate* was under full sail, course west-southwest, in a northeast wind, and under tow by the *Wright*, also under sail. As the wind increased, Scammon signaled his consort to cast off the hawser, knowing Captain Marston would follow standing orders and keep company with the flagship. Nature conspired against orders. A strong squall blew in, churning the seas. The ships lost sight of each other in the heavy mist; then at quarter past eight Scammon's lookout yelled "Breakers ahead!" All heads turned to see a huge mass of rocks on the lee side not five hundred yards away. Quick thinking by Scammon and efficient work by his crew saved the day as the ship hauled her wind to clear what proved to be Halibut Island's shore. Ennis recorded that he had "followed the sea for five years, during which time

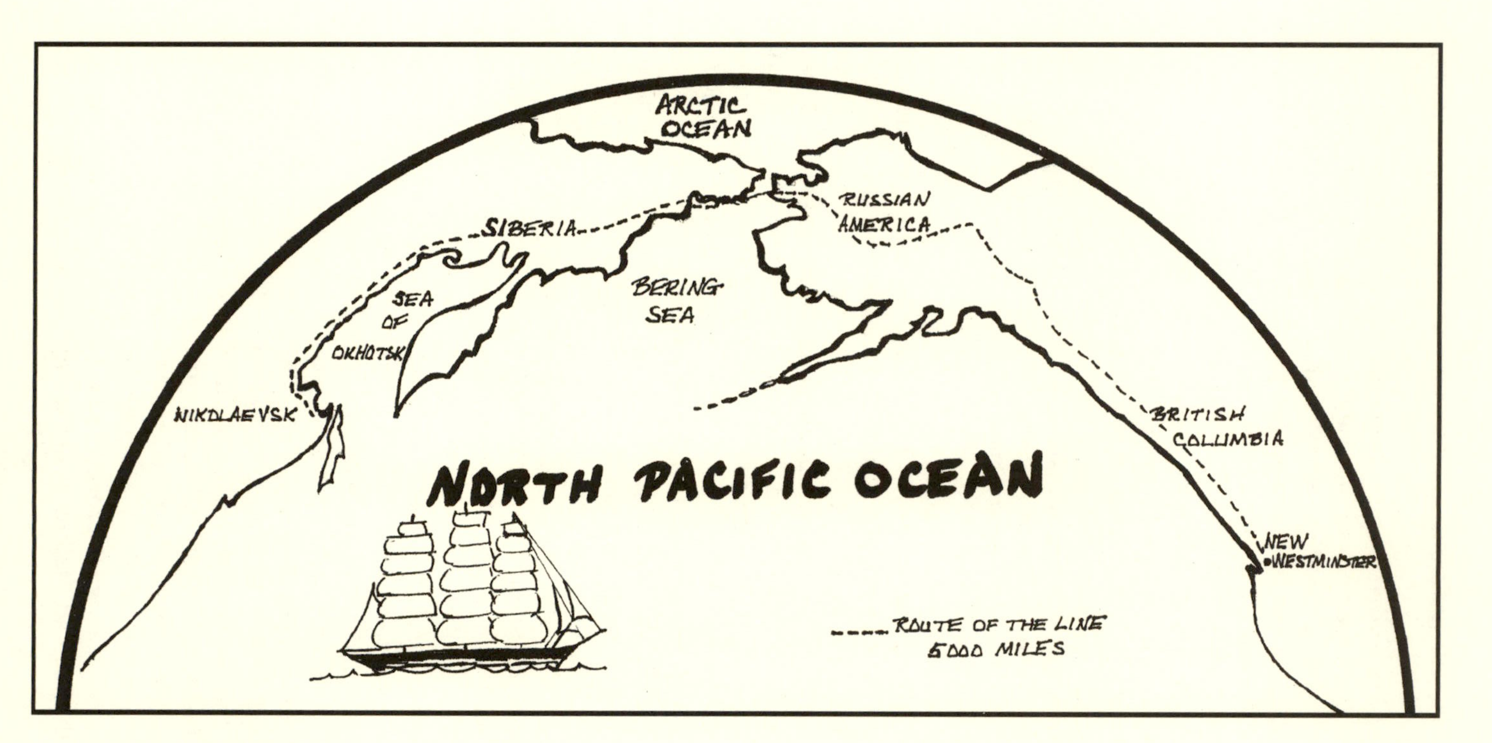

Map 6.1. North Pacific Ocean, drawing by J. B. Dwyer.

I have seen many gales and been in much danger, but never did I see a ship so narrowly escape destruction."[8]

The following day Scammon mustered his officers and crew to tell them he was proud of their performance in saving the ship and the lives of those onboard. Never in his thirty years' experience as a sailor had he seen a ship so near the breakers without going on them.

In the fog that now engulfed everything, the flagship's signal gun was fired at intervals in hopes of hearing from the *Wright*, but all was silence shrouded in gray.

Aboard the exploring steamer on September 4 Bulkley would write:

> Captain Scammon—we arrived this morning at St. Paul's Island and I am leaving this message for you. I am taking some oil & seal beef, also a skin canoe and two Aleuts. We lost sight of you the morning of the 1st inst. when I think you outsailed us. With steam up, our course was set for Unimak Passage, and we despaired of finding you in the thick fog that enveloped us. We made entrance into the passage at sunset and laid by all night, waiting for your coming up astern. In the morning we steamed on back track until noon, firing guns, but heard nothing. Since leaving the strait we have had strong north winds and considerable seas. I shall go directly to Plover Bay for coal, and, failing to find the *Palmetto*, sail over to St. Michael to put Kennicott ashore.[9]

Contrary winds prevented *Golden Gate* from making the Unimak Passage until the date Bulkley had written in his message for Scammon. That evening they moderated, hauling to the west-northwest, then freshening so that the bark brought her sails down to double reefs. That night she stood on opposite tacks under easy sail, a full moon illuminating the Bering Sea. As they sank the land behind them, crew and passengers could still see Shishaldin volcano on Unimak Island, 9,387 feet high, belching smoke.

A north-northwesterly course brought the flagship in sight of the Pribilof Island of St. Paul, but they tacked away to the northeast, and Bulkley's message went unread. On a cloudy September 13, the ship sailed into the bay off the Russian American Company post of Fort St. Michael, situated in Norton Sound, firing her signal gun as she dropped anchor. They were met almost immediately by a boat containing post commander Stepanoff and Kennicott, who brought news that the *Wright* had continued on to Plover Bay after putting him ashore.

Situated where it was, Fort St. Michael was the perfect place to establish a waypoint for the company's Siberian ventures. After the little river steamer *Lizzie Horner* was offloaded from the *Golden Gate*'s deck and the official visit made to Mr. Stepanoff, Scammon designated J. M. Bean as Western Union's storekeeper. His chief duties, however, were to serve in that capacity for Kennicott and his Kviepak Exploring Party.

Consisting of Ennis, Thomas Dennison, Frank Ketchum, Dyer, Charles Pease, Smith, George Adams, and Michael Lebarge, its mission was to explore that river which empties into Norton Sound from its mouth to Fort Yukon, and there, establish contact with Pope's party. The so-called Kviepak River proved to be mythical; it was in fact the Yukon that emptied into Norton Sound about fifty miles southwest of Fort St. Michael.

After the *Wright* departed the post on September 10, she steamed north-northwest up to Port Clarence on what would later be named the Seward Peninsula. Captain Marston reported that he and Bulkley went ashore to "examine for a suitable place to connect the telegraph wire with the telegraph (submarine) cable." Three days later they were approaching Fairway Rock and passing Little Diomede Island on their way to Plover Bay.[10]

Back at Fort St. Michael, good wishes having been made to Kennicott and his men, the *Golden Gate* prepared to get under way on the thirteenth. Scammon gave orders to run a kedge anchor and warped his ship further into the bay, the wind being directly ahead. On her way out, the water level fell so drastically that the bark touched bottom twice, but no damage was sustained.

Outbound on a westerly heading, the weather turned squally with a strong wind from the northwest when at nine o'clock on September 19 Scammon ordered the course changed to southeast by south, a-half south to pass beneath St. Lawrence Island. Three days later, having crossed the International Date Line, on a northerly track, the men sighted land off the port bow. It was Plover Bay at the southern tip of the Chukchi Peninsula. Well known to whalers, it is part of a rocky headland thrusting like a ragged blade into the Bering Sea. The whaling ship *Plover*, Captain Moore commanding, wintered there in 1848–49, and Moore named the bay after his vessel. Dall tells us that the bay is surrounded on all sides by high, rocky hills, "the principal of which, Mount Kennicott, I found to be 2,343 feet high." At the north end of the bay is Snug Harbor, at the other, Emma Harbor.[11]

The weather was cloudy with the wind blowing heavily from the east-northeast as the *Golden Gate* attempted entry into the bay, but when a gale began blowing she was forced to heave to on the port tack under close-reefed topsails. On September 25 Scammon ordered "wear ship," then tacked, and commenced beating into Plover Bay. As his ship dropped anchor, he saw the familiar shape of the *George S. Wright* nearby in Snug Harbor.

It was September at 64 degrees north latitude, and Scammon knew he could not tarry no matter how snug the harbor. Before leaving, however, he heard some grim news. In the harbor was the whaling brig *Victoria* out of Honolulu. Its captain visited the *Golden Gate* and informed Scammon that the Confederate raider *Shenandoah* had been preying upon

America's whaling ships in the Bering Sea. It was a British-built cruiser captained by J. I. Waddell that sailed to the North Pacific in 1865. Just six months before the flagship's arrival at Plover Bay it had destroyed twenty-nine whalers, and one of Scammon's old ships, the *William C. Nye*. By war's end she had inflicted $6 million worth of damage. An embarrassed British government later paid reparations to the United States, which sold the the *Shenandoah* to the Sultan of Zanzibar.[12]

After conferences with Bulkley and Captain Marston, it was decided that the *Wright* continue her explorations of relevant littoral sites. With the *Victoria* in tow, she departed. Scammon remained to take on water. And then, the winds that earlier prevented his entry into the bay came on to delay his exit. While he and the crew waited, they were visited by several natives. Pizzlebo, Enoch, and Knockum brought reindeer and walrus meat, skins, and furs, for the men. Scammon was thankful, especially for the meat, and was impressed with these forthright and intelligent people. He learned that Pizzlebo's father had rendered assistance to Captain Moore when he wintered in the bay, and that Enoch himself had done the same. Scammon wrote that he hoped all company personnel who met them "would treat them kindly as it is of the utmost importance that friendly relations exist along the telegraph line in territory inhabited by these people."

Finally, on September 30, the *Golden Gate* got under way in a northwest wind carrying snow, bound for Petropavlovsk. The ship suffered her first casualty three days later when Boatswain Yale was hit in the temple with a flying jib's block. He was immediately tended to by Dr. Fisher, whose examination revealed no serious injury.

On her southwesterly course, the bark sailed through mostly cloudy weather and heavy cross seas until October 11, when a sudden squall blew out of the south and the ship was struck on her quarter by a heavy sea that sent everything movable onboard flying as she hove up into the wind, her very sails shaking.

Four days later the *Golden Gate* was anchored in Avatcha Bay, Petropavlovsk, for what turned out to be a four-week stay. Official welcomes were extended by the captain of the port, Constantine Chmelofsky. One of the mariners in port at the time, a Captain Hunter of Burlings out of San Francisco, proferred his services as interpreter and was present at official functions with Scammon. Also in port was the American bark *Behring*, which would have cause for thanks that the flagship was there.

On October 20 the *Golden Gate* was reunited with the *Wright*, an occasion Scammon deemed worthy of a twenty-one-gun salute. The next day the governor invited Bulkley, Scammon, and all Western Union Telegraph Expedition officers to dine with him. Their meal was certainly a far cry from the spartan rigors of their last port of call.

Despite little spare time, Scammon wrote to Serge Abasa on November 2:

Col. Bulkley sailed from here the 31st in the *G.S. Wright*. We are lying here windbound, the season is advanced and I am anxious to get southward as soon as possible. We have been entertained here most kindly and for one exceedingly fond of society as I am, I have enjoyed the change from sea life. I have danced with Kamchatka ladies and feasted and frolicked with all who have invited us to their hospitable boards, all of which in my schoolboy days would have seemed highly romantic. It is all over now and again comes the old sea routine. I have read your excellent report and congratulate you on having so many fine officers around you. I am likewise fortunate in having LTs Davidson and Glover. I have fully endorsed your ideas about a steamer and transport vessels and shall insist you be furnished with them. Give my kindest regards to all your officers and tell Kennan that the ladies of Petropavlovsk lost their hearts when he was in town. Tell Mr. Bush I shall call on his sister on my return to San Francisco. I wish you and your command health and success.[13]

What with the generous hospitality being provided by the Russians, it was perhaps inevitable that sailors would overindulge. And some of Scammon's did. While he was ashore a few drank themselves into fisticuffs. After the disturbance was quelled, they were confined in irons and detained in their quarters, to be released later on promises of good behavior.

After some minor repairs to the *Wright* were completed and her coal bunkers filled, she had gotten under way. So had the flagship, with an agreeable wind. It was November in the North Pacific as she sailed out in windy, rainy weather that soon became a violent squall bringing snow and hail. Similar weather had prevented the *Behring* from getting under way, but with the aid of a dozen sailors from the *Golden Gate* under Lieutenants Glover and Davidson, she was able to do so. San Francisco was over five thousand miles away, but the prevailing westerlies that blew from 30 degrees to 60 degrees north latitude would provide favorable winds for the long passage that would take the bark over deep ocean trenches, abyssal plains, and seamounts back to her namesake and into the bay.

What was it like, then, making that passage? Let us hear it in the words of Scammon's private journal for several days in November:

Weather cloudy, blowing fresh from east by north. Heavy lightning in the southwest. During the morning watch the wind continued to increase from the east with rain at 6:30 a.m.; took in sail and hove to on starboard tack. Up to noon it had been blowing a gale from the east-northeast. The wind then hauled to northeast. Wore ship to east-southeast. During remainder of the day it continued to blow from the north-northeast and north-northwest, accompanied by violent squalls and a very heavy sea that continued till midnight when the wind moderated somewhat.

... There being no perceptible abatement either in the violence of the gale or frequency of the squalls it was found necessary to keep two men at the wheel. During the morning watch as the gale began to moderate somewhat, we shipped a heavy sea which filled the gig, unshipped the forward davit and stove the boat amidships. We were compelled to cut away the after tackle to clear the wreck of the boat from the ship. Shortly afterwards, another sea stove in a portion of our starboard bulwarks, doing, however, but little damage. During the entire day the storm continued with more or less severity blowing from west by north to west-northwest.

Then, finally, the entry for November 30, 1865:

During the middle watch, weather thick with light winds from the southwest. At 3:40 a.m. took a sounding and got no bottom at 160 fathoms ... forenoon watch, wind light from the south-southeast. At 10:30 a.m. made North Farallones bearing north east by east a-half east distant 3 miles. At meridian wind increased and weather cleared up. Saw a ship to leeward, outward bound ... at 3:40 p.m. passed Mile Rock. At 4:40 p.m. got anchor off bows and at 4:45 hauled the courses up and took in the royals. At 5:25 shortened sail and came to anchor with 30 fathoms of chain out on starboard anchor. Ordered gig and went on shore accompanied by 3 officers of the Land Service, having been informed of the arrival of Col. Bulkley. Calling on him I learned the *Wright* had arrived earlier the same day in a disabled condition, the storm causing some damage that prevented her from going to her destination, Victoria. All was well aboard the *Wright* and aboard all vessels of the Fleet, which safely arrived in due course having successfully performed the various and arduous duties allotted each.

Indeed they had. The *Clara Bell* had gone to Sitka and beyond; the *Palmetto* to Plover Bay; the *Milton Badger* to the same destination; the Russian brig *Olga* had gone to Petropavlovsk to land Kennan and Bush. And of course the *Golden Gate* made her cruise, but the exploring steamer *George S. Wright* takes the prize for miles covered and places seen. Bulkley's report dated December 1865 describes it all. He tells us that Russian America around Norton Sound is low, rolling country with high mountains to the south, that spurs of the great coastal range stand like a wall on the whole coast, following the Aliaska peninsula to form the Aleutian Islands. North of them the Bering Sea is filled with alluvium from countless rivers, making it quite shallow, while to the south the bottom falls into the depths of the Pacific. North of St. Michael the coast is low and rolling, without timber up to Cape Nome; to the west it is precipitous but not high up to Port Clarence. Here he found a fine bay with a good entrance: ten fathoms deep and a muddy bottom. He thought it a perfect place to land the telegraph cable on the "American side" of the Bering

Strait. The surrounding country was timberless and mossy with ten inches of thawed soil above the frozen ground.

On the Asiatic coast he found St. Lawrence and Mechigme Bays unsuitable for cables due to shallow water, exposure to southeast gales and, especially, driving ice packs that would cut any cable. In this stretch of coast the *Wright* had a difficult time navigating the littoral until she reached Abolesher Bay. Bulkley described this bleak Siberian terrain:

The great masses of sienite that rise in sharp, rough outline at their summits are torn and pushed by the congealing water in every crevice until the avalanche of rocks comes thundering down to the valley, and lies a gentle slope against the mountainside, and in this way these mountains are sinking to hills and crumbling to atoms in the intense cold.

He found the ground in this area thawed to an average depth of three feet. Bulkley rated Plover Bay a good harbor, the coastline to the west being perpendicular cliffs, ragged and serrated with no harbors east of Cape Spanberg. However, directly west of the cape was found a good harbor with sloping beaches at its head whose bottom thirty fathoms down was sandy and muddy. These features continued across Anadyr Bay to the river's mouth. Its ice-free condition also made the bay a good landing site for telegraph cable. South of the Anadyr's mouth, the topography was too rugged for cable landings. Clearly, Bulkley was looking for every possible site where the trans-Bering Sea cable might be brought ashore, and he reported his assessment of that area:

The proposed cable route across Anadyr Bay is 209 miles, which can only be avoided by building a land line north and crossing the Gulf of St. Croix. That coast is rough, a most inhospitable region; from Cape Behring I could see snow-covered ranges stretching far towards the head of the bay on its eastern shore.[14]

So it appears there were going to be two submarine cables: one from the Seward Peninsula across to Plover Bay, then one from there across Anadyr Bay to the river's mouth, where the line would move inland. Bulkley reckoned that the distance under the Bering Strait would be 178 miles, 209 miles for the Anadyr Bay segment. The cables would lie on an even, soft bottom. Ashore, poles would be firmly planted in frozen earth "as if mortised in rock . . . and will stretch over frozen plains unharmed and unmolested."[15]

Back at expedition headquarters, the winter and spring were spent making necessary repairs to telegraph navy ships, conducting administrative business, and planning the 1866 telegraph army campaign. The vessels that had sailed back and forth across the North Pacific, along with the flagship, were brought into the U.S. Navy's Mare Island yard where they were drydocked. Besides receiving required maintenance, their copper bottoms were cleaned.

The *George S. Wright* lost her captain when W. H. Marston resigned his post. He was replaced by Captain J. W. Patterson. Two new ships were added to the fleet: the bark *Onward*, and the *H. L. Rutgers*, another bark which replaced the *Milton Badger*.

When Western Union had purchased the clipper ship *Nightingale* for $23,381 in March 1866, Scammon, as authorized by the secretary of the treasury, shifted his Revenue Service flag to her. From her cabin he issued sailing orders to his captains: *H. L. Rutgers* and *Onward* to Puget Sound to pick up poles and lumber for Russian America and Siberian outposts; *Palmetto* to Petropavlovsk; *Wright*, *Nightingale*, and *Golden Gate* to Plover Bay. The *Mohawk* and *Evelyn Wood* were outbound from England with wire and cable. The U.S. government came through and made its steamer *Saginaw* available for company use. It was ordered to Victoria, British Columbia. And the Russians were doing their part; the *Olga* had already taken Kennan, Bush, Mahood, and their boss, Abasa, to Petropavlovsk; the *Variag* was even then plying the waters of the Okhotsk Sea.[16]

In March, company managing director Perry M. Collins received a letter from I. Tolstoy in St. Petersburg, informing him that his representative, Paul Anasoff, was en route. That gentleman did indeed arrive and booked passage to San Francisco in plenty of time to sail with Scammon on his flagship.[17] Collins, meanwhile, was enlarging the scope of his telegraph vision. He now saw the line connecting China with Japan, the whole of Asia and Europe connected with America. But why stop there? Why not run a line through Mexico, Central America, and South America? The company reported that "many of the governments in South America have already responded to the plan."[18]

While some of the ships were getting under way, others were not, including the *Nightingale*, hampered by maddening delays into May. But the indefatigable Serge Abasa was making perfect use of his time in eastern Siberia. He wrote his brother Basil in February 1866, information surely brought to Western Union's attention by Anasoff, that "the entire extent of the line between the Anadyr and Okhotsk districts has not only been surveyed, but the route of the line has been determined by me in person."[19] More on how Abasa accomplished this feat later.

Western Union vice-president George H. Mumford—he with the under par river steamer named after him—traveled out to San Francisco to become "resident director" of the expedition and spent several days in May using Scammon's gig to visit company ships in the harbor.

Along with her usual cargo, plus a load of coal from the *Jenny Pitts*, the *Nightingale* took aboard the boilers and machinery for the small steamers *Wade* and *Wilder*, named after company executives and destined for distant duty.

On June 1 Scammon received news that America's most notable military figure, General Winfield Scott, had died. He ordered the colors of all fleet ships to fly at half-mast.

Four days later there was a small-scale mutiny aboard *Palmetto*. Scammon dispatched a boat with three officers and some sailors to render assistance. Once aboard they discovered that the bark's officers, aided by Land Force personnel, had quelled the mutineers, though Scammon's men were used to round up the ringleaders hiding in the forecastle. With the culprits in irons, all hands returned to duty.

The days, the precious days, when ships should have been at sea, elapsed. Paul Anasoff arrived on June 23, along with *New York Herald* correspondent William Knox. Then came the Fourth of July matter:

> Having received and accepted invitations from the Grand Marshall to participate in the 4th of July celebrations with the citizens of San Francisco the officers as per orders reported to the executive at 8 o'clock a.m. The *Golden Gate* being the only other vessel of the fleet in port accompanied the officers of the flagship. The flagship and the *Gate* were dressed in commemoration of the day.

On the tenth, Scammon gave his crew liberty prior to departure. Some, perhaps having second or third thoughts about the long voyage, or maybe having had minds changed during Fourth of July celebrations, deserted. That same day the *Nightingale* took 1,766 gallons of water onboard and watched the former flagship leave the harbor with Colonel Wicker and twenty-five Land Service members, bound for Plover Bay.

For his second cruise across the North Pacific, Scammon brought along his family—wife Susan and sons Alexander and Charles, the latter a cadet in the Land Service who would serve with Abasa in Siberia. The clipper ship's crew consisted of six officers, first and second masters mates, and forty-six petty officers, seamen, and boys. Land Service personnel on this voyage, under the command of Major George M. Wright, adjutant, were Chief Quartermaster Scott R. Chappell, Dr. Fisher, Captains Libby, Kelsey, Hartmeyer, and Klinefelter, along with sixty others. After a tow from the steam tug *Lookout*, the *Nightingale* proceeded to sea, bound for eastern Siberia's Chukchi Peninsula. Their course: west by west, then slowly northwest; 36 degrees, 40 degrees, on up to 54 degrees north latitude and the Unimak passage into the Bering Sea, three weeks outbound from San Francisco.

For several days, passengers and crew beheld the clipper under cloud of sail, all of them set, from flying jib and spanker to fore topgallant and main skysail.

Near 48 degrees north the following was recorded in Scammon's journal:

Weather cloudy, wind moderate from westward at 4 a.m. Tacked ship and stood to northward. During forenoon watch wind moderate from W by N; at 12, wind from westward. Tacked ship to southward at 1 p.m. Tacked ship to northward at 7 p.m. With wind fresh from westward tacked ship to southward.

More intensive ship handling ensued en route to Unimak. On Friday, August 3, with the patent sounder indicating depths ranging from 65 to 43 fathoms and a black, sandy bottom, Scammon ordered all sails clewed up and the anchor dropped as a fog set in. Ship's crew and Land Service personnel requested and received permission to try their luck at fishing over the side. The mariners outdid the landlubbers, bringing aboard twenty fine codfish to add some variety to daily meals.

The following day *Nightingale* made sail, passing between Unimak and Akun Islands of the Aleutian archipelago. On Sunday a bark was sighted to windward. She had likewise sighted the flagship and fired a gun indicating her presence, but Scammon and his crew could not make out her colors in the fog. Was she the *Golden Gate*? Scammon hauled the clipper to the wind, backed the main topsail, and ordered the gig lowered to row over and board the bark, but she responded by hauling her wind on the port tack and disappearing into the fog.

Nightingale made St. Lawrence Island on Sunday, August 12. After the usual muster of Marine and Land Force personnel, the ship was visited by a small canoe flotilla from the island which departed thankfully with rations of hard bread and sugar. Two days later the flagship was at anchor in Plover Bay, sails furled and decks cleared. Already present, and nearby, was the *H. L. Rutgers*, which had called at Puget Sound before making towards the bay. Though he was a month ahead of his last visit to Plover, Scammon knew there was no time to be wasted getting things done in those high latitudes. There was much to do: personnel transfers, getting the little steamers ashore, further explorations, and erecting "Kelsey Station."

Company foreman D. C. Norton and an eight-man construction crew reported aboard the *Nightingale* for further assignment. The hulls of the *Wade* and *Wilder* were mated with their boilers and machinery under the supervision of *Wilder's* Captain E. E. Smith to fit them out for riverine and coastal service.

Prior to *Nightingale*'s sailing, Colonel Bulkley had issued orders to Scammon instructing him to reconnoiter the country east and west of Plover Bay and to examine the bay itself. Together and separately, in the flagship's provisioned barge and ashore, Scammon and Major Wright carried out these orders. As senior Land Force officer present, Wright led a party guided by the reliable Knockum that looked for possible telegraph line routes from Plover Bay to Penkique Gulf.[20]

While these activities were under way, the *Wright* was visiting Petropavlovsk and the Anadyr River. Expedition artist and chronicler Frederick Whymper was on board:

> On July 25th we arrived at Petropavlovsk Harbor and found the Russian corvette *Variag* awaiting our arrival. Her commander, Captain Lund, immediately reported to Col. Bulkley. The day of our arrival had been fixed for the celebration of two Russian weddings. The double ceremony was long and fatiguing. It is apparently the fashion for these occasions that a wealthy attendee be master of ceremonies, and that he stand all the expenses! Here, the victim was a M. Phillipeus, a merchant who annually brings his vessels from Hong Kong to Kamchatka and the neighboring coasts. He accepted the burden willingly and provided liberal entertainment to the whole town; the officers of the *Variag*, ourselves, and the captains of several small vessels lying there. After the wedding feast we adjourned by invitation to the house of the Captain of the Port where dancing was kept up with great vigor till the small hours next morning.
>
> We found Petropavlovsk in its brief summer garb; wild flowers, coarse grass and mosquitoes all abundant.
>
> I shall never forget an "international picnic" held during our stay. There were Europeans, Asiatic Russians, Finlanders, Kamchadls, North and South Americans, Frenchmen, Germans and Italians. Chatting in a babel of tongues we walked along till we found a grassy opening overlooking beautiful Avatcha Bay. The weather was perfect and only an occasional mosquito. And then, bliss of bliss, we not only raised a cloud of balmy smoke, but were encouraged therein by our lady friends, some of whom joined us. Here, cigars and cigarettes are always served with tea and coffee, and the ladies retained their seats with us. Would it were so in our own otherwise, more or less happy, land. We did not leave till the stars studded the heavens.

At that stopover, Paul Anasoff and Knox the correspondent made their way down the Okhotsk Sea aboard the *Variag* to Nikolaevsk and from there to various inland destinations.[21]

The *Wright* departed Kamchatka's southeastern port on August 8, bound for Anadyr Bay, over one thousand miles away to the north-northeast. Five days later the exploring steamer entered the bay and proceeded slowly into it until progress was interrupted by visiting Chukchi natives who begged for rum and tobacco. The ship passed an oddly shaped island that her crew decided to dub "Sarcophagus" due to its resemblance, real or imagined, to an ancient stone coffin.

Even before they came to anchor near a Chukchi village, large herds of domesticated reindeer could be seen ashore, grazing peacefully. Bulkley and Captain Patterson immediately bargained for some of the herd to add variety to the ship's menu.

On the fifteenth a boat expedition up into the mouth of the Anadyr River was organized, led by the steamer's second mate, Mr. Labonne, who served as chief interpreter for the expedition. For guidance, the group, consisting of Labonne, Whymper, and three *Wright* crewmen, had only a sketch chart drawn by Bulkley and Captain Marston from their previous reconnaissance. The cutter's mainsail filled with a favoring breeze as the men passed Mt. Dionysius, on the bay's eastern side, steering due west from it in foggy, wet weather. Several hours later the water became quite shallow. The boat touched bottom, now and then grazing sand bars, at times running aground. When that happened the men lowered the sail, jumped out of the boat, and shoved her back into deeper water. After a long, hard day in foul weather, they decided to make camp on a spit of land south of an opening in the coast. Crewmen rigged a tent from the sail and a fire was coaxed from scarce driftwood and brush. Early next morning they continued on the river, searching for Camp MacRae, where they were to leave a message for the leader of the Anadyr exploring party.[22] Earlier, in August 1865, Collins L. MacRae and his men were landed at the mouth of the Anadyr by the *Milton Badger*. They had established a base of operations and began exploring the country to the south and west.

Richard J. Bush and his exploring companion, James Mahood, had traveled hundreds of versts (Russian distance measure equalling two-thirds of a mile) after leaving Serge Abasa and George Kennan at Petropavlovsk. To get to Camp MacRae, they had journeyed all the way up the west coast of the Okhotsk Sea, then north by east, across mountain ranges and rivers to the camp beside the river. As was the case with all Siberian exploring parties, food was never plentiful, especially during the winter months. The specter of starvation was always looming.

In August 1866 MacRae and Bush and those at the camp were surviving on fish and sleeping more hours than normal so fewer meals would be required to sustain them. They had had news of the *Wright* but had no idea when it might arrive, if at all.

On the night of the 14th [Bush's dates do not agree with Whymper's] we were more than ordinarily dubious and retired to our bunks in not the best spirits. Early next morning I was aroused by loud talking and, upon opening my eyes, found the hut full of strangers, and Americans too. Mr. Laborne was the only one I had ever seen before, but acquaintances were rapidly made and during the following half hour there was more information exchanged than ever before in that length of time. The *Wright* lay about 30 miles below, where she had come to get a supply of coal left the previous year. Col. Bulkley was onboard and he had no idea of finding anybody at the mouth of the Anadyr. After eating a "square" meal of cold meat, hard bread and molasses, we joined our friends on their return to the steamer. A salute from the ship's gun welcomed us and shortly afterwards we were surrounded by earnest and curious friends scanning our water-soaked buckskins and asking innumerable questions.

MacRae had come downriver with his boat, which was loaded with provisions. Only after that procedure was completed did the *Wright* get up steam and proceed to Plover Bay where Bush, now a passenger, would obtain more provisions, men, and material.

> Upon entering the bay we found two of the company's vessels awaiting orders, the *Nightingale* and the *Rutgers*. The *Golden Gate*, which was destined more particularly for the Anadyr, did not arrive until two weeks afterwards, so I was detained longer than necessary. Plover Bay is situated at the extremity of a large cape. Here a station was to be erected and a party left during the following winter. As lumber had been brought for the purpose, shortly after the *Wright*'s arrival, the fleet moved to the other end of the bay to select a site for the building. A large number of men had been brought from San Francisco to be landed at different sites along the route, all of whom were put ashore to assist the work. The place was soon alive with busy groups, some carrying stones for foundations, other digging sod, still others carrying lumber from the water's edge to supply the carpenters.[23]

The outpost was completed on August 24. Bulkley ordered a national salute fired aboard the company flagship in recognition of the erection of the first telegraph pole on the Asiatic coast at the place he named "Kelsey Station." Work crews, meanwhile, bustled as more supplies were brought ashore. The *Wright* was sent down the bay to look for the overdue *Golden Gate*.

On Sunday, September 2, there occurred what might be termed the "Kelsey Incident." The Land Force officer in question borrowed the *Nightingale*'s dinghy without first asking permission of the executive officer, a breach of standing orders. He wanted it only a short while to visit friends on the *Wright*. Time passed. No Kelsey. Scammon figured he must have gone ashore and sent some of his officers in his Number Two cutter to retrieve the wayward captain and his ship's dinghy. Not only was Kelsey wayward, he was recalcitrant, refusing the officers' demands that he return the boat. Defiantly, he rowed it right past the flagship, deaf to numerous shouted commands to bring it alongside, and went back over to the *Wright*.

Let us consider this miscreant. Here was a man, who may have talked with Bush, about to be "officially marooned" with a few other hardy souls at a bleak outpost on the Chukchi Peninsula. Should he not be granted a miniscule maritime joyride, no doubt fuelled by clandestine pulls from a liquor bottle provided by friends, before spending a very long winter at Plover Bay? Of course.

The dinghy was returned by *Wright* crewmen. Perhaps Scammon viewed the Kelsey matter in the spirit of forgiveness that must have overcome Bulkley. The captain was not disciplined. He and his twelve men were put ashore September 5. Theirs would be the task of constructing a line along the coast, the route reconnoitered by Scammon and Wright and approved by Bulkley, each of whose ends would then be connected to submarine cables running under the Bering Sea and Gulf of Anadyr.[24]

During his prolonged stay at Plover Bay, Bush had occasion to observe the Chukchi natives while visiting their villages.

The sterility of the neighboring country and total absence of driftwood force them to rely upon other sources of material for habitation and boats. Their tents are made of walrus, seal or reindeer skins and are oval in shape, being held up by curved whale bones. For fuel they burn blubber altogether. They use "bidarras" or skin boats, generally covered with walrus hide, the frames of which are sometimes made of bone. To add bouyancy they attach inflated sealskins to their sides. Their winter costume is of deerskin, with sealskin boots. In summer they wear birdskin garments prepared with feathers and sewn together. For wet weather a kind of overshirt is made from fish skins or whale or walrus intestines, with a hood of the same material. Whale, seal and walrus constitute their only food. They carry on a thriving trade with whalers and traders who visit their coast annually, exchanging walrus tusks, whalebone and blubber for liquor, guns and various kinds of implements.[25]

The most notable Chukchi of course was Knockum. Bush met him during his stay. So did Whymper, who tells us that Bulkley so valued his assistance that he ordered his men to build him a small dwelling place. Major Wright later told Whymper that, during their route of the line reconnaissance, nothing his men did surprised the stoic Knockum, nor caused him to lose his equanimity. Nothing that is except the addition of pepper to food, which elicited the following comment: "Me no sabe white man eat fire on meat."

On one occasion Mrs. Scammon invited Knockum to her cabin aboard the *Nightingale*. Whymper recorded the following scene:

My kind friend, Mrs. Scammon, invited him aboard to look at some pet canaries. Although he had never seen such birds he preserved a gentlemanly apathy, showing no reaction whatsoever. Someone, a little piqued perhaps, informed Knockum that they were worth ten dollars each in San Francisco! "Ah," he replied, shrugging his shoulders, "too muchee!"[26]

By September 12 the *Golden Gate*, late arriving and now loaded with lumber, supplies, and provisions for nine months for twenty-five men, prepared to get under way again, bound for Anadyr Bay. The men on board augmenting Bush and MacRae's exploring and construction personnel included D. C. Norton, foreman, and the following men: Edward Pickett, Edward Brook, W. H. Billady, Patrick Lawlor, Fred Keenan, Eli Henston, John McIntyre, and Charles Brackett.

The sixty-foot steamer *Wade* was towed behind the bark as she made her way back to Camp MacRae, entering the mouth of the Anadyr on September 19.

We steered into the small northern or Golden Gate bay, that having been chosen as the most suitable place for landing the end of the cable to be stretched across the Gulf, but we had only proceeded three or four miles when the *Gate* grounded on a bar. I immediately dispatched Mr. Jared Norton with a boat and crew to go to Camp MacRae and notify the party of our whereabouts, and went with another boat crew to select a site for our station at the mouth of a small river.

The *Wade* was immediately brought up when the *Gate* went aground, but her small engine could not generate sufficient power to pull the bark free. Nature was working overtime to convince all present that this was no place to get anything done, not in late September at 65 degrees north latitude. Ice was beginning to pack the river. Snow was falling. The men decided that the former flagship should be unloaded. Just getting the lumber ashore required tremendous exertions. Extreme weather conditions allowed for only two offloading trips per day. By October 1 "Bush's Station" was completed, though as the artist-explorer notes in his book, it was an inappropriate name, "there being no bushes growing within miles of the spot."

Matters now worsened for the *Gate*. As the tide ebbed in the shallow channel where she lay trapped, the vessel went over on her side, almost on her beam ends. On board her, Bush was trying to sleep and was awakened now and then by loud grating sounds. He could feel the ship quivering. Then it felt as if she had righted herself, only to "fall back with a sound as if nearly every timber in her had broken."

The men found the entire bay frozen over that morning; the *Wade* was now in danger of suffering an icy death. Taking advantage of low tide, they commenced hacking away at the ice with picks and shovels to try to draw up the steamer. They planted posts and had the hauling ropes ready when a massive ice field swept in, caught the *Wade*, and flung her twelve feet up on the beach. Though damaged, the steamer survived the icy toss, and was firmly ensconced for her spring thaw recovery.

Bush and the *Wade* rescue party now became aware of activity near the *Gate*. All her boats were being lowered away and hauled through drifting ice towards the shore.

We assembled on the beach to receive them together with the unwelcome information that the ice had torn open the sides of the ship. They would have to winter at the point. She had onboard but two months' supply of provisions for her crew. I had supplies barely sufficient for my 25 men, and now that number was increased to 46; our supplies would hardly carry us half way through the winter.

So what they did was strengthen their boats with copper brought from the *Gate*, sheathing bottoms against ice damage, then navigate them through the grating chunks to the bark, taking everything off her, in-

Figure 6.1. Dismantling the wreck (*Golden Gate*), drawing by J. B. Dwyer; from the original by Richard J. Bush.

cluding telegraph poles. From these a thirty-six foot long, eighteen foot wide building was constructed under the supervision of Mr. Frost. Together with Bush's Station, it constituted winter quarters for those whom Western Union or whimsical nature put there. For his part, Bush was most grateful that he brought from Plover Bay about a hundred volumes of poetry, romance, and travel books, which became the station's library and provided solace for the ensuing months of hibernation.[27]

Back at Plover Bay, Captain Scammon was all too aware that the kind of weather and sea conditions that wrought near catastrophe on the Anadyr might happen there any day now. A month after *Nightingale*'s arrival, she was still there. The *Golden Gate* and *Wade* had since departed; so had the *H. L. Rutgers*, and the *Wright* with the *Wilder* in tow, the former for Grantley Harbor, the latter for Fort St. Michael. At Grantley, Captain Daniel Libby and his crew, who had helped construct Kelsey Station, would build a similar structure at the Russian American terminus of the trans-Bering Strait submarine cable.

On September 19 the company ship *Evelyn Wood*, completing her multithousand-mile voyage around the Horn from England, arrived from her stop at Victoria, British Columbia, with a cargo of telegraph line and cable. This amounted to fifty tons of cargo that had to be offloaded, further delaying the already delayed departure of the flagship as snow squalls continued. Scammon managed to deal quickly with the situation and got under way for Norton Sound the next day in a freshening breeze from the east-northeast.

Snow, rain, fog, and hail accompanied the brief voyage to Fort St. Michael. Scammon ordered two guns fired to announce the flagship's presence and sent Quartermaster Chappell ashore to report to Mr. Stepanoff. As he had expected, the *Wright* was already in the harbor. When *Nightingale* had anchored, Scammon received Bulkley, Wicker, and Land Service veterans Ennis and Ketchum. The latter brought sad and stunning news: Robert Kennicott was dead.[28] Naturalist William H. Dall was on board at the time.

> Pressing forward as the first man came over the side, my first question was, "Where is Kennicott?" and the answer, "Dead, poor fellow, last May," stunned me with its sudden anguish. I stayed to hear no more, but went to my cabin as one walks in a dream.[29]

When Dall joined the expedition in 1865, he was appointed assistant surgeon, a job he did not want. After resigning that post he stayed on as a scientist without portfolio. Dall, born in Boston in 1845, would become the so-called first scientist of Alaska. After graduation from Boston Latin School, he had pursued studies in zoology under some of the leading lights of the day: Louis Agassiz, Augustus Gould, and Jeffries Wyman. He next traveled to Chicago, where he met and befriended Robert Kennicott at the Academy of Sciences. Kennicott invited him to join the expedition.[30] And now, the man who had been something of a mentor to the twenty-one-year-old Dall was dead. Bulkley understood the situation and decided to replace the deceased Kennicott with Dall as the new Scientific Corps director. The energetic young man immediately submitted his plans for explorations, which were approved by Bulkley.

> I determined to use my best energies to complete the scientific explorations of the northwest extremity of the continent as it had been planned by Mr. Kennicott; the exploration of the region between Ft. Yukon, at the river's junction with the Porcupine, and the Nulato; the region between Nulato and the sea, and west and south of there; and the whole region bordering Norton Sound.[31]

The weather was as stormy as the news during *Nightingale*'s stay as the *Wright* proceeded to Grantley Harbor. The *Wilder* was pressed into service towing lighters and taking personnel ashore at Fort St. Michael. Threatening skies, heavy snows, and strong winds prevailed. Scammon's journal entry for September 29:

> Came in with a strong gale from the north attended at intervals with violent squalls. Ship commenced pitching heavily, taking aboard considerable water. At

6 a.m. turned the men to and cleared decks of snow and pumped ship. At 7 a.m. she commenced striking heavily on the bottom. At 9 a.m. gave her 30 fathoms more chain on each anchor. She continued striking with more or less violence until 5 p.m. when the wind veered to the northwest. The storm abated and she rode easier.

Two days later, with Kennicott's preserved body onboard, the flagship got under way for Plover Bay in a heavy snowstorm and suddenly veering winds that forced Scammon to wear ship. Heavy seas made for an uncomfortable return to the bay with the clipper shipping water and pitching. Scammon ordered continuous soundings be taken during the crossing. To make matters worse, the water supply was running low. Ingenuity wasn't, however. Scammon's executive officer, Mr. Norton, and Land Service member Mr. Ryder rigged an apparatus in the galley to condense water, producing enough so that each person would have one quart per day.

The *Wright*, already arrived from Grantley Harbor, was in the bay as *Nightingale* entered, along with the *H. L. Rutgers* and *Evelyn Wood*. It was a good thing the *Rutgers* was there; she supplied four water casks that were filled ashore to compensate for the flagship's ruined water tanks.

On October 15 all ships in Plover Bay put to sea; the *Nightingale*, towed by *Wright*, was bound for Avatcha Bay. At sea she plowed through an ocean that was anything but pacific. Ship handling was, of course, more dangerous in those conditions as Seaman John Dillon might have told us after he fell from the foreyard to the deck. Amazingly, he sustained no serious injuries.

En route, Scammon notes in his journal that the color of the seawater changed dramatically from blue to dark green on a day marked by heavy ground swells. This was probably caused by the Japan Current, whose warm waters flowed into the North Pacific from the Philippine Sea. The ground swells continued the next day as land was sighted, bearing north-northeast, the ship under all sail and standing in from the north. In the cold, rainy distance the men could see the Avatcha Bay Light. Scammon ordered four guns fired to alert its keeper to their presence, then furled all light sails, backed the main topsail, and hove to. But no light shone forth. Early next morning, lightning flashed from an angry sky. Scammon wore ship to westward, set all sails, and stood in towards the bay with no light guiding his ship. Continuous soundings were taken as she proceeded. They showed eight fathoms under her stern and two fathoms beneath her bow as she went aground. Scammon immediately backed all sail and got an anchor out astern. Every effort was made to heave off, but to no avail. As a heavy snow began falling, the ship swung around, broadside on. All hands, sweating in the frigid weather as they strove to free her, knew they must wait for high water.

On November 7 they were ready. The anchor was out off the starboard bow, the hawser on the windlass. At high water, highly motivated sailors strained as the words "heave and heave again!" were shouted. At 1 P.M. Scammon set his topsails aback as the seabed loosened its grip and the clipper was once again free in deep water. The carpenter informed Scammon that the ship had suffered no damage or injury, so *Nightingale* made for the anchorage off Petropavlovsk. It was a very brief stay, supervised by Mr. Norton, whose chief concern was getting more water aboard. Captain Scammon notes in his journal that he was sick and confined to his cabin for several days.

But he was completely recovered and back on the quarterdeck by November 13, when the flagship got under way with all sail set, homeward bound. The passage was marked by gales, squalls, rain, and heavy seas. One of the most severe squalls carried away the topmast studding sail boom. Hours were spent on the pumps. Winds shrieked through long nights. Here is Scammon's journal entry for Sunday, November 18:

> Weather cloudy. Wind veered to west south-west. Gale continued attended by violent squalls in quick succession and heavy seas. At 3:30 P.M. wind changed to the west. Set fore topmast staysail, squared yards and kept ship on her course. Set foresail, lower foresail and upper main topsail. At 8 P.M. wind fresh from west by north. Weather clear with occasional light hail squalls.

On her way home, the *Nightingale* sang a swift song, making an average of 200 miles per day. She recorded her best distance November 25. With winds from the west in cloudy, squally weather, the clipper logged 234 miles. But the sea is a capricious force. Just two days later, a severe rainstorm struck the ship with unexpected fury, splitting her royals. These conditions presented no problem, though, for a veteran crew. The next day she logged 192 miles.

The oddest event of the passage occurred one week before *Nightingale* reached home.

> Weather cloudy, blowing a gale from the southward attended with severe hail squalls and occasional sharp flashes of lightning. At 3 o'clock A.M. a meteor struck the main topsail sheets midway from the deck, exploded with a loud report, and disappeared without doing any damage or leaving any trace whatsoever.

Presumably, Scammon is referring to a bolt of lightning hitting *Nightingale*'s main topsail sheets since that phenomenon is listed as an obsolete definition of "meteor."

On December 8, 1866, twenty-five days outbound from Petropavlovsk, *Nightingale* entered San Francisco harbor, crossed the bar, and dropped anchor, home at last. The other company ships had already returned. Men, supplies, and, material had been delivered across the North Pacific to places few people had ever heard of before: Fort St. Michael, Grantley Harbor, the Anadyr River, and Gizhiga, tucked inside the northern arm of the Okhotsk Sea. Outposts had been established in British Columbia, Russian America, and eastern Siberia. The route of the line had been explored, poles had been planted, and wire had been strung in conditions and terrain that would have challenged the stoutest of hearts. Wiring the world was well under way, though in Siberia and Russian America, especially the former, endurance and perseverance were sorely tested.[32]

NOTES

1. Private Journal, Western Union Telegraph Expedition, Flagship *Golden Gate*, Captain Charles M. Scammon, in the Scammon Papers, Bancroft Library, Berkeley, Cal. (hereinafter, Scammon *Golden Gate* journal), pp. 3–11.

2. "Journal of William H. Ennis, Member, Russian-American Telegraph Exploring Expedition," *California Historical Society Quarterly* 33 (March 1954): p. 7. (Hereinafter, Ennis journal.)

3. George R. Adams, *Life on the Yukon, 1865–1867* (Kingston, Ontario, Canada: The Limestone Press, 1982), p. 24.

4. Ennis journal, pp. 8–9.

5. Scammon *Golden Gate* journal, pp. 10–11.

6. Walter A. McDougall, *Let the Sea Make a Noise* (New York: Avon Books, 1993), pp. 118–21.

7. Scammon *Golden Gate* journal, pp. 11 and 18, and Ennis journal, pp. 148–49.

8. Scammon *Golden Gate* journal, pp. 10–20, and Ennis journal, p. 151.

9. Ennis journal, p. 151, and Letter Book, Flagship *Golden Gate*, from June 1865 to March 1866, p. 18, in the Scammon Papers.

10. Scammon *Golden Gate* journal, pp. 29–34, and "Cruise and Explorations made by the Exploring Steamer *George S. Wright*," Captain W. H. Marston, Scammon Papers, pp. 36–37.

11. William H. Dall, *Alaska and Its Resources* (Boston: Lee & Shepard, 1870; reprint, New York: Arno Press, 1970), pp. 511–12.

12. Scammon *Golden Gate* journal, pp. 40–42, and Theodore Roscoe, *Picture History of the U.S. Navy* (New York: Charles Scribner's Sons, 1956), nos. 900–901.

13. Scammon *Golden Gate* journal, pp. 43–50, and Letter, Scammon to Abasa dated Oct. 21, 1865, in Scammon's Letter Book.

14. Scammon *Golden Gate* journal, pp. 51–63, and Bulkley's official report, dated December 18, 1865, in "Origin, Organization, and Progress of the Russian-American Telegraph," Western Union Telegraph Company, Rochester, N.Y., 1866, p. 122.

15. Bulkley report, p. 124.

16. Private Journal, Western Union Telegraph Expedition, Flagship *Nightingale*, Captain Charles M. Scammon (hereinafter, Scammon *Nightingale* journal), pp. 71–75.

17. "Origin, Organization, and Progress of the Russian-American Telegraph," Western Union Telegraph Company, Rochester, N.Y., 1866, p. 105.

18. Ibid., p. 15.

19. Ibid., p. 129.

20. Scammon *Nightingale* journal, pp. 80–102.

21. Frederick Whymper, *Travel and Adventure in the Territory of Alaska* (Ann Arbor: University of Michigan Microfilms, 1966), pp. 107–10.

22. Ibid., pp. 115–18.

23. Richard J. Bush, *Reindeer, Dogs, and Snowshoes: A Journal of Siberian Travel and Explorations* (New York: Harper and Brothers, 1871), pp. 431–35.

24. Scammon *Nightingale* journal, pp. 105–12.

25. Bush, *Reindeer, Dogs, and Snowshoes*, pp. 435–36.

26. Whymper, *Travel and Adventure*, p. 122.

27. Order Book, Col. Charles S. Bulkley, Engineer-in-Chief, Western Union Telegraph Expedition, Scammon Papers, Special Order No. 7, Aug. 29, 1866, and Bush, *Reindeer, Dogs, and Snowshoes*, pp. 441–47.

28. Scammon *Nightingale* journal, pp. 114–22.

29. Dall, *Alaska and Its Resources*, p. 5.

30. Smithsonian Institution Archives, William H. Dall Papers, Finding Aid, p. 1.

31. Dall, *Alaska and Its Resources*, p. 6.

32. Scammon *Nightingale* journal, pp. 118–59.

CHAPTER SEVEN

UP THE YUKON IN RUSSIAN AMERICA

A look at the map shows the gigantic land mass of Alaska, formerly Russian America, 586,400 square miles of rugged, mountainous, wintry terrain stretching from the Aleutians, at 52 degrees north latitude, to Point Barrow, at about 72 degrees north latitude; the Arctic Ocean lapping its northern shores, the Chukchi and Bering Seas its western ones; its more temperate archipelagic appendage stretching westward into North Pacific waters to 173 degrees east longitude.

Even on a map, the country seems forbidding, inhospitable. Its coastline is jagged, at times knifelike, seemingly broken out of some primeval ice pack and thrust at random into its surrounding waters. Bisecting this glacially aloof giant from west to east is the mighty Yukon River, the most obvious natural path to follow for the route of Western Union's world-wiring telegraph line. Collins and Bulkley had no choice other than starting near the silted bulge of its delta and relying on assistance from Russian American Company employees and native peoples. They had already secured the former from Governor Gavrischeff.

It will be remembered that Robert Kennicott, landed in stormy weather with his exploring party at Fort St. Michael September 13, had journeyed into the Yukon Territory on previous expeditions. While still back in San Francisco, he had written Bulkley a long memo telling him he had met

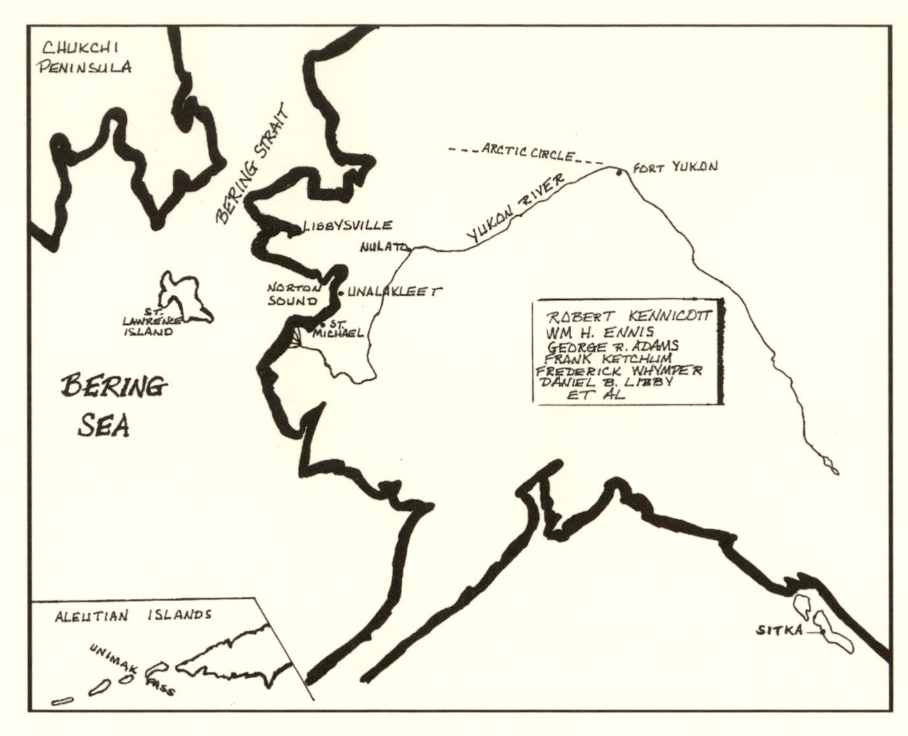

Map 7.1. Russian America, drawing by J. B. Dwyer,

several people with first-hand knowledge of the Yukon River and the Russian American littoral. Based on their testimonies, and his own experiences, the bearded, buckskinned explorer stated, "There has never been any doubt in my mind that the Yukon and the Kvihpak are the same river." (The spelling of the native word *Kvihpak* varies with every writer, some spelling it *Kviepak* or otherwise.)

This information was of major interest for Bulkley and for Kennicott since it would be much easier ascending and descending one waterway rather than two when transporting men and supplies. Captain Klingofstrom, a whaler that Kennicott had interviewed, told him about large native canoes he had seen in the Norton Sound area that could carry fifty men and heavy loads. Kennicott was interested in any boat that might be used to ascend the Yukon, one that could survive rapids, rough going, portaging, and hauling. The principal impediment to this ascent was powerful rapids at the junction of the Tanana and Yukon Rivers. This was as far as Imperial Russian Navy Lieutenant Zagoskin and his party had gotten in 1841. He declared the river impassable beyond that point. But Kennicott was convinced that "with proper appliances, a boat

Figure 7.1. Robert Kennicott, Chief, Scientific Corps, Western Union Telegraph Expedition, drawing by J. B. Dwyer; adapted from photo in *The First Scientific Exploration of Russian America*, by James Alton James, 1942.

might easily be tracked up a rapid where it could not be poled or rowed against the current."

He wrote Bulkley that he believed, other than such a native craft as Kennicott had described, a small steamer might ascend the river "at least as far as Ft. Yukon."[1] No doubt it was this observation that led to the *Lizzie Horner* being trans-shipped to Russian America, where, unfortunately, it proved to be useless. Native craft, whether kayaks or *bidarkas* of various sizes, with or without small sails, performed very well for Kennicott and his men.

Fort St. Michael is situated at a small point on an island of the same name between Point Romanoff and Tolstoy Point on the southern flank of Norton Sound. The shore is rocky and the water shallow, so the Russians built a landing stage out into water deep enough to allow loaded boats with no more than a five-foot draft to come in at high tide. Nearby is a small, sandy beach on which boats may be landed. No wonder then that one of the boats carrying arms, ammunition, and supplies for the expedition capsized during stormy weather. One of the men who was there recalls it this way:

> The goods were immediately unloaded from the ship and landed as the tides would admit, promiscuously on the beach. A few boatloads only were landed at the steps in consequence of the nature of the bottom and beach.[2]

This account comes to us from Otto de Bendeleben. He had been a member of Captain Scammon's marine service aboard the *Wright*, acting as Colonel Bulkley's secretary. When he informed the engineer in chief that he would like to join the expedition, Bulkley signed a transfer, effective immediately. The secretary became Pioneer First Lieutenant de Bendeleben. Little is known of his background, but he achieved a modicum of immortality by having a mountain range northeast of Nome named after him.

We know a bit more about some of the others in Kennicott's group. George R. Adams, who published a diary of his experiences, we have already met briefly. He was born and raised in Farmington, New York, near Rochester and tells us he had four years of school and some college education. He had a gift for languages and knew Greek, Latin, and Spanish; this was a gift he would put to good use in Russian America. And we have already met William Ennis, who became leader of the Norton Sound Exploring Party.

Adams supplies the following information on six of his fellow explorers. Thomas Denison, their quartermaster, hailed from Galveston, Texas, though he had lived most of his life in San Francisco. Auburn, New York, was home to Jay B. Chappell and his brother, Scott. The latter was chief quartermaster, a generous soul fluent in the Malamute language and unexcelled as an Indian trader. Adams doesn't tell us where Fred W. Smith called home, only that he was well liked by all the others. Though he was born in New Haven, Connecticut, Frederick Westdahl's parents had taken him back to Sweden, where he was raised and educated. He had been a first officer aboard the *Golden Gate* before transferring to the Land Service. His fields of expertise were astronomy and navigation, as well as surveying, which he performed in Russian America. Adams tells us that W. W. Smith was a veteran telegraph line builder and an expert operator but provides no further details. We can assume, then, that he was a U.S. Military Telegraph Corps veteran.[3]

The place where they landed was a typical Russian fortified outpost consisting of log buildings surrounded by a rectangular ten-foot-high palisade of pointed logs with a guard tower in one corner.[4] But those who came ashore that stormy September did not stay there. The foul weather compelled them to pitch tents on a spit of land northeast of the fort.

Kennicott was forced to delay his plans to explore the Yukon and the route of the line and had to settle for an initial outposting at Unalakleet, sixty-five miles up the coast. From there he would make the two-hundred-mile trip to Nulato to establish another expedition base.

Figure 7.2. Fort St. Michael, drawing by J. B. Dwyer; from the original by William H. Dall.

The voyage to Unalakleet was made aboard a forty-foot-long, thirty-foot-wide sail barge provided by St. Michael commander Sergei Stepanoff. Kennicott and ten of his men embarked the unwieldy vessel on September 27 with a favorable wind blowing. Also blowing were equinoctical gales. Twenty miles outbound, the barge was almost slammed against the rocky coast, but fate decided the voyage must be completed; Kennicott, his men, and the eleven-man crew were instead shoved into the mouth of a creek on whose banks they camped overnight.[5]

The evening of the second day we arrived at Unalakleet. This fort was built like the one at Ft. St. Michael, only smaller, with no room for us inside. We were given two log houses nearby, 14' by 20' in size, for dwellings, and a smaller one for our kitchen.[6]

Of course the men were grateful for the shelter. Their dwellings, however had been built for fish storage, not habitation. Large cracks between logs let in abundant cold air. However, the cabins were soon cleaned, the cracks caulked, and a huge mud, moss, and stone fireplace built to provide needed warmth.

The morning after our arrival, some of us were standing on the high river bank watching an Eskimo beach his little skin kayak below. We went down to examine it. It was what the Russians call a one-man bidarka. Its frame was made from strips of birch lashed together with sealskin thongs covered with sealskins that had been soaked in water until pliable, cut to proper shape, sewn together with seal sinews and stretched over the frame still wet. When dried it was as taut as a drum then smeared with seal oil to make it watertight.

As the group stood around admiring the ten-foot craft, one of the men opined that only a person taught from childhood could handle it. That was all the prompting young Adams needed. With a boastful "I don't know about that," he inserted his legs and waist into the cockpit, grabbed the paddle, and shoved himself out into the water.

It was pretty wiggly under me at first and I thought I would have to give it up, but putting the paddle in the water, found that I could steady the boat and soon gained more confidence as the wiggling stopped. Turning the boat upstream, I paddled a hundred feet or more, then turned to go downstream. When opposite the party ashore I waved to them proudly with the paddle and asked "Any mail for Frisco?" Taking the paddle from the water was my undoing. With that my pride departed and over I went head first into the (frigid) water with the boat on top of me. I couldn't free myself from the snug-fitting boat and swam the fifty yards to shore with half my body in it.

Adams, who happened to be an excellent swimmer, survived the cold dunking, the jibes of his friends, and the expected reprimand. But it was that boldness that Kennicott admired and so, on the evening of October 3 he went to the lieutenant's quarters to inform him that he had selected him to make the first expedition into Russian American territory.

Adams, I want you to go up the Unalakleet River as far as you can in a canoe and find out all you can from the Indians there about the portage from its head across to the Yukon River, how long it takes and any information available about the country between, its food, fish and game. How soon can you be ready?

Adams, of course, replied "Immediately," but Kennicott told him next morning would be just fine. Rushing down to the riverbank with his bedroll, kit bag, and revolver, Adams found Kennicott and two others waiting for him. After warning his youngest explorer that the river's rapids and snags made it dangerous and that the Russians would not vouch for the friendliness of natives, Kennicott introduced him to his expedition partners. One was an Eskimo, already ensconced in the bow hole of a three-hole *bidarka*. This was an 18-foot-long, 2½-foot-wide version of the kayak. Its holes featured raised rims. If the crew then put on a *camlaker*, a waterproof hooded shirt made from seal intestines whose waist was bound snugly to the rims, complete watertightness was achieved.[7]

The other boat mate was a Russian half-breed named Ivan Simonsen Lukine, not a run-of-the-mill company employee. Lukine had been taken to Sitka as a youth and educated by a Greek Orthodox priest. Besides learning how to read and write Russian, he mastered several Indian languages, including Ingalik, spoken by the people who inhabited the upper Unalakleet region. While in the employ of Stepanoff, Lukine had conducted what amounted to commercial espionage. Stepanoff's HBC counterpart up at Fort Yukon had sent an expedition downriver to a point north of Nulato. The Russian was determined to find out what his rival was up to, so he sent Lukine, in the guise of a runaway employee, to Fort Yukon to learn what he could. At the outpost on the Arctic Circle, Lukine was received sympathetically as a victim of those cruel Russians. His curiosity was comprehensive. All his questions were answered. Loaded with information, he stole away in the dead of night, launched his canoe, and returned safely to St. Michael with intelligence for Stepanoff.[8]

With a "good luck" from Kennicott, Adams stowed his kit bag in the *bidarka*'s center hole, arranged his blankets for a seat, got in, and helped launch the boat. Under way, Lukine and the Eskimo commenced a running conversation in native tongue regarding navigation and directions as they paddled upriver. Adams began to feel superfluous. He grabbed a paddle. Lukine vetoed his assistance, which would be allowed only when they experienced rapids or swift currents. It occurred to Adams that he should take this opportunity to learn Lukine's language. Employing the only Russian phrase he knew, "How do you say that in Russian?" he began pointing to various objects such as rocks and posing the question. Lukine caught on and played along, improving his command of English in the process. By noon that first day Adams had fifty Russian words listed in his notebook.

The great adventure turned into an abortive effort as freezing temperatures, river icing, and lack of provisions forced the men back to camp after a week's difficult travel. But it was not a wasted journey. Besides improving his language skills, which in time enabled him to act as interpreter, Adams learned from the Indians at Ulukuk village about a short cut to Nulato. Kennicott decided to travel there as soon as was practicable. First, provisions, proper clothing, and dogsleds had to be procured. Solutions translated into survival for the major and his men; real exploration was replaced by a series of trips back and forth from Unalakleet and St. Michael to Ulukuk and Nulato, which was reached November 10 by Kennicott, Adams, Lebarge, and Lukine. Dogsleds had been procured from Stepanoff. They were used to carry supplies only; the men walked or ran behind. Mostly they ran in order to try to keep warm inside their parkas in freezing or subzero temperatures. As all Arctic travelers before them had discovered, they learned to take good care of their feet. They learned how to treat frostbite and that a hot cup of tea tasted better than vintage wine; that hungry sled dogs will eat just about anything and will break into the food supply if it isn't properly secured. They learned how dependent they were on the kindness of the various Indians they met along the way who welcomed them into their camps and fed them. The men were split up into smaller groups by Kennicott to maintain the supply lifeline. He planned their trips and his trips and dealt with maddening details and insubordinate Russian workers. Perhaps he dreamt of days when alone or with a single companion he had journeyed into the wilderness.

Adams tells us that when he and the others arrived at Nulato in the middle of the afternoon, "our faces were a mass of ice, both of my cheeks and my nose were badly frozen."[9] The Russian fort, whose large yard was enclosed by several buildings and a stockade, situated near the confluence of the Yukon and Nulato Rivers, had a violent history. When the Russian explorer Malakoff came to the site in 1838, he erected a small trading post which was inhabited until that winter, when lack of provisions forced his party back to St. Michael. In their absence, the local Indians burned the place to the ground. Malakoff and his men rebuilt it on their return the following year. The Indians repeated their arson and made off with everything stored in the post.

From 1841 to 1851 the newly fortified outpost survived amidst an uneasy truce with the Indians. Then in the spring of 1851 Lieutenant Barnard of the H.M.S. *Enterprise* arrived in search of information as to the fate of Sir John Franklin, an arctic explorer who had disappeared. Being ignorant of local customs and tribes, he sent a peremptory message demanding the presence of the chief of the Koyukuns. Taking this as an affront to his honor and influence, the chief decided to take his warriors to Nulato and settle the matter. One of the victims of the ensuing massacre was Lieutenant Barnard. His grave and that of the post commander, or *bidarshik*, Derabin, were still there behind the fort when Kennicott and his party arrived.[10]

The major remained at Nulato only five days, securing available information on the surrounding territory, then returned once again to Unalakleet. Before leaving, he left a message for Adams.

> You will, during my absence [of 40 days] with Mike Lebarge and Lukine, make such explorations on or near the proposed telegraph route from Koyukuk westward as your limited means will permit. You will also do any work you deem expedient to facilitate the progress of this expedition towards Fort Yukon. . . . I would advise you to proceed first to Koyukuk then penetrate the country westward towards Norton Bay, striking southward at the Yukon in time to reach this post before exhausting your provisions.[11]

Soon after his return to Unalakleet, Kennicott dispatched the Norton Sound Exploring Party. Headed by Lieutenant William Ennis, it consisted of Otto de Bendeleben, Richard Cotter, Jay Chappell, and two men Ennis identifies as T. Nefaker and V. Hanson. Otto describes the former as a "Russo-Californian with 37 years service in the Russian-American Company." Accompanying the party as far as Inglutalik were an old Malemute Indian chief, his wives and children, their dogsleds both ahead of and behind the Ennis group.

With their two sleds ready to go, the men set out on their northerly journey, traveling over the ice and snowy roads.

> Our second day was spent at the village of Shaktolik where we were received with ceremonies and singing. Then commenced the dancing and distribution of presents in the large dance-house where we were given whale blubber and frozen fish together with dried reindeer meat. . . . [I]t was now our turn, and presenting them with tobacco, we told them through our interpreter that we promised them good treatment as long as they behaved themselves towards us. Afterwards, there was nothing for it but to give them a song, so we all struck up the much admired "Marching Through Georgia" so well known and liked by the natives of the whole territory.

The Eskimos provided the men with sleeping quarters and food for their dogs. They had to lay over the following day to repair one of their sleds and secure rations of dried fish for the next leg of their trip.

> On our departure we experienced rough roads and extreme cold weather with strong head winds, but by making long marches we finally arrived at Inglutalik.

Compelled to lay over yet another day, Ennis and his group proceeded towards Kwik-mute, on Norton Sound's eastern shore. Here they encountered an Eskimo who had been to San Francisco and knew a little English. He informed them that if they followed their intended route they would find no food. However, Ennis did learn important information about their intended destination: that there was no continuous water from Kwik-mute to Grantley Harbor as was indicated on their maps; that the rivers from Golovin Sound (to the west) to Grantley Harbor were not navigable. But Ennis wanted to investigate the river just to the west that emptied into the sound.

> With that intention I left with Mr. de Bendeleben, two Russians and one sled lightly loaded and proceeded on the road. We traveled but a short distance when a south-east gale with snow came upon us. The sleet and water it also produced falling on the icy road rendered it impossible for four men pushing and 7 dogs pulling to make any headway.

Ennis returned to Kwik-mute, where he was able to gather a bit more information about the surrounding area. The country between the village and Golovin Sound was moderately level, sprinkled with Indian settlements, and well suited for a telegraph line route. And there were, he was informed by natives who had been there, sufficient trees further west for poles.

In his report dated December 23, 1865, Ennis recommended that Richard Cotter, who had some mountaineering experience, be put in charge of an expedition the following spring to explore the country from Nulato north up the Koyukuk River, then westward across the mountains to Inglutalik, where Ennis would have a cache of provisions for him and his men. He further suggested to Kennicott that he, Ennis, should explore the country west all the way to Grantley Harbor, either by dogsleds in March or by *bidarkas* in May. No wonder Kennicott put Ennis in charge of all future explorations "for the telegraph line between Grantley Harbor and the Yukon River. I leave the manner of carrying them out entirely to your own judgement," he wrote.

The return trip to Unalakleet by Ennis and his men was an endurance contest. One forty-mile stretch in particular remained frozen in the leader's memory.

> The day was bitter cold with a gale force wind blowing directly in our faces and the thermometer standing at 34 degrees below zero. From early morning till late at night did we trudge along, our dogs completely worn out and ourselves almost frozen. We finally arrived at our destination only to find that all members of the party were badly frozen. Mr. Cotter was so badly frostbitten that he lay down and cried in anguish. . . . I have since experienced colder weather, having been on the road with the thermometer at 52 degrees below zero.[12]

All the men survived to explore again.

George Adams, Lebarge, and Lukine had departed for Koyukuk on November 17 with a strong head wind drifting snow in their faces and a temperature of 32 degrees below zero. "Our faces were a mass of ice and the wind seemed to blow right through me," wrote Adams in his diary. Three days later he and the others were back in Nulato, having accomplished little except to make observations from a mountaintop.

Several days later they set out again, this time hoping to learn more about a trail from the Yukon across to Norton Sound at a village named Koltog. There, Adams learned that the Indian who had promised to guide him was gone. No doubt he figured if some crazy American really wanted to travel all that way in the dead of winter, he could do so without his help. Adams suspected it was just an excuse, that he was afraid to go. An Indian at the village informed the brash young man that a journey now would take thirty days, but if he waited until March it could be done in ten. Confronted with such logic, such prudence, Adams settled for traveling to a nearby village to buy as much dried fish as he could. With a sledload of that Russian America staple he and his party returned to Nulato on November 28.

> It was a great relief to get back to comfortable quarters with plenty of edible food, a Russian [steam] bath and a change of clothes; also to get rid of a colony of companions I had accumulated in Indian houses that had kept me scratching. Every Russian fort and trading post has a steam bath where its men and women bathe every Saturday. The Nulato bath house had two rooms. The first, 10' square, was where you undressed. This opened to a 10' by 20' room containing a pile of large boulders heated by a fire beneath them. Buckets of water are thrown on the fire to create steam. Bathers sit or lie upon platforms, one above the other, at the end of the room while steaming. When through with this process, there was a barrel of water or float ice from which the bather dipped and poured to cool off.

The *bidarshik* at Nulato took inventory not long after Adams had returned and discovered his provisions were getting dangerously low. Adams decided to return to Unalakleet, spend Christmas there, and return with more provisions. During the wintry journey, Adams figured he would make use of the wind. Using poles cut from birch trees and a blanket, he rigged a "square sail" and attached it to the sled. Thus assisted, the dogs expended less energy and the sled glided more swiftly down the frozen river.

Five days into their journey Adams and Smith heard someone chopping wood in the near distance. Curious, they trudged through deep snow in the direction of the sounds and hallooed. Out of the woods came two men they recognized immediately, Frank Ketchum and Joe Dyer. (In his diary Adams identifies the other as Dyer; in his narrative account, written later, as Charles Pease. If it was Pease, we know that he was a member of the Scientific Corps. Another of its members, Henry M. Bannister, would soon be joining the expedition.)

Perhaps Kennicott was being haunted by the specter of insufficient provisions, or maybe he was just taking prudent precautions based on experiences to date. Whatever the case, he had dispatched Ketchum with two sleighloads of provisions for Nulato. After feasting on reindeer steaks and flapjacks, the groups parted company the following morning. Adams and Smith completed their journey on the run, their sled slotted in the frozen tracks of Ketchum's sleighs.[13]

Nulato now became the cynosure of Kennicott's efforts. He had to stock it as fully as he could for his proposed spring ascent of the Yukon, having vetoed the idea of attempting the trip by dogsled. Most of his men were employed in the enterprise, including Cotter, Dennison, Pease, and Bannister as 1866 began. The young Bannister wrote of some of his experiences in a letter home.

I left Unalakleet on the 30th of December with Mr. Bendeleben and two natives. Our load was a very heavy one and one of the dogs dropped dead at the start. The wind soon increased to a perfect gale [so] we moved very slowly, hardly able to make the dogs face the wind, all of us either pushing or pulling the sled. . . . [B]efore long my face swelled and my eyes nearly closed so I had to fall back. The others pushed on. I followed, guiding myself by the moon, the one thing I could see distinctly, keeping it directly behind me. [Finally] I was met by an Eskimo sent out to find me, who took me directly to the village where I thawed out with cold water.[14]

Ennis, among others, heard of Bannister's plight and wrote about it in his journal.

Stepanoff immediately sent his own sled to bring him back to St. Michael where he was attended to most faithfully. At one time it was feared he might lose his nose and ears, but owing to the kind attention of those around him, he recovered, no doubt a "wiser" and better man, and greatly disgusted with the Arctic.[15]

One of the trips took Adams, Ketchum, Smith, and Pease to St. Michael to transport two skin boats back to Nulato. One was a three-hole *bidarka*. The other was a *bidarra*, or *umiak*, as the Eskimos called it. Open at the top with no deck, it was twenty feet long and five feet wide with a birchwood frame lashed together with sealskin thongs and covered with waterproofed sealskins sewn together.[16]

Kennicott also acquired four new sleds, different in construction from the ones he and the others had been using. These were Ingerlik sleds. Made of birchwood lashed together, they featured light, flexible frames that would bend going around corners or over obstacles. Though they did not appear strong, the twelve-foot sleds could hold up to six hundred pounds.[17] The sled most utilized was the Malemute type. It was made from sprucewood, the runners constructed from the jawbones of bowhead whales. They could carry up to eight hundred pounds. While expedition members often walked or ran behind their sleds, they could of course, conditions permitting, stand on the runners and ride.[18] The men also wore snowshoes when necessary during their wintertime journeys.

The parka was an essential item of clothing in this climate. This was a knee-length garment of dressed deerskin, belted and hooded, trimmed around wrists, skirt, and hood with strips of white deerskin, wolverine, or wolfskin. The trim around the hood used the animal's longest hairs so that when it was drawn up it covered the face completely.

Boots were made of reindeer leg skin, where the hair was short, smooth, and stiff. Knee length, they had sealskin soles that were waterproofed in the manner of skin for boats. The sole was turned over at heel and toe and gathered so as to better protect those parts. If necessary, the soles could be replaced in a half-hour's time. A pad of dry grass was worn under the feet and shaped to the sole as a shock and moisture absorber. Strings were tied around the boots at the ankle to secure them to the lower leg.[19]

Major Kennicott reached Nulato on January 24 with Smith, Adams, Lukine, an Eskimo, and three dogsleds. The trip was made in stages. On one of them, Adams found himself feeling drowsy, so he lay down on his sled and fell asleep. It was 45 degrees below zero. His Eskimo companion tried to wake him.

> I paid no attention to him [so] when we came to a sliding place he tipped the sled enough to roll me off into the snow which awakened me as I floundered out of it. The Indian was saying "big cold, sleep soon die," since which time I have thought that freezing would be a comfortable way to die.[20]

Kennicott was able to make one short trip up the Yukon in February. With Adams, Lebarge, Lukine, three Eskimos, two sleds, and eight dogs he traveled for ten days, visiting villages and gathering pertinent information. It was some of that information that compelled his decision to abandon further exploration up the river until the spring thaw. Even the most ardent of his group, including Adams, conceded that such a journey would kill men and dogs. Of the sixteen dogs they had brought to the post, only nine survived. Instead, it was decided to bring the *bidarra* and *bidarka* the rest of the way to Nulato, along with sufficient equipment and provisions, and be ready at the first sign of open water to board them and proceed upriver.

Adams observed his twenty-first birthday on March 20, noting in his diary:

> Do not feel in very high spirits. The living here [he was back at St. Michael] is "high toned" and I don't feel much like leaving. The year is going fast. The ships and letters will soon be here and the time passes much faster while we are at work. We leave for Unalakleet tomorrow.[21]

In the meantime, Kennicott had made a brief reconnaissance of the country to the northwest where Cotter and his party, sent over by Ennis, would soon be exploring all the way to the mountains. Ennis was busy preparing for a return to Norton Sound, fretting about insufficient dogs and food. His target date for getting under way was April 1. Whether he prayed for help or not we do not know. If he did, they were answered when a group dispatched by Kennicott arrived to transport more supplies back to Nulato. Frank Ketchum was in charge. He had instructions from his boss to give Ennis any dogs he might need. Just like that, twenty healthy canines were his. The lieutenant might have had cause to feel optimistic with this turn of events had it not been for the letters from Kennicott that Ketchum gave him. They were gloomy, "written in a most dispiriting manner; the failure to penetrate to Ft. Yukon preyed greatly upon his mind."

Ennis replied with encouragement, reminding Kennicott of the spring thaw, making possible an ascent by boat. Yet even as he wrote, there lay open on his desk another document, dated February 21, 1866. It read: "In case of my death before the arrival of Col. Bulkley, or of orders superseding those given me, Lieut. Wm. H. Ennis will take command of this expedition."[22]

Kennicott had suffered what was thought to have been a mild heart attack while still in San Francisco. No doubt his exertions, frustrations, and dashed hopes combined to activate his inner voice, which told him he might not survive his tour as expedition leader.

Ennis allowed none of this to prey upon his mind. He had a mission to accomplish. At noon on April 1, in company with de Bendeleben, Dyer, Cotter, Chappell, Hanson the interpreter, and five Eskimos, he set out with three sleds, twenty-one dogs, and provisions for two months.

> When my expedition left Unalakleet, the Russians, in a body, turned out and gave us a salute of 17 guns.
>
> The first day out was good, but on the second a heavy drift of snow commenced, increasing in fury by the hour. We toiled along however, facing the cold north wind, and although at one point I thought we could not find the village of Shaktulik . . . we at last saw it, hailing it with delight, for all hands were weary and hungry.

The snowstorm that accompanied them to the village forced them to remain in it for four days, and it was still snowing heavily when they recommenced their journey. Their next camp was a small, lonely hut on Norton Sound, from which they had to excavate the snow that had filled it. No fire was built. They survived a dismal night on body warmth, huddled together.

The following morning, Ennis made the decision to divide his party. Cotter and Dyer were sent eastward, through the Koyukuk country to Nulato with letters for Kennicott. Bidding them good-bye on April 7, Ennis and company struck westward across the bay to Kwik-mute. Here, Ennis ordered Chappell to sound through the ice, purchase whatever food and supplies that he could from the natives, then explore a pass through the mountains to the west.

On the ninth, Ennis, with de Bendeleben and Hanson, continued his explorations.

Our course followed the coast. That night we camped in a deserted village we called Two Hut Camp, 30 miles distant. Here are arctic furs in profusion and the scenery is very refreshing to the eye. Some natives came to visit us, bringing a species of sea crawfish, which we ate at our evening meal. Next day we made the large village called Athnockemute. Here we met with a good reception and distributed the usual presents of leaf tobacco. Up to this point we found no impediment to our telegraph line. From here however, the timber ceased until we reached Golovin Sound. There, we saw firs as far as 60 miles up the "Irathlul" river.

From there the party struck northward across the mountains, then traveled back in the direction of the sound until they scaled a mountain overlooking it. After staying the night in a village at the base of the mountain, they continued on to another village ten miles away where Ennis was supposed to meet the man who would guide him to the Bering Strait. The guide was there all right, but he wasn't going anywhere. "The road too long," he said, "no dog feed, no Indians; my dogs will die, my provisions become exhausted." Undeterred by this flat, unequivocal statement, Ennis offered to give the man his single-barrel shotgun. He still refused. Then, an Indian detached himself from a group nearby who had been listening to all this and said he would serve as guide for the shotgun. He wasn't just any man. Their guide was in fact the chief of the local tribe and proved to be the best guide and companion Ennis ever had.[23]

For the next fourteen days Ennis, de Bendeleben, and Attalk, as Otto rendered the chief's name in his account, trekked in a west-northwesterly direction across mountains and frozen rivers.

We met no more natives in the villages until we reached Tuk-suk-mute in the channel leading from Grantley Harbor to the inland bay called Irr-maghe-zuk. Here we feasted on delicious fish. Next day we arrived at Nook, the spot which divides Grantley Harbor from Port Clarence [probably Teller on current maps]. Here were many natives fishing. Mr. Ennis went out onto the ice to take soundings. I was unable to stir much, having been affected by snow blindness ever since we left Golovin Sound.[24]

They remained at Nook for two days before retracing their path back to Kwik-mute. The weather continued its barrages of snowstorms and gales. For the last stage of the journey they were able to travel by *bidarra*, which carried them, their dogs, and sled on a thawed river back to camp, where a lonely Chappell greeted them enthusiastically.

In his journal Ennis had effusive praise for his guide, the Indian chief, and penned this encomium:

He fed our dogs by hunting, made our camps and campfires [when wood was plenty] and in fact did everything a man could possibly do. "Al-seek-Al-Seek" [as Ennis rendered his name] I shall never fail to remember thee as long as I am living in this infernal country.[25]

Their round-trip of over four hundred miles was the longest yet completed by any of Kennicott's explorers.

By May 1 the days in Russian America were still long ones; the weather had become mild, rendering snow trails impassable by dogsled. So when Adams, Dyer, and two natives departed Nulato for another exploration of the country to the north and west to determine the best route for the line, they conducted their surveys at night, sleds running easily over the crusted snow and ice.

Adams was looking forward to their first stop, a village he had visited the previous November and had flirted with the chief's pretty young wife. His happiness upon arrival was increased when he learned that the Indians had snared hundreds of grouse, 260 of which he purchased. That night in the village was spent with Adams and Dyer parrying each other's flirtations with the chief's wife.[26]

A week after the return of this survey expedition, the men at Nulato watched the ice breaking up in the river, noting that it had risen six feet that morning. No longer were they facing knifelike north winds and killer blizzards. Now and then they spotted geese and ducks on the wing. Their spirits had risen sufficiently by May 12 that they spent part of the evening sitting outside the fort singing. And yet, Kennicott remained moody.

While I was writing last night the major came in and stood beside me for a while and then said he was tired and would turn in. When I had finished writing I looked at him and thought he was asleep and said to myself, "Good, he can forget his troubles for a while."[27]

In the morning six of the expedition members then at Nulato went down to breakfast as usual: hot cakes, bacon, whitefish, and coffee. Halfway through the meal they noticed the seventh member was missing. Where was the major? An hour later it occurred to them that they ought to look for him.

I was in the fort yard and some women came running up and said that the major was lying on the beach. I ran down with the rest and saw him about 500 yards south of the fort, stretched out on his back. His hands were folded across his chest. Wondering what he was doing in that position we went down and spoke to him. Getting no answer, we examined him and discovered he was cold and rigid, probably dead for several hours. There were no marks on his body and we thought he had died of stroke or heart disease. But that evening, after bringing his body back to the fort, we noticed a white froth coming from his mouth. We then realized he had committed suicide. We knew that he carried strychnine to poison wild animals for Smithsonian collecting. We found none of the poison on him or in his personal effects and concluded that he had taken it and thrown the bottle into the river, hoping to cover the cause of his death and further mystify us. The feelings of all of us today cannot be imagined by those not here and I could not describe them. They are too awful.

Near his body they found a circle, one foot in diameter, drawn in the sand with his small pocket compass, opened, placed in the center. And there were some lines traced in the sand from that compass, pointing towards the river. The men presumed Kennicott had been taking bearings even as he died. If there was any other meaning to the compass, circle, and lines in the sand, no one ever divined them. Perhaps they had some runic importance to the dying Kennicott.[28]

As for his death being a suicide, that was the conclusion of those who were there. But they were not doctors. This author could not find any official report as to the cause of death, so it may indeed have been a heart attack, or something else. His friend, Dall, did not believe he had taken his own life. Nor did others. There being no final, conclusive word on the matter, it will have to remain an arctic mystery.

The thirty-one-year-old explorer-scientist had died, as de Bendeleben says in his obituary, facing his favorite direction, north. "His kindness of heart could not be excelled. His memory will be ever dear to every one of the pioneers of his party."[29] Dall further memorialized him by seeing to it that a town in southeastern Alaska (as it then was), situated in the glaciated fastness of the Wrangell Mountains, was named after his departed colleague.

Upon returning to their quarters Adams, Ketchum, Lukine, and Lebarge found a note written by Kennicott, presumably that morning. It said that in case of his death, Ketchum, the oldest member of the group, should take charge. A meeting was convened and they decided to carry on and that Ketchum, Lebarge, and Lukine should ascend the Yukon in the *bidarka* up to the fort. Adams, accompanied by Smith and Pease, would take Kennicott's body in the *bidarra* back to St. Michael.[30]

So it seems that Kennicott wanted Ketchum to take charge of immediate exploration and Ennis to be in overall command. Dall was selected by Bulkley to take over as Scientific Corps director. At times these efforts would, of course, overlap.

A coffin was constructed of whipsawed boards caulked with moss and pitch. Adams wrapped it in his rubber blanket and tacked down the seams; he and Smith sat up with the body that first night.

On June 1 we left Nulato in our skin boat on what was probably one of the longest and most perilous funeral trips [five hundred miles] ever attempted. We had put a mast in the boat upon which a square sail could be hoisted for sailing before the wind. We expected to be carried downriver by a 5 mile per hour current, needing the oars only for landings or to avoid obstacles. The coffin was placed aft of the mast leaving just room enough for one person to sit and steer. Charles Pease, who had once been a sailor, acted as pilot and took the helm.

Eight days later the coffin boat arrived at St. Michael, where they were greeted by Ennis, de Bendeleben, Dennison, Bannister, and Bean, all having been informed of Kennicott's death by Dyer. They placed the body of their deceased leader in a vault beneath the watchtower and held funeral services. In the middle of the difficult downriver journey, Adams wrote in his diary: "Hope I have seen the Yukon for the last time." That was not to be the case.[31]

In due course Kennicott's body was placed aboard the *Wilder* and taken out to the *Nightingale* for transportation back to San Francisco. The flagship brought the new Scientific Corps leader, William H. Dall, and Whymper, the artist, who had previously volunteered to join Kennicott's party. By that time it had already been organized.

I was, however, determined to visit the unknown Yukon territory which had been, from the commencement of our explorations, more spoken about than any other. Ketchum . . . had promised me every assistance and kept his word. And I am indebted to the other officers, especially Messrs. Ennis, Dennison, Dyer, Lebarge and of course, Ketchum.[32]

Ketchum was a thirty-four-year-old native of St. John, New Brunswick, Canada. Family records provide scant information on his activities prior to joining the expedition. From comments made by his comrades, we know he was an experienced outdoorsman.[33] His Yukon ascent partner, Michael (or Michel) Lebarge, was born on the south bank of the St. Lawrence river in Chateauguay, Quebec, below Montreal, to French-Canadian parents. According to Dall, he was on the same ship as Kennicott and other expedition members traveling from New York to San Francisco in 1865. In those days people making the trip had two choices: take about six months and sail around Cape Horn, or sail down to the Panamanian isthmus, make the uncomfortable overland trip across it, then book passage aboard a ship plying the route from its Pacific coast to California, cutting travel time in half.[34] Apparently, Kennicott's group encountered several "lively incidents," as Dall describes them, crossing the isthmus during which Lebarge showed courage and initiative. Impressed, Kennicott asked him if he would like to join the expedition. And he did.

In October 1866, Dall, Whymper, Ketchum, Lebarge, *Wilder* engineer Mr. Francis, Dyer, and a line constructor called Scratchett made a dog-sled journey up to Nulato.[35] The previous month, hundreds of miles to the west in the "jaw" of the Seward Peninsula, Dan Libby and his men were landed by the *H. L. Rutgers* at Port Clarence. The camp they established was dubbed "Libbysville" in honor of their leader, who had selected the site for his Grantley Harbor Division.

One of its members was an enterprising Irishman named J. J. Harrington. He decided to produce a newspaper called *The Esquimaux*. Being the only such publication of its kind, a look at the editor's opening remarks in the first edition, dated Sunday, October 14, 1866, is in order.

> The Esquimaux will be published the first Sunday of each month. It is devoted to the interests of the foreign population in and around Libbysville. It will contain a summary of passing events and all intelligence of interest to the denizens of this neighborhood. Original and selected miscellany, correspondence & etc. will form a prominent feature. The terms of subscription will be nothing for the first year, and if the enterprise meets with encouragement, this price will be doubled after the expiration of its first anniversary.

Libby and his men wasted no time planting poles and stringing wire, as we learn from Harrington. "The first dispatch over our portion of the line, 2½ miles long, was received at this office on Wednesday last week . . . and the first click of the magnetic talker sounded in Russian America. How soon will it be before it is answered from 'Frisco?" Or, in modern terminology, one could make "local calls only." Unbeknownst to them, the expedition members had erected the first telegraph line in Russian America. In fairness to the constructors elsewhere in the territory, it should be noted that their Libbysville colleagues had precut poles and wire right there, ready to go after the material was offloaded from the *H. L. Rutgers*.

In the November edition of *The Esquimaux*, Harrington reported that "the telegraph line is now built a distance of 15 miles from this point [the main building]. The way station, where most of the party camped [for] a week was named Tentopolis." That same November edition carried the stunning news of Lee's surrender, that Cornwallis had been defeated, and a dispatch from Noah's ark, "We are still afloat." Harrington knew full well that a dose of humor would do the lads a world of good and help sustain morale.

The December edition carried a letter from Capt. Libby to all members of the Grantley Harbor Division.

> The construction of the line from Port Clarence to Grantley Harbor, though but 15 miles, was part of the work I did not hope to see completed this fall, nor under such favorable circumstances. . . . [I]t will even surprise the Engineer-in-Chief. It has been my wish and aim to construct as much line as possible in the least amount of time. To that end . . . you have labored with much energy, for which I most sincerely thank you. Presumably, we can commence operations

> again in early March or April of the coming year. I hope before another winter sets in to have the largest section of this line, 200 miles from Port Clarence to Golovin Sound, completed. It would be pleasing to have it said that we did the most and best work of any party attached to this expedition.[36]

Elsewhere, preliminary exploration was just getting under way.

Dall and his party arrived at Nulato on November 27. Enroute, the scientist decided to strike out on his own, ignoring the remonstrances of his comrades. He was determined, in spite of the weather, to push ahead to the next village. The wind, sweeping across treeless terrain, slammed sleet into his face as he tried to traverse country near the Unalakleet River. Dall was forced to walk sideways. He soon lost his way, but discovered his error in time to retrace his steps, and he reached a wooded part of the river in late afternoon.

> I found the ice rather soft and covered in places with drifted snow so that traveling was very laborious. To add to my annoyances it soon became very dark and I had to grope my way over icy hummocks and through snow drifts until nearly worn out by exertion. Passing round a bend in the river the ice gave way under me. I just had time to throw myself on one side, where it was more solid, and I got off, wet to the knees. Taking off my boots and socks I wrung out the water and put them on again. They froze immediately. . . . I trudged along and to my great delight, about eight o'clock, the moon rose, and I soon saw the village standing out against the sky.[37]

While wintering at Nulato, the group decided on plans for the coming season. Whymper and Dall would ascend the Yukon by water as far as Fort Yukon. Ketchum and Lebarge would make the same journey with dogsleds over the ice in February. Dyer would descend the river and investigate its delta.

Christmas was celebrated with due ceremony and attention to the holiday meal. In Dall's words, "our knowledge of chemistry and the domestic arts was taxed to the utmost in the production of pies, gingerbread and cranberry dumplings." The men feasted on reindeer meat, a brace of roasted ptarmigan, green peas, tomatoes, and other preserved vegetables.[38]

What of the Yukon River itself? What did these men think of it? "Stolid indeed must he be, who surveys the broad expanse of the Missouri of the North for the first time without emotion," Dall relates.[39] A village youngster once exclaimed, "It is not a river, it is a sea!"

Whymper tells us that he "was prepared to see a large stream but had no conception of the reality. Neither pen nor pencil can give any idea of the dreary grandeur, the vast monotony, or the unlimited expanse we saw before us."[40] The word *Yukon,* which translates as "big river," was certainly that. Its width varied from less than a mile to five miles. Its course covers territory from 57 degrees, 45 minutes north latitude at its source in British Columbia to the Arctic Circle at 66 degrees, 33 minutes north latitude, to its deltic mouth at 63 degrees north latitude. Fed by numerous tributaries, the river runs through every variety of terrain, placid and lakelike or boiling with treacherous rapids, its waters dotted with islands or clear and deceptively shallow. At the Ramparts, the river is very wide and tortuous, full of sloughs, islands, and cut-offs. Here the country is low and flat with many small rivers, concealed by myriad islands, flowing into the Yukon. Anyone venturing upon the waters of the Big River must be ever alert for snags, logs, and other obstacles that could easily rip a hole in a boat or destroy it entirely.[41]

On February 11, 1867, Dall and the others observed a spectacular display of the aurora borealis, the northern lights. The men first noticed the lights in a gap between some hills north of Nulato. They seemed to approach in a cloudlike shape with a rising wind. As a luminous cloud it manifested itself in successive waves, resembling rings of smoke from a pipe, one within the other, gradually expanding.

> The inner or focal rings were more intense [in color] than the outer ones. As the waves or ripples advanced they were compressed into oval form by the wind, the longer diameter being east and west . . . from the brighter portions of the rings, light streams of the same medium occasionally dripped, then dissipated. . . . [I]t followed the air currents entirely; all its motions guided entirely by them. It covered the whole sky in about 2 hours. As it spread and enlarged, the light became fainter; not a positive light, but a mildly luminous appearance like phosphorescence.[42]

A month after this ethereal event, Ketchum, Lebarge, and their party with four loaded sleds departed for their trip to Fort Yukon. As they did so, a group of Indians and Russians from the fort stood shaking their heads, knowing they did not have sufficient provisions or dog food. The intrepid explorers knew this as well but were confident they could kill or trap enough food for them and their dogs. So, in Dall's estimation, "it was unquestionably one of the most remarkable journeys undertaken by modern explorers."

In the meantime, Dall and the others were planning to build a new headquarters for the Yukon division, a one hundred- by sixty-five-foot enclosure containing a barracks, officer's quarters, bath house, cook house, and several store houses. After haggling with the local Russian constructor, Dall was relieved when work began at a location near the Klatkakhatne River on Fort Kennicott.

Between Fort Kennicott and Nulato, a distance of about a mile and a half, they decided to erect a telegraph line, even though, as Dall notes, "it was not strictly in our line of duty." They cut down thirty "pole trees" and planted them along a route twelve feet wide that had been cleared by hired Russian labor. By mid-April the men were in their shirt sleeves. The following month, the ice broke on the Yukon and its tributary rivers. On the anniversary of Kennicott's death, at the fort named after him, a cross was erected bearing a tablet which read: "In memory of Robert Kennicott, naturalist, who died near this place May 13, 1866, aged thirty."

With his memory alive in their minds, Dall and the others set about getting the *bidarra* ready for its long ascent to Fort Yukon. As they readied the fifteen-foot-long, four-and-one-half-foot-wide boat, they endured the jibes of Russians, whose larger craft was all ready to launch: "You can't row that against the current; it won't hold a sail; you will fail." While taking to heart the words of these experienced people, the Americans only redoubled their resolve to persevere and prevail, even, as Dall states, "if the boat had to be replaced by a raft." A mast was fabricated and secured. A square sail made of stout linen toweling purchased from the Russians was attached. Two small tents were folded and loaded aboard along with the other equipment. Too small to take a rudder, the *bidarra* would be propelled and guided with several oars and a large paddle cut from seasoned spruce. The Indian doing all the work and carving, Kurilla, decorated oars and paddle with stripes of red ochre.

On the morning of May 26, Dall and Whymper helped Joe Dyer and his two Indian companions into their three-hole *bidarka* for the trip downriver to the Yukon delta. Then the pair, along with Kurilla, Mikaishka, and a Koyukun they called Tom, added their weight to the eight hundred pounds already loaded in the *bidarra* to begin the riverine adventure of a lifetime. The whole enterprise had been conceived after Collins descended the Amur; their colleagues had been on the Fraser; others worked along the Anadyr. Now it was their turn.[43]

Elsewhere in Russian America the telegraph army had not been idle. In late January, Ennis, Fred Smith, two Indians, and a Russian departed Unalakleet with two sleds and fourteen dogs for a trip to Libbysville. Ennis wanted to visit his counterpart and bring back some of his men to augment his meager work force. Before leaving, he assigned Adams and Chappel to command districts through which the line was to be built: Chappel was put in charge of the Golovin Sound to Unalakleet section; Adams, the section from Unalakleet to Nulato.[44]

The arrival of Ennis and party in Libbysville was headline material in *The Esquimaux*. Its previous edition had reported what could have been traumatic news. "Our latest dates from San Francisco are to the 7th of August, by the bark *Evelyn Wood* via the steamer *Wright*. The intelligence brought by her is, however, to be doubted. She reports completion of the Atlantic cable."[45]

It had, in fact, been completed. On July 27, 1866, the steamship *Great*

Eastern entered Newfoundland's Heart's Content Harbor, bringing ashore a cable that stretched all the way to Ireland. Yet Western Union proceeded with work in British Columbia, where the verified news was first received, until October 1866. Not until March of the following year did the company order cessation of operations. That information, like the news about the Atlantic cable, traveled slowly to Russian American personnel and their brethren across the Bering Strait in Siberia.

Certainly the stalwarts in Libbysville had good reasons to be skeptical. Hadn't Cyrus Field's cable efforts failed time after time? Dan Libby's men worked doggedly on.

Our camp was pitched under the most propitious weather on the 14th of March and all looked forward to the speedy completion of that portion of the line extending to Lake Marizuk. Five days later we were reminded of the fickleness of the weather. The thermometer suddenly changed from 4 degrees above zero to 20 below; a furious storm of cutting wind and snow from the north proclaimed the elements at war with everything perishable . . . the storm continued unabated for 7 days, when it suddenly hushed to a calm with the thermometer at 55 degrees below zero. It was only a lull. For on the second day, Aeolus in his equinoctical fury again opened his heaviest artillery and from the chilly north hurled his penetrating blasts in fearful gusts, testing the pregnability of all before it, drifting the snow in dense clouds, obstructing vision and piercing every aperture in cabin and tent.

Two men from this work party were caught in the storm while hauling poles with dogsleds about five miles from camp. The dogs panicked and ran headlong over a cliff, the men releasing their hold just in time. Below that cliff was a receptive cushion of deep snow. The dogs survived and made their way back to camp before their masters did. The pair, guided by a compass, battled wind and snow and frostbite, at times digging holes with their snowshoes into drifts for shelter. After five hours their ordeal ended and they rejoined their comrades in their ten by twelve foot cabin.[46]

By the time Ennis returned to Unalakleet he discovered that Adams and Company had been making good progress cutting and planting poles, though as the twenty-one-year-old notes in his diary: "Building a telegraph line with dogs and sleds your only transportation in the frigid zone is not as much fun as it is cracked up to be." Yet he and his boon companion, Fred Smith, along with the rest maintained high morale through it all, cutting, planting, and building new camps as they advanced. By early February, they were five miles beyond Unalakleet, working on frozen ground. Sometimes they had to stop and clear a road. By month's end they were fifteen miles from their starting point. Adams passed yet another birthday on March 20. "Wish I was home. Nearly finished the 22nd mile today. This morning had the hardest snow storm we have had this year." On April 26 he wrote:

> Lt. Westdahl and myself have been doing the hardest work on the line viz. hauling poles since most of the men are unable to work. It is hard to work on little or no grub and they are completely played out. We are almost entirely out of provisions.

It was so bad that Adams's natural resilience faltered. "This is the last hard work I shall do while I stay in this country." But Ennis had not forgotten them. A sleigh with three hundred pounds of deer meat arrived at their camp. Then, as if on cue, huge herds of reindeer began moving through the area, easy targets. Well fed and rested, the men continued, only to discover that the spring thaw made work even less enjoyable. The snows became rains. Frozen ground became muddy morasses. Dug holes filled with water immediately. Yet they persevered.[47]

So had Dall, Whymper, and their *bidarra* mates. By June 7 they had reached the confluence of the Yukon and Tanana Rivers, about 240 miles upstream from Nulato, paddling, tracking, and avoiding dangerous obstacles the whole way. At the confluence was a tongue of land called Nuklukahyet, a major trading rendezvous site. Indian tribes from the surrounding country, even some from Fort Yukon, would gather annually for bartering and socializing. When the explorers arrived, they had to endure what Whymper described as a "ceremony." Indians, whooping, yelling, and brandishing guns, advanced on them, stopped, then fired their guns into the air.

> We, with the Indians just arrived, returned the compliment, and then the chief whose acquaintance we had made during the winter, came forward and welcomed us. This man had treated Ketchum and Lebarge very well on their winter trip and they had left a letter for us, asking us to give him powder, etc. We found this place almost bare of provisions; the Indians dancing and singing all the same with empty stomachs, knowing that moose hunting season was at hand.

Three days after departing Nuklukahyet, the voyagers encountered the Yukon's rapids, beyond which Zagoskin alleged it was impossible to travel. Here the river was relatively narrow with a long, rocky archipelago of sometimes submerged boulders around which the water rushed, boiled, and foamed at a seven-knot clip.

> For the greater part of the way we tracked from rocks on the west side, occasionally having to take our Indians onboard and paddle with great vigor. It would be easy to make this a sensational affair, but in truth, we passed them without great difficulty. A steamer could go through them, except for the first fortnight in June, when the water is at its strongest.

The country through which they were passing was, and still is, called the Ramparts, due to the high, craggy rocks which rise from the surrounding banks. Whymper may have chosen not to describe this part of their journey as sensational, but it was wearying; they were still negotiating it five days later. As they emerged from the gorge, they found themselves on a stretch of river that opened out into lagoons and shallows, dotted with numerous islands and populated with the lumbering forms of moose. In the air a pestiferous profusion of mosquitoes.

> [They were] like smoke in the air. Through constant and enforced observation, I came to distinguish four kinds—a large, gray one, another with white leg joints, a very small dust-colored one which held its proboscis horizontally in the advance, and another small one which carried its probe in the orthodox manner. All were distinguished from the civilized species by the reckless daring of their attack.

Buckskin and netting over the head proved to be the only armor against them. Exposed hands were bitten relentlessly and became raw. The airborne tormentors drove bear, moose, and deer into the river. "All Nature," wrote Dall, "rejoices when the end of July comes and their reign is at an end."

A map of this part of the Yukon northeast of the Ramparts will show geographic tributes to Whymper's companion: the Dall River, and north of it, Dall Mountain. Both were now on the home stretch of their ascent. On the nineteenth and twentieth of June they found the water alternately strong and shallow, sometimes both. And then, torrential rain fell upon them. But they all knew they were getting closer and closer to their destination and paddled along with even greater intensity. The night of the twenty-first–twenty-second was the shortest of the year; the sun set a few minutes after 11 P.M. and rose forty-five minutes later. The following day brought a view of the mouth of the Porcupine River, which empties into the Yukon from the north. Now they *knew* they were very near. Just half a mile more and there it was, Fort Yukon. They expressed their jubilation in a volley of gunfire. "Kurilla blazed away till we were all deaf." A large group of Indians had gathered at the landing. An old French Canadian and two Scotsmen came down to greet them, telling them that the post commander, Mr. MacDougall, was expected back any day. The 630-mile, twenty-nine-day journey was over. Shown a room in the commander's house after pulling their boat ashore, they stowed their baggage, found their beds, and slept.[48]

McDougall returned on the twenty-sixth and welcomed the men warmly, bringing with him the "latest" news. Whymper records in his book, without comment, that some of this news was "the successful working of the Atlantic cable." He was much more interested in the

Lucullan feasts served him and the others consisting of "moose meat boiled, varied by boiled moose meat, alternating with the meat of boiled moose."[49]

The twenty-ninth was made memorable by the return of Ketchum and Lebarge from their "descending ascent" of the Yukon, the first explorers to have made the journey. They had arrived at Fort Yukon on May 9, traveling over steadily melting ice and snow with their dogsleds. Remaining at the fort until the ice broke, they went the rest of the way, six hundred miles to the burnt-out remains of Fort Selkirk, by canoe. The compound on the west bank of the river near Pelly Crossing had been torched by warring Indians years before and never rebuilt. Though the Yukon sometimes ran through rugged country, Ketchum told Whymper, it was navigable the whole way. All the Indians they encountered were friendly and expressed a desire to see more white men in the region. Why Ketchum and Lebarge did not descend the river to its source is not known.[50] The hoped-for linking of Russian American and British Columbia telegraph army pioneers never occurred. In the meantime, Russian America had been sold to the United States, and there is every reason to believe that Secretary of State Seward, reading reports of explorations and findings there, was all the more eager to conclude the deal.

In March 1867 Russian Minister Edouard de Stoeckl, who had been rescued from the *Novick* four years earlier by Scammon's *Shubrick* crew, actively pursued the sale with Seward, who had just received a letter from Western Union vice-president William Orton informing him that the company's board of directors, now convinced of the Atlantic cable's success, had decided to cease work on the Collins Overland Line despite an expenditure of $3 million. Seward replied in part:

> I am not one of those who have been disappointed by the magnificent success of the Atlantic Telegraph. I regard it as tributary to an expansion of our national commerce. . . . Nevertheless, I confess a profound disappointment in the suspension of the Inter-Continental Pacific Telegraph enterprise. . . . I abate not a jot my former estimates of the importance of that enterprise. I do not believe that the United States and Russia have given their faith to each other, and to the world, for its prosecution in vain.[51]

Seward, ardent backer of wiring the world and manifest destinarian *par excellence*, was not going to begrudge Cyrus Field's achievement, and he saw clearly that the defunct telegraph expedition had bonded his country and Russia together to their mutual benefit. He was not about to squander the diplomatic and geo-political possibilities thus engendered. His counterpart wanted to sell. He wanted to buy. De Stoeckl wanted $10 million. Seward countered with $5 million. They settled on $7.2 million. Ironically enough, the tsar's authorization for the sale was transmitted over the Atlantic cable, motivated by his desire to offload the financially and logistically burdensome colony and to increase the imperial coffers.

Neither side wasted any time since Congress was preparing to adjourn. Agreed to on March 29, the treaty of sale was signed the next day. Overcoming some congressional opposition and the jeers of men such as Horace Greeley, Seward engaged in intense lobbying of Senator Charles Sumner's Foreign Relations Committee, President Andrew Johnson, and others to help ensure approval of the sale. He got his wish, a bit delayed by the abortive impeachment of Johnson, on July 14, 1868.[52]

Adams was probably the first of the expedition members to receive the cease work order. His diary entry for June 26 notes that the *Clara Bell* had arrived from San Francisco with the news, relayed to him by St. Michael storekeeper Bean, who had traveled to Nulato, then on up to their work camp, where Adams and his men had just completed a new log house. "We are all ordered home (much joy) . . . intense excitement among the men, who ask all sorts of questions, e.g., will we be paid?"[53]

Colonel Bulkley had dispatched the *Clara Bell*, Captain John Norton commanding, to convey the order to the Russian American outposts, along with news of the Big Sale. Upon completion of its messenger service, the bark sailed across the Bering Strait to Plover Bay, landed the men it had picked up to await arrival of the *Nightingale*, then proceeded to the Anadyr to bring out the stranded crew of the *Golden Gate*.

Two days before receipt of this sensational information, Captain W. W. Smith, a former sailor, and Westdahl had departed for a thorough reconnaissance of the harbor in Golovin Bay. The steamer *Wilder* had just been freed from a sand bar where she had grounded. Adams and his men had completed about forty miles of line. They had built their own launch and named it the *Pioneer*. This was all old news now. Ennis, back up around Kwik-mute, had to be notified of the new situation. Unable to convince local Indians to make the trip, Adams and Jay Chappell readied the single-masted *bidarra* for the voyage across Norton Sound. It was an unpleasant one, featuring tricky winds, clouds of mosquitoes, and little sleep. Yet, Adams remained appreciative of natural phenomena.

> The bluffs at the end of Auc Point are 75 to 100 feet high straight down to the sea and look like they have been sliced by a knife. The cracks and crevices are covered with sea fowl of all colors—millions of them. The air was full of them flying backwards and forwards. It was one of the prettiest sights I ever saw.

On July 6 the nearly exhausted pair arrived at Kwik-mute, only to learn that Ennis and his party had left the day before. Two days later, they were all reunited at Unalakleet, where they learned that most of the men once there had departed for St. Michael aboard the *Wilder*. Ennis, Adams, Chappell, Fred Smith, W. W. Smith, and constructor George Dow followed in *bidarras*, coming ashore the thirteenth. Twelve days later, Dall, Whymper, Ketchum, and Lebarge joined their comrades at the fort.[54]

Their trip down the Yukon had been a rapid one. Leaving Fort Yukon with a volley of *bon voyage* musketry ringing in their ears, they made one hundred miles per day, reaching Nulato on July 13. A message awaited them there: Bring everything portable down to St. Michael. After procuring a larger *bidarra* and the assistance of two more Indians, the quartet proceeded into the lower Yukon. Traveling exclusively on the west side of the river, they passed many Indian villages, where most residents were busy drying fish. The idea of going home spurred them on and gave rise to musical expression.

Our Indians, as well as ourselves, made the hills and riverbanks echo with songs, all of us feeling gay and festive, as the Americans say, and cheerfully looking forward to seeing our ships.

On the night of the twentieth, they found themselves fogbound, unable to see the bow of their boat, and entrusted their fate to the course of the current. It delivered them into a fine, sunny morning. Five days later they sailed into the next chapter of their lives, all but Dall, that is.[55]

The scientist, having loaded big boxes of specimens collected for the Smithsonian aboard the *Clara Bell*, volunteered to stay on another year to complete his work investigating Alaska's wildlife. We learn from him that the Russians did not tell their own people of the sale until February 1868, and that the news was received by one and all with great joy. For his part, Dall had already raised the Stars and Stripes on the flagstaff in front of Fort St. Michael. During his year in the new American territory he lived among the Inuit, learning more about their customs, speaking their language as well as Russian, filling more kegs with specimens, ably assisted by the faithful Kurilla. Then on June 27 one of his assistants came running up with the news: two American ships were at St. Michael. Taking the swiftest *bidarka* to be had, Dall and his Indian friends rowed with a vengeance to the fort.

I hastened to the house on the point which was evidently occupied. Entering, I nearly stumbled over a sleeper on the floor. He rose and came out into the light, and I was soon shaking hands and exchanging hurried interrogatories with Mike Lebarge. The unmixed delight at seeing his familiar face can hardly be appreciated. I found to my own astonishment that speaking English after a year of nothing but Russian and Indian dialects was anything but easy.

What was Lebarge doing there? He was now a businessman, a founding partner of the Pioneer American Fur Company, one of several such concerns rushing in to fill the vacuum created by the departed Russian American Company.

On August 9, 1868, William H. Dall and his collected specimens shipped out aboard the schooner *Frances L. Steele,* bound for San Francisco. There he was welcomed so warmly that he was moved to write that "The friendship of Californians, so easily acquired, is as precious as their own gold and as enduring as the Sierras. When I stepped aboard the eastbound steamer, I felt almost as if I were leaving rather than approaching home."[56]

Arriving at Port Clarence on July 28 was the *Clara Bell* with the order and the news, the latter still viewed with suspicion by John J. Harrington's *Esquimaux.*

It is strange news to us, for all looked forward to successful completion of the transcontinental telegraph. The reason for the suspension [of work] is a mystery. Private word points to continued working of the Atlantic cable. The erected line will not be disturbed.

The Libbysville constructors had built twenty-two miles of line in the worst possible conditions, subsisting on "food from which the appetites of the civilized shrink." They departed with regret mixed with pride. The original forty-one, including Goble, Klinefelter, prose stylist William Walker, Dan Shea, Charley Tourtellot, Jud Watson, Tom Yates, and George Perrin, had been reduced to thirty-nine. George O'Callaghan and M. L. Slavan had died, inspiring Harrington to versify.

Amid the frozen Arctic, where summer's but a day,
And brings the flowers to blossom for a winter's quick decay,
The white man's venturous footsteps have pressed the snowy sod,
And they are laid beneath it, in communion with their God.
The years pass by unheeded, they feel not the northern blast,
Or the icy snows which winter above their dwelling cast.
Their mourners are the ocean and the mountains towering high,
Mute sentinels who never tire of watching where we lie.

And so the men bade good-bye to Libbysville, leaving behind a brief statement of their mission in the main building and a sign painted on the tower house which read: "Libby Station. Established September 17, 1866. Vacated July 2, 1867." Commending the structures and completed line of the not-so-tender mercies of "the drear power of the Arctic seasons,"[57] they took their leave and boarded the *Clara Bell,* joining the St.

Michael's contingent for the brief voyage to Plover Bay and an anticlimactic sojourn at that Chukchi Peninsula outpost.

The reader will recall that Captain Kelsey, erstwhile dinghy joyrider, and a dozen telegraph line constructors were put ashore inside Plover Bay on September 5, 1866, at the newly built Kelsey Station. They had spent a winter not unlike the one experienced by their Russian America colleagues: stormy weather and temperatures dipping to 45 degrees below zero. The bay froze solid on November 25. It was not open to ship traffic until the following July. Some of Kelsey's men suffered frost bite and showed signs of scurvy. One of them, Robert Lawton, constructor, reached the end of his tether on March 11, and hung himself in the davits of the *Victoria*. It was the same Honolulu-based *Victoria* that, two years previously, had had to be towed out of the bay by the *Wright*, had continued her whaling cruise in search of the bowfin, and subsequently returned to Plover Bay, where she was fated to become icebound during the winter of 1866–67. She sustained sufficient damage to render her unseaworthy.

By the time the *Clara Bell* arrived at Kelsey Station on July 9, its persevering workers had managed to build thirteen miles of line. They were as happy to see their comrades from across the Bering Strait as those going ashore were to see them. Once again, however, the problem of insufficient provisions imposed its exigent presence. But first, the men needed shelter. A tent city sprang up along the shores of Emma Harbor, tents made from the disabled *Victoria*'s sailcloth. In one of those temporary abodes, boreal journalist J. J. Harrington set up shop and began publishing a Plover Bay edition of *The Esquimaux*. From him we learn that Captain Redfield of the *Manuella* took his ship out to visit whalers in regional waters to buy provisions from them for the residents of "Tentopolis." Some of its better hunters went out in search of game. Others tried to catch salmon. Dan Libby and four of his men took a boat out into the bay, visiting whalers in search of extra food. The crew of the *Victoria*, living aboard, invited some former Libbysville denizens to dine with them. Knowing the meal would consist exclusively of "whale food," they declined. In due course the brig was surveyed to determine her condition, condemned as unfit for service, and sold at auction to Captain Redfield.[58]

All those gathered at Tentopolis had foresworn the use of "spiritous liquors" during their tours of duty in Russian America in accordance with company policy. Now with time on their hands and boredom eroding self-discipline, some of them ventured forth in search of alcohol, or a reasonable substitute.

Some of our men found a keg of specimens preserved in alcohol belonging to one of our Smithsonian collectors. . . . [T]he temptation was too much for them, and they proceeded to imbibe the contents. After drinking to their hearts' content, and becoming visibly affected thereby, they thought it a pity to waste the remaining contents of the barrel, and, feeling hungry, went on to eat the lizards, snakes and fish which had been put up for a rather different purpose.[59]

We are told that all the miscreants survived, though all suffered bad cases of what was then called the inward gripes.

A different sort of unpleasantness befell the carpenter of one of the barks lying in the harbor. Aboard the *David Crockett*, he was rehooping the cask in which was preserved the body of his late captain. Suddenly, the bung loosened and struck him in the forehead. "Since then," J. J. Harrington reported, "he suffers under the singular illusion that it was the body of the dead man that inflicted the blow."

Some of the long hours of waiting in the camp were eased by singing and storytelling and the musical renditions of a pair known only as Frank and Ned, who regaled audiences with violin and banjo performances.[60] They had been members of the Anadyr river party from Camp Macrae. Led by Bush, they were picked up by the busy *Clara Bell*, joining expedition brethren at Tentopolis. They too had lost several of their group after surviving extreme privations in eastern Siberia. Charles Geddes, who had been carpenter on the *Golden Gate*, and constructor John Robinson were buried near their camp. For them, Bush wrote the following:

Fierce wolves shall dash over the spot in pursuit of their prey; wild reindeer shall come to crop frozen lichens from their tombs; the partridge to build her nest between them; and the startled hare shall take shelter behind them; but nothing can disturb the departed in this their long, last sleep.

Sailcloth from the ice-crushed former flagship served as tent material for Bush and his men. Not long after their arrival, they and the others witnessed first-hand the capture of a bowhead whale by the crew of the brig *Pfeil*. Before their eyes, the seventy-foot cetacean was harpooned, brought alongside, and cut up. Bush records his amazement at the size of the jaw, "with 1700 pounds of black whalebone clinging to it." The ship's captain, addressing his captive audience of onlookers, told them:

There gentleman, look at that. Did you ever see anything on shore as handsome as that. And pointing to the huge mass of greasy blubber heaped upon the deck he said, there's something that may look dirty and worthless to you landsmen, but it is gold to us.[61]

And so the days passed for company employees in Emma Harbor, waiting for word that the *Nightingale*, on her last voyage for Western Union, had been sighted. We can only wonder whether Bush, gazing out to sea, might have imagined the sails of another ship, the outline of another shore he had seen two years ago.

NOTES

1. Smithsonian Institution Archives, William H. Dall Papers, Record Unit 7073, Box 18, Letter, Robert Kennicott to Col. Charles S. Bulkley, dated June 28, 1865.
2. Otto de Bendeleben, "Sketches of the First Telegraph Explorations in Russian America," *The Esquimaux*, April 4, 1867.
3. George R. Adams, *Life on the Yukon, 1865–1867* (Kingston, Ontario, Canada: The Limestone Press, 1982), pp. 176–78.
4. William H. Dall, *Alaska and Its Resources* (Boston: Lee & Shepard, 1870; reprint, New York: Arno Press, 1970), p. 10.
5. Op. Cit., note 2.
6. Adams, *Life on the Yukon*, p. 30.
7. Ibid., pp. 30–31.
8. Dall, *Alaska and its Resources*, pp. 276–77.
9. Adams, *Life*, pp. 121–30.
10. Dall, *Alaska*, pp. 48–51.
11. Adams, *Life*, p. 131.
12. "Journal of William H. Ennis, Member, Russian-American Telegraph Exploring Expedition," *California Historical Society Quarterly* 33 (March 1954): pp. 153–57, and Otto de Bendeleben, "Sketches, Part 2", *The Esquimaux*, May 5, 1867.
13. Adams, *Life*, pp. 132–36 and pp. 44–68.
14. James Alton James, *The First Scientific Exploration of Russian America* (Evanston, Ill.: Northwestern University, 1942), pp. 268–69.
15. Ennis journal, p. 159.
16. Dall, *Alaska*, p. 15
17. Adams, *Life*, pp. 141–42.
18. Dall, *Alaska*, p. 25
19. Ibid., pp. 21–22.
20. Adams, *Life*, p. 83.
21. Ibid., p. 152.
22. Ennis journal, p. 163.
23. Ibid., pp. 163–65, and de Bendeleben, "Sketches, Part 2."
24. de Bendeleben, "Sketches, Part 2."
25. Ennis journal, p. 165.
26. Adams, *Life*, p. 86.
27. Ibid., p. 161.
28. Ibid., pp. 90–91 and p. 161.
29. "Memoir of the Late Robert Kennicott," *The Esquimaux*, November 4, 1866.
30. Adams, *Life*, p. 91.
31. Ibid., pp. 91–92 and pp. 161–66.
32. Frederick Whymper, *Travel and Adventure in the Territory of Alaska* (Ann Arbor: University of Michigan Microfilms, 1966), p. 146.
33. Biographical data from Harriet Irving Library, University of New Brunswick's Ketchum genealogy.

34. *Biographies of Alaska-Yukon Pioneers, 1850–1950,* vol. 2, comp. and ed. Ed Ferrell (Bowie, Md.: Heritage Books, 1997), p. 182.

35. Dall, *Alaska,* p. 25.

36. *The Esquimaux,* October 14, 1866, vol. 1, no. 1, "City Intelligence," November 4, 1866, and "Congratulatory Letter," *The Esquimaux,* December 9, 1866.

37. Dall, *Alaska,* pp. 33–34.

38. Ibid., p. 58.

39. Ibid., p. 41.

40. Whymper, *Travel and Adventure,* p. 164.

41. Dall, *Alaska,* pp. 279–81.

42. Ibid., p. 60.

43. Ibid., pp. 63–73.

44. Adams, *Life,* pp. 187–88.

45. "The Blank in our News from the Outside World," *The Esquimaux,* January 6, 1867.

46. "Letter From Yankee Jim," *The Esquimaux,* April 7, 1867.

47. Adams, *Life,* pp. 109–12 and pp. 189–98.

48. Whymper, *Travel,* pp. 210–16, and Dall, *Alaska,* pp. 100–2.

49. Whymper, *Travel,* p. 219.

50. Ibid., pp. 227–28.

51. James D. Reid, *The Telegraph in America* (New York: John Polhemus Publisher, 1886), pp. 516–17.

52. Walter A. McDougall, *Let the Sea Make a Noise* (New York: Avon Books, 1993), pp. 306–7.

53. Adams, *Life,* p. 207.

54. Ibid., pp. 208–9.

55. Whymper, *Travel,* pp. 233–39.

56. Dall, *Alaska,* pp. 239–42.

57. "Our Arctic Home" and "The Three Graves," *The Esquimaux,* July 7, 1867.

58. "City Intelligence" and "Libbysville Items," *The Esquimaux,* July 14, 1867.

59. Whymper, *Travel,* p. 242.

60. "City Intelligence," *The Esquimaux,* September 1, 1867.

61. Richard J. Bush, *Reindeer, Dogs, and Snowshoes* (New York: Harper and Brothers, 1871), pp. 515–17.

CHAPTER EIGHT

ORDEAL IN SIBERIA

Land ho! came the long-awaited cry from the *Olga's* foremast lookout. The Russian brig had been at sea forty-seven days since sailing through San Francisco's Golden Gate on July 3, 1865, sometimes under close-reefed topsails or becalmed in gently rocking swells, or dashing ahead with a fine breeze off the quarter, with neither a sail nor land sighted the entire voyage.

Serge Abasa, Richard J. Bush, George Kennan, and James A. Mahood rushed up on deck and peered through obscuring shrouds of fog for a glimpse of terra firma. Piercing the occluded vista and catching the rising sun's streaking rays were snowcapped volcanic peaks: the 7,000-foot Mt. Villenchinski and 11,554-foot Mt. Avatcha, according to Bush's guidebook. Avatcha Bay, Petropavlovsk, Kamchatka Peninsula, the first step in the quartet's Siberian adventures, had been reached.

At its narrowest point Avatcha Bay was one-and-a-half miles wide. As the *Olga* proceeded, watchers on deck noticed its engirding cliffs decreasing in altitude, the unfolding view now one of verdant slopes and small, sheltered bays. High upon its northern flank stood a wooden lighthouse, lashed firmly to the ground, in front of which a trio of jagged monoliths jutted from the water—the Three Brothers. Old earthworks could be discerned on either side of the bay from which Russian defenders, including the crews of *Avrova* and *Dvina*, had repelled attacks by British and French ships under Admiral Price during the Crimean War.

The peninsula itself smoked and smoldered. At any given time it might grumble and rumble. Kamchatka was, and is, a land of active volcanoes and potential earthquakes. Bush tells us that Mt. Avatcha erupted in 1861, that in February of that year a strong quake inflicted widespread damage in the southern region. The place is situated on the western rim of the North Pacific's "ring of fire," along whose perimeter massive tectonic plates grind and shift.

But the scene was peaceful and surprisingly lush, with trees, foliage, and gardens greeting the eyes of the Americans as they were led by Mr. Fengler, a local fur merchant, to his house. All along the way the newcomers were greeted with shouted salutations from young Kamchadals, as the natives were called. Bush notes this was wholly unexpected, that "it was a pleasure to return their salutations . . . that this was a custom that ought to be introduced into countries pretending to much greater civilization."

In Fengler's comfortable home, pride of place was demonstrated by the center of domestic Russian culture, the samovar.

> In a moment's notice it yielded delicious draughts of Siberian nectar. The tea we drank in this country was unsurpassed. One sip was sufficient to remove all previously acquired prejudice against the beverage. It is the universal drink among all classes and is always kept in readiness for the visitor.

Major Abasa and his men remained in Petropavlovsk, making plans for their explorations, gathering every bit of useful information, and doing a little sightseeing. They were impressed by the monuments erected to North Pacific explorer-navigators Bering and La Perouse and amazed at the proliferation of wildflowers carpeting the hillsides—wild roses, tiger lilies, and "Solomon's seal" among them. And they were happy to discover a number of Americans at this distant location: Pierce, Hunter, Fronefield, and Dodd. While the first pair were quite content to stay put, James Dodd, for seven years a fur trapper in country, and Fronefield volunteered to join the expedition.

Initially, Abasa's plan was to travel to Gizhiga, tucked up into the Okhotsk Sea's northern coast, and make it his starting point for further explorations of the route of the line. But it was now too late in the season to risk a sea voyage. How were the hundreds of miles of little-known or unknown territory going to be reconnoitered? The major finally realized that he would have to break up his telegraph army squad and assign them specific areas. Bush and Mahood would go by ship to Nikolaevsk on the mouth of the Amur, then trek through Romanoff's "woody and

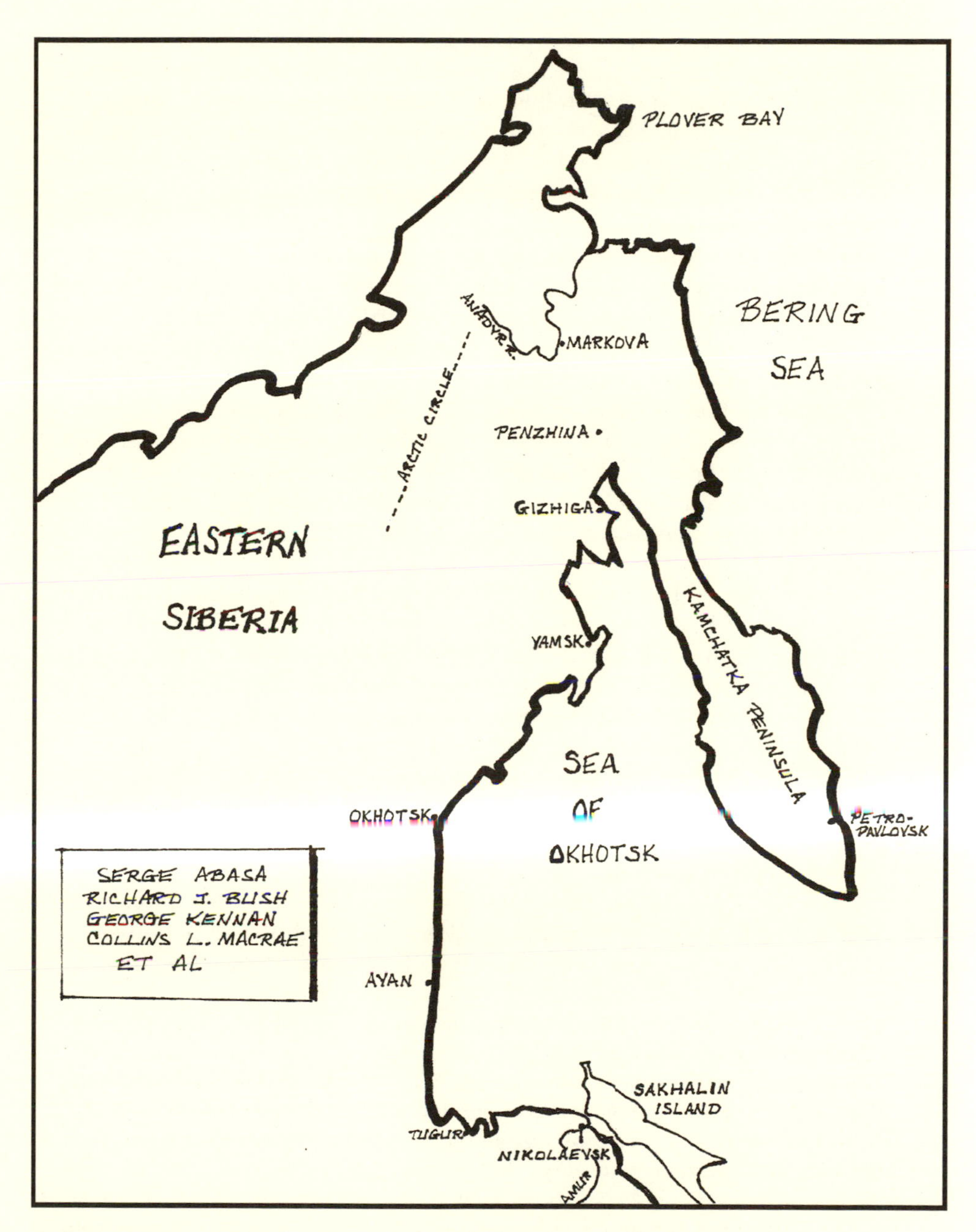

Map 8.1. Eastern Siberia, drawing by J. B. Dwyer.

morasty desert" a thousand miles northward to Okhotsk town. The major and Kennan would traverse the peninsula, then make a hard-left turn down to Gizhiga, where the pair, plus Dodd, would part company. Abasa assigned to himself the mission of exploring towards Okhotsk and a hoped-for rendezvous with Bush and Mahood. Kennan and Dodd were to proceed north-northwest up to Penzhina, then continue on in an attempt to establish contact with Macrae's Anadyr river party.[1]

The natural dangers awaiting the explorers were viewed and accepted as risks they were willing to take. These risks included encountering the potentially hostile Korak tribesmen inhabiting Kamchatka's northern sector. (Kennan's spelling is used here. The name of these natives is also spelled *Koriak* and *Koryak*.) In Kennan's words, "It was no pleasure excursion upon which we were about to enter." And it would be up to the exploring parties, traveling with guides and indigenous peoples, to subsist on what the country afforded them. Russian authorities at Petropavlovsk were highly skeptical about their chances at success. The supremely confident and resourceful Abasa shrugged off their attitude with a typical comment, "We'll show you what we can do." While plans matured for the peninsular transit, Bush and Mahood were preparing to sail west.[2]

On Friday, August 25, the day before they had to go back aboard the *Olga*, Bush and Mahood purchased proper clothing for their travels—kuklankers, torbassas, chazees, malachis, and archaniks: a knee-length, hooded garment made from two layers of reindeer skin; knee-length fur boots made from reindeer leg skins; reindeer, wolf, or dog fur socks; fur bonnets worn under the kuklanker hood; and black tippets made from Siberian squirrel tails to be carried between the teeth as protection for the lower face while heading into frigid winds. The first Americans to penetrate the interior of Okhotsk's western coast would be well protected against Siberian weather.

Their tobacco supplies fully stocked and armed with letters for various officials and others in Nikolaevsk, Bush and Mahood departed on a warm, pleasant day amidst heartfelt goodbyes from their comrades.

> The lofty volcanoes stood forth in all their majesty, attired in a gorgeous array of blue and silver, cleaving the bright blue firmament with their towering crests. The grass-covered slopes of the adjoining shore were still damp with morning dew, and the sun's slanting rays transformed it all into myriad sparkling gems. All nature seemed to have conspired in rendering this, our last glimpse of Avatcha Bay, unsurpassable in beauty.

The little brig coasted south around Kamchatka's acicular extremity through fog and tricky currents, seeking the passage between it and Paramushir, the northernmost Kuril island. On they went until August 29, when the lookout shouted the dread cry, "Breaker's ahead!" Surrounded on three sides by rocks against which boisterous surf splashed thirty feet skyward, *Olga* barely managed to escape destruction by adroit ship handling. The exclamations of relief were short-lived. As favorable winds died, strong currents began pushing the brig inexorably back towards the rocks. Surely all hands would have to abandon ship. Boats were being readied. Bush and Mahood had their sealskin bags packed and ready to go on deck. "There's a puff!" cried one of the sailors . . . then another; the wind increased and held, filling sails so *Olga* could sustain headway against the current and move out of harm's way. She was now halfway down the archipelago and able to navigate the Boussole Channel around Simushir Island, westward into the Okhotsk Sea. Ahead was La Perouse Strait, between Hokkaido and Sakhalin Island's southern tip, then a northern transit of the Gulf of Tartary (Tatar Strait today) to de Castries, 150 miles below Nikolaevsk on the Manchurian coast. At this place, named by the great French explorer Comte de la Perouse after his Minister of Marine, all ships awaited pilots or a tow to shepherd them through the shallow, constricted strait towards Nikolaevsk. Bush and Mahood, faced now with a choice between an indeterminate wait for their water passage or an overland trip of fifty miles to the Amur and a northward river voyage to their destination, chose the latter. Had they been able to obtain timely information by telegraph from Nikolaevsk, they might have decided to wait, but the line to de Castries, an extension of Romanoff's Amur River project, was down.

The first leg of their journey was on horseback over a corduroy road to the shores of Lake Kidzi. From there, they crossed in a flat-bottomed, square-sided boat ever in danger of capsizing, reached the far shore, traveled more cross-country, and finally, reached the banks of the Amur.

All along the way they were assisted by Cossack soldiery and indigenous Gilak tribesmen. The latter provided a unique libation, "brick tea." It consisted of pulverized tea plant leaves and stems mixed with bullock's blood, baked or dried into brick-shaped cakes, hence the name. Never mind how this sounds. They loved it.[3] They were now in Marinsk, two hundred miles away from Nikolaevsk. The seat of government for eastern Siberia was situated on the Amur's north bank where the mile-wide river begins its rush into the Tatar Strait after completing a west to east oxbow. Perry M. Collins had arrived here eight years earlier on the last stretch of his exploratory descent of the waterway. Arriving on July 11 aboard a government vessel in company with Imperial Navy Captain Fulyhelm, he paid his respects to Governor-General Admiral Kosakevitch, presenting letters from Muraviev to the man in charge of Siberia's maritime provinces. Afterwards, taking in the view before him, Collins was heartened to see the Stars and Stripes flying from the masts of several schooners and barks anchored in the river. Two of them, the *Lewis Perry* and *Behring*, represented the major commercial houses of Carlton and Burling, San Francisco, and W. H. Boardman and Company, Boston, eager to expand their Asian commerce. This is exactly what Collins had in mind, trade enhanced by world wiring telegraph.[4]

Bush and Mahood came to Nikolaevsk on September 15 aboard a borrowed barge.

> The left shore was a continuous meadow on which were stacked thousands of tons of hay; on the right, an abrupt range of hills. . . . [A]s we neared the town, the river's edge was lined with seines and fish traps, suggestive of the diet awaiting us.

They presented themselves and introductory letters to outgoing Governor-General Kosakevitch. The old admiral was still there, soon to be replaced by the well-traveled, multilingual Admiral Fulyhelm, Collins's former river trip companion. The town, with its rows of one-story log buildings, disappointed Bush's expectations, though the bustling water traffic of native *lotka* craft invigorated his interest.

The pair next visited the resident American commercial agent, Mr. Chase, in whose office were gathered more fellow countrymen. Among these businessmen was a Mr. Barr, who supervised the port's manufacturing center, the sawmills, foundry, and other enterprises. He had the distinction of being awarded a Russian gold medal for having transported two Philadelphia-built river steamers to Nikolaevsk. One of them, the *Amur*, was preparing for its maiden ascent when Collins was in town.

And while Bush and Mahood were made welcome everywhere they went, attending several social events, and introduced to "vodki, immense quantities of which are consumed," they failed to secure any useful information about their route of exploration. This and other matters resulted in a longer than expected stay.

Finally, by October 21, they were ready to depart. The decision to make Tugur, about two hundred miles to the west, their initial destination was based on discussions with Admiral Fulyhelm, his staff, and Mr. Lindholm, who operated the whaling station at that village tucked inside Okhotsk's serrated southern coast. Another European they met, Russian American Fur Company veteran and Polish national Mr. Swartz, volunteered to join the expedition as interpreter.

The country to be traversed was swampy, marshy terrain, so the one animal suited for journeying there, reindeer, had to be procured. Eventually, fourteen were rounded up and herded to a rendezvous point on the other side of Lake Orell, which had to be crossed first.

Before boarding the government's river steamer *Gonets*, Bush and Mahood packed only the essentials. The rest, they were told, would be provided when they reached Tugur. The essentials included, as was the case for all Western Union explorers, Colt pistols, double-barreled shotguns, and Sharp's carbines.

It was the steamer's first crossing of the shallow, twenty-mile-long lake that, in October, lay before them blanketed with snow. The *Gonets* worked its way ahead in stages at first, having to back off when impeded by the snow. After miles of slow progress, the crew was in a mood to give up, but Bush and Mahood urged them forward.

When we had reached the middle, a strong northerly wind arose, which tried the strength of our little steamer greatly, and, though her thin iron hull shook and yielded to the pressure of the waves like an India-rubber boat, she brought us safely to our destination.

It was a Gilak village where they expected to find one of their Cossacks, Yakov, with the reindeer. They were nowhere to be seen, and the villagers knew nothing about them. Mahood and Swartz were sent out to search for the missing and much-needed deer as the *Gonets* disappeared over the horizon. A short while later, Bush was just pitching his tent when he heard the searchers halooing from a distance. Coming into camp, Mahood reported that they had detected far away sounds but decided to fortify themselves before continuing ahead. None of the men had eaten anything substantial since morning and were happy to sit down to a meal of fried salmon provided by the Gilaks. Immediately afterwards, the reindeer search resumed. Many hours later, Mahood, tired and miserable from rowing the *lotka* in the rain, returned with the news that Yakov and the deer were ten versts (one verst=two-thirds of a mile) distant. It was a thoroughly soaked group of travelers that heard the shouts of "Alane, alane!" on October 24. They had acquired sufficient knowledge of Russian to know this meant their deer were in sight. Bush's long-imagined animals pulling Santa's sleigh, his expected vision, was at odds with reality as he viewed the "awkward, clumsy looking, mostly white animals one could have mistaken for cows at a distance."

On closer inspection he found them a "regular Falstaff's brigade" as far as uniformity was concerned; "some with brown backs, others with fine sets of antlers, still others missing horns." On the shoulders of the lead deer, clothed in layers of heavy fur, was Michael, a Tungustian herdsman Bush and Mahood had met back in Nikolaevsk, member of one of the nomadic Tungu tribes of eastern Siberia who followed migrating reindeer and depended on the animals for their existence.

The bucks of the herd had been trained for riding; the rest served as pack animals. Pack and riding saddles were quite similar: buckskin pads stuffed with moss or hair joined together with curved deer horns. The riding saddle's pads were wider and stood out more from the animal's shoulders. There were no stirrups or any kind of foot support. Halters were made exactly like their American counterparts but from seal thongs or braided strands of buckskin.

October 26 marked the first day of the westward trek on deer back; actually riders rode on the reindeers' shoulders due to their weak backs. A small group of natives gathered round to watch Bush and Mahood and Swartz attempt saddle-borne positions.

> To mount a reindeer is by no means a simple operation for the beginner. Great care must be taken not to injure the beast. Besides, it requires a good deal of agility which I, for one, did not possess.

They were instructed to take the halter in the right hand, placing that same hand on the saddle, while resting the left hand on the top of the five-foot staff or "polka." Then they were to place the right foot on the saddle, gain a balance point, and jump onto the saddle. This was easier said than done. Too forceful or too weak a jump landed one back on the ground. Once aboard, the rider then had to continuously lean left and right to counteract the swaying gait of the deer.

Swartz's first attempt was too athletic and he flew over the deer's saddle. Mahood had a good start, but as soon as his right foot touched the saddle, his deer started off and he fell. We don't know how tall or short Bush was, but he tells us that he couldn't kick high enough to get his foot over the saddle. After four failures, he had to be lifted into his saddle. He notes that the Gilak children were especially amused at the impromptu comedy routine.

Once under way, progress became a matter of staying in the saddle. By the time they reached their campsite for the night, the trio was averaging one fall per verst. Bush marveled at the expertise with which their Tungu companions dismounted upon reaching the campsite, cut down about thirty slim larch branches, planting them in a twelve-foot diameter circle so that the ends were all self-supporting. Over this framework their tent was spread. Boughs were strewn on the ground for natural mattresses.

Temperatures continued unseasonably warm, and rainy weather persisted, at times forcing the men to dismount so their deer wouldn't become enmired. All were surprised, emerging from their tents November 1, to find the ground covered with snow.

> At 1:30 p.m. we came in sight of a range of mountains higher than any we had seen before in the vicinity of the Amur. They were about 15 versts south of our trail, and attained an elevation of nearly three thousand feet.

Bush was probably seeing the foothills of the Dzhagdy range. Three days later, a foot of snow covered the ground, making for much improved traveling conditions. Temperatures were averaging a near perfect 20 degrees farenheit. Nevertheless, it took them a week to reach Tugur, crossing the dreary, mossy Sololoucan barrens and fording several rivers. Finally their deer crunched across crusted ground as they approached the whaling station.

> [The ground] was covered with a thick coating of beautiful frost work which prevented the deer from slipping. This frost work carpet was superb in its beauty, consisting of innumerable, transparent, leaf-like crystals standing on edge, most of them two inches in height and sparkling in the brilliant sunlight like a sea of gems.

Tugur had been fortified by exploring Cossacks in the seventeenth century as those daring adventurers expanded Russia's domain to North Pacific shores. The reindeer riders were looking forward to the provisions promised by Lindholm in the face of contrary information offered by neighboring Tungustians that the station had been deserted. They were, unfortunately, correct. On the main door of the station house was a note stating that, due to lack of supplies, all personnel had gone to Mamga, another whaling station one hundred versts away. From both of them, coastal whaling was practiced, natives going out in skin boats to harpoon the mammals, row them inshore, then cut them apart.

From an old woman living in one of the nearby huts, they learned of a Yakut village only five versts distant. Though the dwelling they entered upon arrival there was miserable looking, the venison steaks and milk presented to them might well have been ambrosia. Refreshed and energized, the men set out again for the whaling station, where they were greeted by about fifty men, women, and children, mostly Yakuts, whom Bush describes as "mild, inoffensive people, industrious, ingenious, and gifted with natural business tact. They might, with propriety, be called the Yankees of Siberia." Their dress was a mixture of Russian peasant and the skin clothing of other tribes: a large, gray cloth overcoat, well-tanned buckskin pants, and heavy, tanned buckskin boots. The dwelling Bush thought miserable was the Yakut's native abode, the yourt. Built of small split logs standing on end and sloping inward, its roof supported by heavy posts and the whole banked over by clay, the structure reminded the Civil War veteran of a Mississippi ironclad. A small, deerskin-lined door provided access to a ten-by-twenty-foot square interior, whose principle feature was the *chual,* or fireplace-chimney made of long, light poles bound together and plastered over with concave layers of baked, hardened clay. Two small apertures admitted light. Some Yakuts covered the openings with glass obtained from whalers, though most had transluscent fish skins affixed with wet snow that froze on application. Others had ice windows, known to last for months during Siberian winters.

To the extent possible, the men replenished their provisions, which now included thirty-six pounds of fresh beef. They also bought eight new reindeer after hard bargaining with the local headman, with more to be brought in by Vasilly and Eoff, the two Tungustians who were to serve as guides-herders.

On November 15, with the thermometer reading 10 degrees below zero, the explorers ventured forth again, heading toward the Uda River, which flows into the Okhotsk at its southwest corner. For several hours they followed the beach until a strong north wind, vanguard of a snow and ice storm, forced them to detour inland a while until conditions permitted a return to Okhotsk's shore. Two days later, as they were looking at the four-thousand-foot range known as the Arla Hills, deepening snow began hampering their deer's progress. Snowshoes seemed to be the answer, but they had none. Eoff, however, chopped down a tree near the camp and began hacking off branches with his hatchet to make some. The finished shoes were five feet long and ten inches wide, with very thinly hewn wood bent upwards at the toe. The snow was now so heavy that one of the men had to slog ahead, breaking trail for the reindeer to follow. But after a while, "riding [was] generally impossible, and we had to flounder through paths made by the deer [meaning] we had to take longer than normal steps with high, long strides."

Bush's mount, though a very spirited animal, had shorter legs than his cervine brethren, and as he descended a ridge, his rider realized he had lost sight of the rest of the party.

> By this time my deer had become frantic at being left alone; it was impossible to restrain him. We had gone about 200 yards when both of us fell, and another long walk succeeded. After climbing three trees in attempts to sight my companions and falling out of each one, I finally overtook the train an hour later. . . . Should anyone be desirous of becoming proficient in the use of words and phrases suitable only for such occasions, I heartily recommend a winter trip across the Arla Hills on a short-legged deer.

Their immediate destination, chosen by Eoff, was Solavoff's yourt, which was reached on November 21. Bush and Mahood and Swartz were informed that the great man had provided vital assistance to the Russians during the Crimean War in the form of a large herd of cattle. For this patriotic deed, the tsar sent Solavoff a coat profusely decorated with gold and silver lace and fringe. It only wanted proper measurements, being many sizes too large for its honored wearer. Here they soujourned for several days. Twelve pounds of beef had been added to their provisions when they set out again on a trail featuring numerous wolf tracks. The natives assured them that the wolves rarely attacked men, and that, this time of year, they prowled the seashore, subsisting on the carcasses of seals or whales that drifted ashore.

In due course they gained the summit of the Tela hills. Bush described the panorama that lay before them:

> The view from the summit was superb, though desolate in the extreme. On our right lay the Arla valley, patched with white barrens, through which that river and the Torum wind to the sea. On our right lay the Tela valley, extending to the Uda River, far to the west. Looking out over the valley we beheld Elbow Island of the whalers, while to the northwest lay Oudskoi bay, bounded on the farther side by the high, ragged, snow-covered peaks of the Dzhugdzhur range.

Anglicized as the Juggur Mountains, the massive cordilleria stretched all the way north to Okhotsk town. According to Bush, "Our friends in Nikolaevsk predicted we would never emerge from their mazy, intricate depths."

Camping the following evening on the five-hundred-foot-wide Uda River at the village of Algasee, the men had finished their tea and sat around the fire smoking their pipes when, to their amazement, a Tungustian lad of eight began singing the American tune "John Brown." Though the words were mangled, the air was unmistakable. Musing on how this could be, Bush decided the boy had learned the song from American whalers who used to frequent Oudskoi and Tugur Bays. The next leg of the journey, eighty versts to Oudskoi, would have to be made with dogsleds.

The eastern Siberian sled, or *narta*, was eight to ten feet long and two feet wide, with a railing on either side to keep the load in place. Its four-inch-wide runners were constructed of the same material as the sled itself, of white birch or another suitable wood. Rawhide was used to secure the joints. A strong, bow-shaped piece of wood was attached to sled front to which seal thongs were tied for hitching up the dog team. Whips were never used on the animals. Drivers carried *ostles*, four-foot-long wooden staffs spiked at their lower ends that were used to brake and maintain equilibrium when under way.

After the sleds were loaded and frozen-fish dog food packed up, fur blankets and bedding was spread on top "making quite a comfortable couch for us to lie upon." Off they went! The teams were excited and eager to move out and went dashing down the trail in the dim twilight, barely missing huge trees.

Racing beneath low branches, Bush's team suddenly vanished and the next thing he knew, the sled was plunging ten feet down to the snow and ice-covered river Uda, which they followed to Oudskoi. They arrived at the small Russian outpost several days later, much to the amazement of its inhabitants whose only contact with the outside world was a yearly visit by a Russian supply steamer. One of the inhabitants happened to be an American whaler, Captain Hutchinson, who knew Swartz from their days as Russian-American Company employees. Their hearty greeting completed, the men were all introduced to the *ispravnik*, or chief government official, who at thirty years of age looked like a drinker. "Consuming vodki figured largely in the social enjoyments of Oudskoi society." Bush, Mahood, and Swartz hardly had their coats off before a bottle was produced and "piat nadsat carplets"—fifteen drops of vodka—were being drunk all round. Russian etiquette required them to toss back at least one glassful, but the *ispravnik* set a pace they declined to match. Enter the local priest, a long-haired and robed gentleman, who surprised the company, Bush tells us, "with the amazing agility with which he emptied glass after glass that would have done credit to any Bacchanalian association."

The travelers were stuck in Oudskoi for a month, awaiting more reindeer for the journey north to Ayan, so they had the opportunity to experience Russian customs first-hand, among them the *vechourka*, or dance. Held in the house of one of the village Cossacks, with a lively Cossack orchestra providing the music, the event occurred in a room with benches arranged along either side. Tea drunk and a national song played, everyone was encouraged to stand and sing, at which point the ladies tossed their handkerchiefs on the partner of their choice, challenging him to dance. The Americans found themselves hauled onto the floor, along with Swartz, where, Bush tells us, "I participated in the longest song and dance of my life." Suddenly, the band stopped playing. All the ladies turned to their partners, faces lifted upwards expectantly for the kisses that were then bestowed. This routine was repeated, with diluted vodka drunk after every second dance, tea after the fourth. The hardened travelers retired at eleven o'clock that evening, totally exhausted.

Bush and his companions took advantage of their stay by practicing snow shoeing, using the polka as a stabilizer and as a brake when descending. These were the type of snowshoe that had flat wooden bottoms soled with hairy animal leg skins that aided forward gliding and prevented backsliding.

Finally, by December 20, the men were ready to recommence their explorations, sixteen reindeer having been obtained from neighboring Tungustians. Supplies were completely replenished and included beef, sugar, tea, and *sukarie*, black bread dried into small cakes, plus Yakut butter and frozen milk in blocks. Snowshoes, fur socks, and new boots were also packed away. Ahead lay unknown territory, even to the natives, who always took a roundabout route to Ayan, by way of Yakutsk, a mere 480 miles to the west-northwest. After showing doubtful Tungustians their compasses and explaining how they could navigate by them, and offering substantial inducements, the men managed to convince several natives to accompany them. Bush admits that even he,

Mahood, and Swartz harbored serious misgivings about the likely success of exploring a coastal *terra incognita*. They did, however, secure useful information from a Tungustian hunter who knew of a serviceable trail about two hundred versts northward to his village.

Bush and Swartz reconnoitered ahead on snowshoes once the party reached Okhotsk's shores. Frozen water as far as the eye could see ended in nearshore clumps and masses of ice above which rose a steep cliff featuring a fifteen-foot ice shelf. Fifteen versts of tortuous travel and several pairs of broken snowshoes later, the men reached the beginning of the hunter's trail. Christmas 1865 found them proceeding up the Goram River into ever more mountainous country.

This river winds through an immense chasm; on both sides, high, rugged, mountains rise thousands of feet. Their bases are clothed with dense forests of larch, their summits bald and snow clad. In many places the river bed is bordered by high cliffs and frowning precipices to pass which we had to drag our deer over the smooth ice.

They had lost the hunter's trail. Frigid temperatures and knifing winds foreshadowed possible poorgaw storms. Deer food had run out and they were spending more and more energy pushing and pulling them along. Coming upon what looked like probable feeding ground for the deer, the men found only charred remains of forests and undergrowth. Respite from this purgatory came on the twenty-eighth and they let their deer feed for two hours while they, their underclothing having become damp, had to engage in violent exercise to prevent that inner layer from freezing. Bush records his dislike for these calisthenics because he had sprained his ankle the previous day. At the following evening's campsite, he tells us, his companions were virtually unrecognizable; beards and mustaches were frozen over, eyebrows and eyelashes frosted with ice, "making us look more like a troop of patriarchs on a pilgrimage than a band of young explorers." By this time they had developed a practiced routine of pitching a tent, getting a fire going, the tea brewing and their pipes aglow. Then they consumed a meal of boiled deer meat or beef, black bread, and butter.

On December 31 they were atop the Juggurs, eastern Siberia's highest mountains. Their ridge marked the main divide for eastward- and westward-flowing rivers. The view was both magnificent and discouraging, revealing seemingly impassable terrain in every direction. After descending into a wide, shallow, wooded basin and forging ahead several versts, they came across fresh deer tracks. A short while further on, a trail revealed itself. Their deer practically charged down it and into a Tungustian encampment, the hunter's home village. New Year's Day was celebrated with a change of clothes and the opening of a can of roast turkey that had been buried in their provisions. That evening nature treated them to the sight of a magnificent display of the *aurora borealis*. But, most welcome of all, they learned from a villager that, if they only retraced the course of a stream Bush and Swartz had noticed the previous Wednesday, they would reach Ayan.

Two-and-a-half weeks later they did reach their destination, only to discover it almost totally abandoned. Nearby they found a yourt stuffed with hapless natives waiting for the mail courier from Yakutsk. And in the whaling station itself they met the two remaining inhabitants, Mr. Popoff, the *ispravnik*, and the last Russian-American Company employee, Mr. Sleigerstroff, residing in a surprisingly large, comfortable house. Here they were treated to excellent tea and Havana cigars and replenishment of provisions. However, they were warned severely against their proposed attempt to journey directly up the coast. Even the hardiest of native hunters, they were told, had failed to penetrate the country. But Bush and the others were determined to continue their northward explorations. They were happy that their one remaining Cossack, Ivan, agreed to accompany them. As had been the case in Oudskoi, they were forced to remain in the village until more deer were procured. Not until the first week of February were they able to get under way, having hired an extra Tungustian to break trail for the deer. Through deep snows, narrow gorges, over ridges and the Juggur Mountains for the second time they rode and snowshoed. Though the going was rough, the extreme physical exertion was now something to which they had become enured. And as Bush relates, the wide-open spaces offered singular opportunities:

> We enjoyed perfect freedom. Cold formalities are abandoned and a person displays the generous free impulses of his nature, unfettered by customs and etiquette. Many times a party of bearded men might have been seen tumbling about in deep snow or making the woods ring with hideous howls and noises without fear of odious comparisons. Often at night, emerging from our tent into the still, clear atmosphere, we whooped and shouted, pausing to hear the echo as it bounded from mountain to mountain, finally losing itself among the loftiest peaks.

Sober matters also occupied their thoughts. What if one of them became seriously ill or had a bad accident? It was decided that a stretcherlike contrivance would be borne by two deer, one following the other. For the most part, they trusted in their youth and fitness, the pure cold air, and vigorous exercise to see them through.

February 13 found them camped in misty conditions amidst what they thought was mostly level ground. But the rising sun, dispelling mists, revealed the roseate peak of a distant mountain. Learning from their native companions that it had no name, they decided to call it Bulkley Mountain. It was, in fact, the eastern terminus of a high range running westward to form the northern boundary of the large basin they had been traversing since crossing the Juggurs.

February 20 brought them to a Yakut village whose "superior and very domestic" inhabitants lived in more spacious, much cleaner yourts than the Tungustians. Here, Bush, Mahood, and Swartz secured fresh reindeer for the last leg of their journey, reaching Okhotsk on March 2.

> Never was a devout Mussulman, on his approach to Mecca, more elated at the prospect of fulfilling his life's dream and terminating his pilgrimage than I was at the sight of Okhotsk. . . . [T]he distance was not over 1200 miles, but the time consumed and obstacles overcome made it seem three times as great.

The town itself was a jumble of thirty houses and one church, home to some three hundred Russians, Cossacks, and Yakuts. In one of the houses, Abasa greeted the explorers with news that, after waiting two weeks for them, he had traveled over four hundred miles west to Yakutsk to hire laborers, then returned to Okhotsk. He was now preparing to go back to Gizhiga, where he had left Kennan and Dodd.

When on March 15 the major asked Bush if he would like to join him for the return trip, he could not have been happier. He didn't think he would miss the rigors and adventures of winter travel in frozen wastes, but he did. Besides, this time they would go by *pavoshkas*, long, narrow sleds thickly lined with furs that had semicircular covers for the passenger, bundled snugly beneath those furs. The driver, who sat forward completely exposed to the elements, was in command of a twenty-dog team. In eastern Siberia, however, comfort is a highly relative concept.

The morning of March 17 was darker and milder than usual. The lead driver looked at the skies and warned Abasa that a poorgaw was imminent. Soon, its steady, violent winds began blowing. That afternoon the sled train was facing a high, mountain ridge. As a body, the sled drivers begged the major to stop at the nearby yourts. Abasa refused. Employing his distinct version of foul language and threatening the use of his Cossacks, he forced them to continue. It soon became apparent even to the iron-willed major, amidst white-out conditions and sleds whacking into trees and other obstacles, that a halt must be called. When the lead driver informed him that he was lost, Abasa gave orders to stop. Suddenly, the winds abated. Abasa sent some men ahead on snowshoes to reconnoiter. Bush and the others began to haul and drag the sleds up the ridge, doing their imitations of dog teams. Shouts from the scouts told them the ridge top was near; gaining it they found themselves facing a downhill run on the sheltered lee of the slope.

There followed a heedless, headlong descent, *pavoshkas* careening near the brinks of fifty-foot precipices, then into a narrow gorge where the snow was one hundred feet deep, blown there from neighboring summits. By eight o'clock that evening they were grateful to have survived the wild, dangerous ride that almost claimed several sleds and dog teams and were looking forward to the warmth of Yakut yourts.

Their next objective was Yamsk, lying to the east on the Pyagina Peninsula in Shelikov Bay. Enroute they encountered a new tribal group, the Lamuts who, though resembling Tungustians, relied on fish for their diet, though reindeer were plentiful enough to meet the needs of the exploring party. The local chiefs were willing to sell Abasa as many reindeer as he needed but did not want them used to build a telegraph line.

> The major explained it to them, telling them it would consist of a simple line of poles extending through the country with a small wire stretched over the top. Still skeptical, they were told how they would benefit from the forts and stations that would be built to support and maintain the line. One of them then asked which direction would the line run. On being told he became very gloomy. The pall was broken when another asked how far apart would they be, and, upon being told, they all cheered up, for they believed it would be a solid line that would obstruct their normal travel routes.

The party reached Yamsk on March 24. Nine days later they were in Gizhiga, the seat of government for northeastern Siberia and site of the annual rendezvous of regional fur trappers and traders. Its log buildings were well constructed and spacious, some having carpeting and wallpaper. Bush notes that its people were "intelligent and industrious, much given to nightly entertainments." The inhabitants were focusing that industriousness on preparations for the coming celebration of Easter. And when they weren't doing that, some of the residents strolled down to the riverbank, where large swings hung from trees.

> They were large, each capable of holding a dozen people. They were propelled by Cossacks in their gray uniforms and the natives sang their melodious airs while swinging back and forth.

Not quite the scene one imagines when thinking about eastern Siberia.[5]

The three exploring parties were reunited in Gizhiga, relating their adventures to one another, celebrating the fact that the entire route of the line had been reconnoitered. Kennan and Dodd, along with Abasa and his Cossack, Vushine, had begun their Kamchatka Peninsula "ascent" September 4, 1865. Up its volcanic spine they went, first on horseback, then in Kamchadal boats, lastly on sleds pulled by reindeer,

Figure 8.1. Gizhiga, drawing by J. B. Dwyer; from the original by Richard J. Bush.

coming into Gizhiga November 26. Kennan was much impressed with the natural, though sometimes stark, beauty of the peninsula and, like his colleague Bush, could become rapturous.

> It was a warm, beautiful Indian summer's day; a peculiar stillness and Sabbath-like quality seemed to pervade all Nature. The leaves of the scattering birches and alders along the trail hung motionless in the warm sunshine, the drowsy cawing of crows upon a distant larch came to our ears with a strange distinctness, and we even imagined we could hear the regular throbbing of the surf upon the far-away coast. A faint murmurous hum of bees was in the air, and a rich, fruity fragrance came up from the purple clusters of blueberries which our horses crushed underfoot.

But no matter how appealing the pastoral scenes or description-defying the panoramas, Major Abasa remained focused and impatient, perforating the air with machine gun bursts of profanity. His favorite expletive was "Chort!" which he delivered so that the recipient felt as if a nail was being driven into his heart. Kennan tells us that he was rivaled in his explosive virtuosity by the party's chief driver, Maximof, whose language "would have excited the envy and admiration of the most profane trooper in the army."

Two incidents marked the journey. One was Abasa's severe illness, which rendered him delirious at times and lasted over a week. The other was a breakneck gallop of thirty miles along a beach, racing the oncoming tide to gain reentry to their trail at its other end. Halfway across, their way was blocked by what appeared in the closing distance to be bears. They stopped and readied their rifles as the creatures drew near. Suddenly, Vushine straightened up as they crouched behind some rocks shouting "Loode, they are people!" Natives dressed in fur coats and pants approached yelling "Don't shoot" in Russian. Remounting their horses, the party continued the race, which they won with ten minutes to spare.

In Gizhiga, the recovered Abasa formulated further plans. Since Macrae, who was supposed to have rendezvoused with them earlier, never arrived, Abasa dispatched Kennan and Dodd towards Anadyrsk, eight hundred miles away, to find out what had happened to the Anadyr River party. The major would travel to Okhotsk to link up with Bush and Mahood. With full cooperation from Gizhiga's *ispravnik,* who ordered six of his Cossacks to transport the men by dogsleds to the Korak village of Shestakova, where more sleds and teams would await them, Kennan and Dodd left on December 13 for their journey northward.

> Our short stay in Shestakova was dismal and lonesome beyond expression. It began to storm furiously about noon on the 20th, and the violent winds swept up such tremendous clouds of snow from the great steppe north of the village, that the whole earth was darkened as if by an eclipse.

They reached Penzhina, a small grouping of log houses, yourts, and four-legged structures called *bologans,* on December 29, 1865. After gathering information on telegraph-pole lumber and hiring sixteen men to cut it, Kennan and Dodd continued their search. Three weeks into the new year they attained their objective. Anadyrsk contained about two hundred people living in four small villages, Markova being the central one, whose log houses had blocks of ice for windows.

Inquiries concerning the whereabouts of their missing comrades brought the pair news from Chukchi natives that a small band of white men had been landed by "fire ship" or steamer the previous fall.[6] Three months into the new year they heard the story first-hand after Macrae and A. S. Arnold straggled into Markova.

Collins L. Macrae and his exploring party had been landed by the *Milton Badger* inside the mouth of the Anadyr River in August 1865. They had just enough time to bring their stores ashore and construct their "hibernation den" before winter imposed its icy reign. The only wood in sight was of the drift variety along the riverbank, so they dug a five foot deep, nine foot by eighteen foot pit framed with drift logs and pine boughs. Outside of these, they made a sod and dirt embankment. Their

Figure 8.2. Headquarters, Markova (Anadyrsk), drawing by J. B. Dwyer; from the original by Richard J. Bush.

roof consisted of the few boards they were able to obtain from the ship. With their cooking stove in place, ample provisions stowed away, and sufficient fuel at hand, their exploring whaleboat nearby, the men believed they were ready to face the worst. No sooner had they hibernated when violent winds accompanied by heavy snows blasted the already bleak Siberian landscape.

Little by little they were sealed off by surrounding ice. They were five men on an unknown shore in eastern Siberia surrounded by a reputedly hostile tribe, the Chukchis. Not a pleasant prospect when their mission was to proceed to the head of the Anadyr and then, if possible, work their way down the Okhotsk Sea to link up with Major Abasa's party. Not having any winter transportation, this, of course, was impossible. So Macrae decided they had to hunker down and await contact with local natives. In due course a band of Chukchis arrived, and friendly relations were established. Their chief, Okakrae, after being made to understand that the men wished to ascend the river, told them that he would return with deer in several moons. Macrae's attempts to buy the animals outright failed. During early winter, Macrae and Robinson decided to walk to the Chukchi village twenty-five miles away, only to find it deserted. Though tired and hungry, they had no choice but to retrace

Figure 8.3. A Yakut yourt, drawing by J. B. Dwyer; from the original by Richard J. Bush.

their steps back to camp. Nature conspired to make the trip an ordeal as a slicing wind cut through their clothing, threatening to solidify damp undergarments. Headway was nearly impossible on the slick footing. By nightfall they were stumbling along. Robinson declared his intention to stop and freeze to death; he could not go on. Macrae would have none of it and, taking Robinson's revolver and carbine, helped him to his feet. Onward they struggled. Wind and cold increased, followed by that deadly drowsiness from which no man awakes. Supporting one another, persevering beyond human endurance, the pair at long last reached camp. Inside their burrow, anxious comrades tended the half-dead men, appalled at the thick coating of frost beneath their garments. Robinson did not fully recover for three weeks.

Okakrae finally appeared. However, he informed Macrae that he could only take two of the party on the Anadyr trip. Since Arnold understood Russian, he accompanied his boss on what was to be an unecessarily long journey, prolonged by Chukchi intransigence and mistrust; they thought the pair might be spies and did not want to incur the wrath of Russian officials. On several occasions Macrae and Arnold seriously considered resorting to firearm coercion but desisted. Sixty-four days after leaving the Chukchi village they walked into Anadyrsk, where they were delighted to find the comrades they had left behind, plus Kennan, Dodd, Bush, and Mahood.[7] There followed a welcome hiatus of days filled with dance parties, card playing, sled rides, and snowshoe excursions as the explorers restored themselves and waited for spring.

In April, Bush was appointed superintendent of the Gizhiga to Bering Sea section of the line, with Macrae in charge of the Anadyr River district. Abasa ordered both men to Anadyrsk, there to descend the river to its mouth and meet company ships expected to arrive shortly. The major, accompanying them, would stay in town and hire fifty or sixty native laborers to begin the construction of station houses and the cutting and distribution of poles along the river.

Kennan and Dodd remained in Gizhiga with very little to do. The former was optimistic.

> The country, although by no means favorable to the construction of a telegraph, presented no obstacles which energy and perseverance could not overcome, and, as we reviewed our winter's work, we felt satisfied that the enterprise in which we were engaged, if not altogether an easy one, held out at least a fair prospect of success.

Abasa returned to Gizhiga in May, having hired the laborers, and, with Kennan and Dodd, rented a log house overlooking the Gizhiga River. From there, Kennan became a close observer of Arctic summer with its constant daylight. Yet nature's clock was still working and there was a "strange, mysterious stillness pervading heaven and earth like that which accompanies a solar eclipse." A song sparrow in a nearby thicket dreamt that it was morning and "broke into an unconscious trill of melody." Waking, it uttered a few perplexed peeps, then went back to sleep. By the end of June, trees were in full bloom, along with primroses, cinquefoil, cowslips, buttercups, valerian, and Labrador tea flowers. Bird life that would have kept ornithologists awake for days on end filled the skies and populated the rocky coastline.

On June 18 the W. H. Boardman company brig *Hallie Jackson* entered the gulf, bringing the first news from the outside world the men had had in eleven months. Though she brought no word of Western Union ships, she did bring stores the men had left at Petropavlovsk the previous fall as well as cargoes of those three essential items—tobacco, tea, and sugar.

In mosquito-maddened July, most Gizhiga residents moved to their summer fishing stations along the river. Well-rested telegraph army officers chafed at their enforced inactivity.

Cries of "Soodna, soodna!" rent the air on August 14. A ship had been sighted. All eyes focused on the bark with an American flag flying from her peak. Her first boat ashore brought Captain Sutton of the *Clara Bell*, two months out of San Francisco, carrying men and supplies for line construction.[8]

That same month Bush's party had reached their objective on the Anadyr and were waiting for a company ship to arrive. Getting there had taken three months of sometimes very tough going, but the men hardly expected anything less based on previous experiences.

It had begun April 18, 1866, as a dogsled journey. Several days later they were in trackless tundra.

> The dreary solitude and awful silence that reigned over this rigid, lifeless expanse produced a feeling of strangeness I could not overcome—a feeling that some dread calamity was about to befall us. I felt as if I could only see some motion, a fluttering leaf, anything against the brilliant, blinding snow, what a relief it would be. But no, there it lay, cold, stark, stiff and motionless, the very corpse of Nature.

Into Korak country they went, Bush describing the three different types of natives as "civilized," "settled," and "reindeer" Koraks. Or, those living in coastal villages, those living in permanent abodes along Penzhina Gulf, and the nomadic tribe that herded and lived off reindeer.

Poorgaws accompanied them to Penzhina just as their dog food was running out. The small settlement of fifty souls was four days' hard travel from Anadyrsk, but Bush selected a different route, one along which a telegraph line could be built. He and Macrae would go east towards the Myan River, a large tributary of the Anadyr which flowed north, and explore to its mouth. By choosing this route, Bush had picked a region that was largely unknown, even to the natives. Choosing the best dogs from their train, Bush and Macrae set out, with Vassily their Cossack and their drivers, steering for the Polpol River, which they ascended to a reindeer Korak encampment. The explorers found them to be superior to the others of their tribe, "ignorant of the tricks and deceptions of their settled brethren, characterized by generous, unsuspecting natures."

May was a month that Bush and Macrae had eagerly anticipated, with its blue skies and balmy breezes, or at least the version of this clement weather one might expect at 64 degrees north latitude. But no, they were forced to warm themselves by dearly imagined visions of May as relentless poorgaw winds roared and shrieked "as if bent upon the destruction of every living thing in its path."

On the fifth they were in wooded country following a branch of the Myan they dubbed the Abasa River when they came to the three hundred-foot-wide main river, the deep snow along its banks marked with fresh bear tracks. Climbing a bluff that afternoon Bush was encouraged by the sight of numerous trees which could produce sufficient poles for the entire line. Two days later a six-thousand-foot-high elevation that Macrae recognized, and which they named Telegraph Bluff, came into view. They had twenty-four hours to go. On May eighth they arrived at Anadyrsk.

> Our journey had been severe, but our discoveries had far exceeded our expectations and pointed to the Myan and Abasa rivers as the natural course of the line.

In the main village of Markova, Bush and Macrae found fellow expeditioneers Dodd, Robinson, Harder, and Smith. Abasa was with the local *ispravnik* and informed Bush that he was returning to Gizhiga the next day. Before doing so, he approved Bush's plan to begin cutting and distributing poles along the Anadyr to have them in readiness should the expected supply ship arrive with wire, brackets, and insulators.

Not only did Bush plan to raft poles down the river, he intended to transport a dozen yourts to be erected at strategic sites for winter shelters. The boats to be used were *vetkas*, flat-bottomed, fifteen feet long and two feet wide, boards sealed with pitch and bound with deer sinews. The operator would sit in the bottom and propel the craft with a light, double-bladed paddle.

There followed a month of difficult travel, frustration, and hard work, with few poles being cut. The experience was capped by a return to Markova that required a dangerous final leg of thirty-six straight hours of travel over melting snows and river ice. As always, Bush the artist could be inspired by nature no matter the circumstances, and he describes the most beautiful sunset he had ever seen.

> The northern heavens were aglow with gorgeous displays of gold, crimson, purple, orange and numerous tints, blending into one harmonious whole and casting a luster of indescribable beauty over the cold, cheerless landscape. And then, a heavy thundercloud rolled majestically across the heavens, darting its forked tongues of vivid lightning athwart the variegated curtain of light suspended beyond.

By June 22 the rivers had subsided sufficiently to allow boat travel; Bush prepared to raft down the Anadyr. The water was high and fast, and a strong north wind threatened to shove the rafters onto the lee shore. Three versts downstream, Bush's *vetka* was thrown against the point of an island with great force, but the boat held together and their journey down the wild river continued. On the thirtieth they had ventured beyond the confluence of the Myan and Anadyr and into a mile-wide section of the latter, whose peaceful waters gave way several days later to boiling, rushing, island-crowded rapids. July 13 brought them to Macrae's old campsite, vandalized since last he saw it. The burrow they had dug was half-filled with water on which floated torn, rotten U.S.

Army blankets. Here they pitched a tent and proceeded to build a new log house at the site Bush named Camp Macrae. As hordes of Siberian mosquitoes made the men's lives wretched, they could yet find certain satisfaction in having completed their mission; all the yourt station houses had been erected and they were ready for the next stage of construction. There were now thirteen men at Camp Macrae, subsisting primarily on fish caught with seines made from horsehair. Their diet included deer meat after Macrae's old native friends, hearing of his return, brought some into camp. Then, an amazing coincidence occurred. On August 14, the same day the *Clara Bell*'s boats visited Gizhiga, a boat from the *George S. Wright*, carrying Whymper and Labonne, arrived at Camp Macrae. As described in an earlier chapter, Bush went back to the *Wright* and Plover Bay after stores for Macrae had been offloaded.[9]

Back at Gizhiga, Kennan was listening to Abasa demand explanations from Captain Sutton, who patiently told him that his ship had been unavoidably detained in Petropavlovsk. Asked "What steamer is that anchored beyond the *Clara Bell*?" the captain replied, "The *Variag*, a Russian corvette." "But, what is she doing here?" "Why, major, you should know. She has been detailed by your government to assist in line construction. And she brings an American correspondent and a Russian commissioner."

A loaded bark, a steam corvette, a correspondent and a commissioner. It certainly looked like business and we congratulated ourselves and each other upon the improving prospects of the Siberian Division.

Morale was further heightened by the arrival of long-delayed mail from home and reports from Colonel Bulkley on progress of the enterprise to date, as well as the men, ships, and supplies transitting the Bering Sea. They would get no assistance, however, from the *Variag*. At twenty-two feet her draft was too deep for Okhotsk Sea operations; she could come no closer than fifteen miles to its coast. Major Abasa decided to wait in Gizhiga, delaying a planned labor-hiring trip to Yakutsk, until the supply ships *Palmetto* and *Onward* arrived. Instead, he detailed Mr. Arnold to take charge of the five constructors who came aboard the *Clara Bell* and travel to Yamsk to hire pole-cutting work gangs there. He sent the *Variag* to Okhotsk with stores and dispatches for Mahood, who had been living alone there for five months. Presumably, the offshore waters were deep enough to allow the corvette to navigate them.

The *Palmetto*, accompanied by the Russian supply steamer *Sakhalin*, arrived September 19. Her power source and draft allowed the *Sakhalin* to cross the bar into the river's mouth. A strengthening storm produced a close-reefed topsail gale from the southeast that sent a heavy, rolling sea into the wide open gulf, imperiling the *Palmetto*, which would have to await another high tide if she did not perish beforehand. By the twenty-third her sheet anchor cable had broken. There was no alternative for Captain Arthur. He would have to weigh anchor, get under way, and stand directly in for the river's mouth. She came in nicely at first, then about a half-mile from the lighthouse she ran aground in seven feet of water, with spray breaking over her quarterdeck as she was bounced again and again against the bottom. High tide rescued her from being bashed to bits and lifted her further into the river's mouth. The receding tide revealed no more damage than some copper sheathing sections missing and her false keel gone. With her decks canted at a forty-five-degree angle and the ship on her beam ends, offloading her vital cargo was going to be difficult, but with welcomed help from the *Sakhalin*'s boats and crew, most of it was brought ashore. Not until October 12 did the *Palmetto* cut her kedge anchor cables, furl her sails, and recross the bar out to sea.

Besides her cargo, the *Palmetto* brought fourteen men and their construction tools. Abasa, having gone back to Yakutsk to hire more men and buy three hundred horses, left Kennan in charge. He sent Mr. Sandford and twelve men with axes, snowshoes, and dogsleds into the Gizhiga River woods to cut poles and build station houses between the town and the shores of Penzhina Gulf; and he sent Mr. Wheeler with a native work gang, six sled loads of provisions and axes, plus dispatches for Abasa, to Mr. Arnold at Yamsk. Kennan now followed Abasa's last order and prepared to travel the first winter road to Anadyrsk to learn what had happened to Bush's party and whether or not the supply ship ever arrived at the river's mouth. There followed what Kennan describes as the "most lonely, most dismal expedition of my Siberian experience," for he went without any fellow Americans, and after several days, without his one Cossack. It went even slower than normal due to deep, soft snow and shortened days. Frigid temperatures froze soup and other foods before they could be ingested. On reaching the town of Penzhina in late November, Kennan fully expected Bush to have sent word there per prior agreement. There was none. He feared the worst. His grim presentiment only deepened when a priest from Anadyrsk arrived, replying to Kennan's "Where's Bush?" with "Bokh yevo zniet" (God only knows). He told Kennan he had last seen Bush in July at the mouth of the Anadyr and that there was famine in that region. Assuming the worst, Kennan purchased sufficient dog food to last five teams forty days; he convinced the local Korak chief to drive his reindeer herd to Anadyrsk to feed the local populace. He also sent natives to Gizhiga to alert the *ispravnik* about the famine and dispatched a letter to Dodd telling him to transport all available provisions to Penzhina, then started for the blighted town himself on November 20.[10]

When we left Bush in chapter 6 he and his men and the crew of the wrecked *Golden Gate* had gone into winter quarters at "Bush's Station" in October 1866. There were barely enough provisions to feed the inhabitants for six months and no resupply could be expected until the following spring. Bush and his quartermaster Mr. Farnum devised a strict eating schedule with equally strict portions.

> In a short time the proper names for days of the week were never heard, but, by general consent, designated by the most prominent food item for that day according to our bill of fare, e.g., "bean day," "sugar day," "soft bread day," etc.

Bush had his hospital steward/medical advisor, Mr. Dixon, take temperature and barometric pressure readings at morning, noon, and night every day. He commended *Golden Gate* passengers Stoddard, Smith, Leggett, and Kelly for their cheerful stoicism in sharing the enforced survival conditions at Bush's Station.

As Bush saw it, there were two possible means of assistance: Chukchis making their southern trek or dogsleds he had previously arranged to be sent from Anadyrsk when winter travel season opened. But, he mused, even if the dogsled drivers ventured forth, they would find Camp Macrea, forty-five miles away, abandoned, and would probably return to Anadyrsk. So on October 20 he sent a party led by Mr. Smith to Camp Macrae with instructions to remain as long as possible. Only a few days later, some of the Smith party returned with three Chukchis, who explained that their people were avoiding the white men, fearing they had come to make war on them. "After all," they stated, "if you come in peace, why didn't you bring your women and children with you?"

Made aware of the grim situation the white men faced, the Chukchi chief readily agreed to bring over the deer herd, one hundred fifty of which Bush managed to purchase. "This was a day of rejoicing for all hands," Bush tells us.

On the thirty-first, dogsleds arrived from Anadyrsk with news of the famine conditions there. No salmon had ascended the river. Their dogs were suffering a form of distemper. Bush was undoubtedly sympathetic, but he had his own problems and a telegraph line to build.

Since no poles had been rafted on the Anadyr, no work was yet possible along its shores. Commencement of construction looked most promising for the Myan River section, but first, Bush would have to obtain transportation and dog food to sustain operations. He decided to travel to Gizhiga, by way of Anadyrsk, to secure supplies and relay news that the *Golden Gate* had been lost, but her crew saved. Leaving Macrae in command, he started for Anadyrsk on November 5, accompanied by construction foreman D. C. Norton, Harder, and two others. Five days later they arrived at the Telegraph Bluff yourt; twelve days after that they came to Markova, Anadyrsk, where they discovered that news of starvation conditions had not been exaggerated. Delayed one week by a storm, Bush continued on to Gizhiga.[11]

The lonely Kennan persevered on his northern journey and was ascending a mountain through clouds of flying snow south of Anadyrsk.

> Gaining the summit we stopped for a moment to rest our dogs when we were startled by the sight of a long line of dark objects passing swiftly across the bare mountaintop a few yards away, plunging down the ravine from which we had just come. They seemed to be dog sleds and we with a great shout began pursuing them. As we drew nearer I recognized among them the old, sealskin-covered pavoshka I had left at Anadyrsk the previous winter. I knew it must be occupied by an American. With heart beating fast I sprang from my sled, ran up to it and demanded in English, "Who is it?" Out of the darkness came a voice I knew well that answered "Bush!" Never was a voice more welcome.

The reunited friends went back to the camp Kennan had just left on the mountain's south side, blew the embers of the still smouldering fire to life, spread their bear skins, and exchanged news. They talked through the night, trying to decide what to do next, but reached no decisions, except going together to Anadyrsk. However, realizing he was only eating into his friend's scanty supply of provisions, Kennan left November 29 for Gizhiga.[12]

It must have been a cheerless Christmas and a less than happy New Year of 1867 for Bush, but at least he had the 1,100 dried fish Kennan had left him. He used some of this supply to feed a train of thirteen native dog teams dispatched on January 13 to bring back Jared Norton and five workmen to begin pole cutting and distribution along the Myan River. On February 2, eight sledloads of supplies from Penzhina, by way of Gizhiga, arrived at Anadyrsk. Bush sent them immediately to the mouth of the Anadyr to bring back Macrae, telegraph operator Baxter, the *Golden Gate*'s first officer, Mr. Frost, and six other men. Jared Norton and his party sledded into Markova on February 5; two days later a construction party under his brother, David, left for the Myan.

Bush had hoped that by waiting until February to send men into the field, they might avoid extreme cold weather. Once again, nature refused to cooperate. Temperatures averaged 50 degrees below zero, and during the coldest nights, David Norton reported that his men, camped outside, dared not go to sleep. The meager food supply was augmented in late February when some Koraks drove their reindeer herd into the village.

Not until March 4 did the sleds sent to bring back Macrae and his party arrive at Markova. Their arduous journey became a funeral one when John Robinson died en route. But there was no time for mourning, no time for anything but accomplishing the job at hand. Macrae started immediately for the lower station on the Myan to cut and distribute poles by hand. He and Bush had given up all hope of securing dogsleds for that work, though Bush was able to send to Macrae more provisions that he had purchased with deer meat from local natives. Bush then proceeded to Penzhina on March 26 to try to procure more dogsleds, only to find the place nearly deserted, so he pushed on south to Gizhiga.[13]

Kennan had arrived there in mid-December 1866 after departing Anadyrsk. Letters and orders from Major Abasa awaited him: eight hundred Yakut laborers had been hired; three hundred horses with pack saddles, along with huge quantities of provisions and equipment, had been purchased. Some of the Yakut men were on their way to Okhotsk. The rest would be deployed in detachments along the route of the line. Abasa instructed Kennan to make arrangements for the transportation of telegraph army officers from the *Onward,* needed to supervise these work parties, from Petropavlovsk to Gizhiga, to prepare to receive sixty Yakut laborers, and to send six hundred army rations to Yamsk for the construction party there.

To fill these requirements I had 15 dog sleds at my disposal. The Russian governor cooperated by sending two Cossack couriers to Petropavlovsk after the Americans presumably left there by the *Onward* and a half-dozen Koraks to carry provisions to Yamsk. With my sleds I was able to supply Mr. Sandford and his party now cutting poles along the Tilghai River, north of Penzhina.

Late that month Kennan and Dodd were surprised by the visit of a Mr. Lewis, a young telegraph operator whom they found in their house calmly drinking tea. This enterprising individual, dispatched by the chief foreman aboard *Onward,* had traveled from Petropavlovsk to Gizhiga, 1,200 miles by dogsleds, accompanied by only a few natives. Kennan rated it "one of the most remarkable journeys ever made by a company employee." Lewis reported that the ship had discharged her cargo and landed most of her passengers; the foreman wished to know what to do next. Not until February 1867 did three of the bark's telegraph army personnel arrive. There was no word on the Atlantic cable's success.

In January, Kennan took fifteen sleds to Sandford's camp, intending to move it further up the river, but a severe storm on the intervening steppe dispersed and separated the party. They wandered around for a week in clouds of drifting snow which even hid their dogs from sight. Sandford managed to return to his old camp with a portion of his men; Kennan led the remainder back to Gizhiga.

Kennan began another trip, this one three hundred versts west to the village of Gamsk to rendezvous with Abasa, in March. With him on this poorgaw-blasted ordeal was one of the Americans from the *Onward,* Mr. Leet, who was an odd individual, prone to reckless behavior. At one point, after refusing to answer his sled driver's questions after a day's frigid travel, his companions feared he might be dead. Kennan shook him. The fur-covered body stirred and a voice said, "Answering that driver of mine was just too much trouble. Besides, I've seen worse storms in the Sierra Nevadas." The last words Kennan recalls him saying were, "What would our mothers say if they could see us now?" After reaching Gamsk, Leet had started for Okhotsk, where Abasa wanted him to supervise a work gang. Once there, he wandered off to the seashore, pulled out his pistol, and killed himself.

The Gamsk journey was Kennan's last sojourn in eastern Siberia. By late May, ice in the gulf was melting; by June, ship navigation was possible, and the New Bedford whaling bark *Sea Breeze* arrived. After greeting Kennan and some of his men, Captain Hamilton asked if they were shipwrecked and was astounded to learn of the telegraph expedition. He then told Kennan that the Atlantic cable venture had been successful and showed him the *San Francisco Bulletin* with news of it.

> All work on the project had been stopped, the enterprise abandoned. The *Onward* arrived July 15 with orders to close down, discharge native laborers, gather all the men and return to America. It seemed hard to give up at once the object to which we had devoted 3 years of our lives; for whose attainment we had suffered all possible hardships of cold, exile and starvation, but we had no alternative and began at once to prepare for departure.

Summing up the work of the Siberian division, Kennan noted they had surveyed the entire 1,500-mile-line route from the Amur River to the Bering Strait, prepared 15,000 telegraph poles, cut fifteen miles of road, and built fifty station houses. There were seventy-five Americans and one hundred fifty natives with sufficient resources for them to keep working another year, but their purpose no longer existed.

When the *Onward* sailed for San Francisco in early October 1867, Kennan, Mahood, and Price, who had just arrived, were not aboard. "We were," Kennan wrote, "the rear guard of the grand army, and intended to go home in winter across Asia and Europe around the world." He does not tell us what became of James A. Mahood, but he and Price began their five-thousand-mile odyssey by dogsled on October 24, and "caught sight of the glittering domes of Moscow" on January 3, 1868. It would not be Kennan's last visit to Russia, or to Siberia.

Serge Abasa returned to St. Petersburg that August. Like his men, he had served his country and his company above and beyond the call of duty.[14] Bush and Macrae up on the Anadyr and Myan Rivers received word to cease work in July 1867 when the inexplicably empty *Clara Bell*—word having been relayed to company headquarters about their perilous condition—sent a boat to Bush's Station with the news. Fortunately, sufficient salmon had been salted away for emergencies, and half-rations sustained the men. The news, it might be imagined, should have been greeted with hearty cheers all round. But no, Bush tells us that it was greeted with quiet resignation, if not disappointment.

> The truth is, we looked upon the project as a great national undertaking that would do credit to any nation. To construct a telegraph line through wild, hitherto unexplored territory, the greater portion of which lay through arctic regions where the severest cold and innumerable privations had to be endured, was an enterprise about which we felt very proud. Now that the walls were sealed, the greater part of our sufferings behind us, the heaviest obstacles overcome, to see our pet project abandoned . . . was by no means gratifying.

Collins L. Macrae and his men seemed to suffer more numerous privations than his Siberian expedition compatriots. Readers may recall that Bush left them at Anadyrsk in March 1867, when he traveled to Penzhina then Gizhiga for more sleds and provisions. He did not return to the stricken settlement until May 21, when he found Macrae and some of his party living with natives, barely surviving. The others, camping along the Myan, were experiencing similar conditions. Then there were the *Golden Gate* survivors who had been left to fend for themselves back at Bush's Station months ago. No one had any idea how they might be faring. Macrae, then D. C. (David) Norton, Myan River party supervisor, reported to Bush.

The first thing Macrae had done after Bush left was build a fifteen-foot-square cabin at Markova. He then deployed Norton and his six-man team to cut and distribute poles along the Myan, and sent another group under Mr. Frost to do the same on another section of that river.

For Macrae, the intervening months resolved themselves into a persistent struggle to kill, catch, find, or transport food for his men and they to do the same for theirs.

D. C. Norton and party built four stations along the river to support their tree-cutting and pole-rafting operations, and he described some of that activity.

> The men found it very hard to work, chopping into the frozen trees and, contrary to their expectations, hardly an axe was nicked, though dozens of hickory axe handles shivered to pieces when jarred by chopping. The severe cold, instead of rendering the axes brittle, appeared to have the opposite effect, though this may be attributable to the excessive electricity in the air, which pervaded the metal.

He and Mason, Nesbit, Smith, Colburn, Burton, and Charles Scammon were ably assisted throughout this period by the native Ilya Deachkoff.

Hearing these reports and assessing the situation, Bush decided to bring back to Markova the men who remained on the Myan. One of those in the dogsled train sent to retrieve these men was a 17-year-old lad by the name of Loveman, who was eager to prove himself. When he returned to Markova, he was a sight to behold: head bare, face dirty with a careworn expression, clad in fur socks and what was left of a parka. It seems he got lost after encountering bears on the trail. "Two of them were sitting on a snow bank," he told his amused audience, "looking at me wondering if I was good enough to eat or not." Avoiding them was his only concern, never mind if he wandered alone for three days. The second night out he decided he was hungry, so he stopped to make a fire, only he had forgotten to bring matches. Hardtack would have to suffice. Having no idea which way to go, he let his dogs take his sled where they pleased while he lay on top of it, sleeping. Next thing he knew he was being pulled through a pond, its ice having broken. He tried to dry his wet clothes. His food had run out. He had given up all hope of ever finding Markova, or of being found. His dogs were dead tired.

Then I got to thinking about starving to death and didn't like the notion. I wished I had never heard of the Telegraph Expedition. Pretty soon I fell asleep, and the next thing I knew I was surrounded by the sleds coming back from the Myan with all the men.

Loveman's tale, told with engaging chagrin, its teller smiling at his audience's laughter, provided welcome humor to men whose morale was normally sustained by pure grit.

In early June, Bush boated down the Myan, reaching its main station on the twelfth. There he made arrangements to travel to the Telegraph Bluff yourt on the Anadyr to secure constructor Robinson's remains and have them buried at the Anadyr bay station. He and his party were gratified to find the body intact in the hut, just as Macrae had left it four months earlier. They gave it a temporary burial on June 21, intending to bring it the rest of the way as soon as possible. Increasing winds and tides began to impede the progress of their boat as they rounded the bend in the east-turning river twelve miles below Camp Macrea. At one point a sudden gale forced them to seek shelter on a small island, where they might pitch their tent.

To our astonishment, the ground was literally covered with gull's nests. Our caps and handkerchiefs were soon filled with eggs, but these, like the goose eggs we had found earlier in our journey, we had to condemn as inedible.

They found Camp Macrae vandalized completely by bears; beef and pork barrels had been ripped open, half the roof was missing, Bush's *vetka* had been clawed to pieces. Finally, on June 26, they reached Bush's

Station, where they were warmly greeted by a cheerful group of *Gate* survivors, commanded by J. H. Robinson, whose spirits that day were raised by the launching of the completely repaired, freshly painted river steamer *Wade*. These men had not only survived, they had prevailed at their remote outpost thanks (again) to the ration strictures of Quartermaster Farnum. There had been several casualties, however. Ship's carpenter Geddes had died and now lay buried beneath a low mound with an appropriate marker. Before all hands departed, Robinson would rest in an adjoining grave. M. J. Kelly, who had been Colonel Wicker's clerk, had several of his fingers amputated by ship's doctor Mr. Dixon after suffering severe frostbite.

To defeat "cabin fever" and stay healthy during the winter months, when temperatures sometimes plunged to 65 degrees below zero, the men exercised whenever possible: hunting, fishing, playing baseball, or running foot races.

For his part, officer-in-charge Robinson managed to construct three miles of line and installed an instrument and battery in the station house. In his estimation, wire stronger than the normal Number 9 type would be required if a line was to be built because his measurements indicated a contraction stress of six feet per mile along his line.

Needless to say, Bush was surprised, if not somewhat amazed, by all this, but he was perhaps happiest and proudest of the little paddle-wheeler *Wade*'s operational status. He put her to work carrying coal for her own use upriver at the small village of Oochostika; from there she would support the line-building program. Animals and natives reacted with alarm and amazement as she chugged up and down the river.

> The little *Wade* was the first steam craft that ever plowed these waters, and will probably be the last. Centuries may roll by . . . before she has a successor. . . . Chukchis scrutinized her carefully from stem to stern, and with our limited knowledge of their language it was impossible to explain its workings to them, but they seemed pleased with the ride we gave them.

It was on the *Wade's* third trip downriver, just as she rounded Cape Large, that expedition members sighted the *Clara Bell*. She brought news of the Atlantic cable's successful completion and orders from Major Wright to pack up everything as soon as possible and proceed to Plover Bay. And so, the *Wade* made her final trip on the Anadyr, under command of Mr. Frost, to pick up Mr. Mason's work party. By the time they arrived on July 26, the *Bell* had been loaded with everything of value, including spars, rigging, anchors, and chains from the doomed *Golden Gate*.

From the deck of the bark, Bush, Macrae, and the others could see the sign painted on a board nailed to their old station, its name, date of erection, and date of abandonment. *Gate* survivors put up their own sign on their quarters, "The House That Jack (tar) Built," with a sketch of its history. Outside the storehouse was another parting note, hoisted on a pole which read "Farnum's Gash—To Let."

The *Wade* performed her last official duty by towing the *Clara Bell* out of the bay. That done, the *Wade* was towed to Plover Bay where the boiler and machinery were put aboard the *Nightingale* and her hulk given to the natives.

Gazing out to sea on September 6, 1867, Bush and the Siberian expeditioneers, the denizens of Kelseyville and of transplanted Libbysville caught sight of a clipper ship.

The long, unexpected delay of Col. Bulkley caused him and *Nightingale's* crew, having come by way of Japan, some anxiety. But they were here now, and we got ready for our homeward voyage. Before long we were gliding under full canvas through the waters of the Bering Sea, bound once more for the world and civilization. These we reached after a short, joyous voyage of twenty-two days.[15]

NOTES

1. Richard J. Bush, *Reindeer, Dogs, and Snowshoes: A Journal of Siberian Travel and Explorations* (New York: Harper and Brothers, 1871), pp. 31–44.
2. George Kennan, *Tent Life in Siberia* (New York: G. P. Putnam's Sons, 1893), pp. 44–46.
3. Bush, *Reindeer, Dogs, and Snowshoes*, pp. 60–85.
4. Perry McDonough Collins, *Siberian Journey: Down the Amur to the Pacific, 1856–1857*, a new edition of *A Voyage down the Amur*, ed. with intro. Charles Vevier (Madison: University of Wisconsin Press, 1962), pp. 279–99.
5. Bush, *Reindeer*, pp. 105–326.
6. Kennan, *Tent Life in Siberia*, pp. 52–338.
7. Bush, *Reindeer*, pp. 340–45.
8. Kennan, *Tent Life*, pp. 343–67.
9. Bush, *Reindeer*, pp. 347–432.
10. Kennan, *Tent Life*, pp. 368–89.
11. Bush, *Reindeer*, pp. 448–57.
12. Kennan, *Tent Life*, pp. 390–98.
13. Bush, *Reindeer*, pp. 461–72.
14. Kennan, *Tent Life*, pp. 400–25.
15. Bush, *Reindeer*, pp. 476–518.

CHAPTER NINE

THE UNFINISHED EPIC

> The anchor is down. We are home again and the bright skies of our country bend over us. Probably, we are together for the last time . . . separated forever, but memories of the past will linger among these associations that no one shall ever forget. . . . The trials and hardships to which you have been exposed are understood; the unfaltering determination to do your duty, appreciated. Though the work in which you were engaged has been abandoned, it does not detract from the credit which belongs to you; no men could have done more; few men so much. . . . For the hearty support you have given me, accept my thanks. If it is in my power to advance your interests, believe me ever ready. . . . The work is finished. Let me welcome you home again. And now we part. Good bye, Good bye.[1]

These valedictory words from Colonel Bulkley were delivered to Western Union Telegraph Expedition personnel returned by the *Nightingale* October 8, 1867.

Readers may recall that he had earlier sent a commendation message to Edward Conway in British Columbia on the fine work his men had done. Their labors ceased in March 1867. A blockhouse was built at the end of the hundreds of miles of completed line and filled with equipment in hopes that the Atlantic cable might yet fail. Fort Stager remained manned until 1869, when John McCutcheon, its last operator, abandoned it, leaving behind thirteen canoes loaded with provisions and clothing.

The line from New Westminster to Quesnel remained in active commercial operation until 1871 when the British Columbian government secured a perpetual lease on all Western Union lines within the colony. When British Columbia became a province in July that year, the Dominion government took over the lease. Nine years later the government purchased all Western Union property and privileges for twenty-four thousand dollars. In his 1874 book *The Wild North Land,* William F. Butler describes what remained of the line between Quesnel and Fort Stager, which was left to nature's whims.

> Crossing the wide Nacharcole River and continuing south for a few miles, we reached a broadly cut trail which bore curious traces of past civilization. Old telegraph poles stood at intervals along the forest-cleared opening, and rusted wires hung in loose festoons from their tops, or lay tangled amid growing brushwood of the cleared space. . . . [W]hen civilization once grasps the wild, lone spaces of the earth it seldom lets go; yet here, having advanced its footsteps, it shrank back again, frightened at her boldness. Even so, this trail, with its ruined wire, told of the wreck of a great enterprise.[2]

The efficient Edward Conway remained in British Columbia and died in Victoria.

Franklin L. Pope returned to New York, where he edited *The Telegrapher* for a year. In 1869 he published a book destined for fifteen editions, *The Modern Practice of the Electric Telegraph.* After working on improvements in the stock ticker machine, he partnered with Thomas A. Edison and James N. Ashley to form Pope, Edison and Company, and on June 7, 1870, Edison and Pope took out a joint patent for a single-wire printing telegraph, which they sold to the Gold and Stock Telegraph Company. The pair did not get along. Their company was dissolved in 1870. Pope turned to private practice as a patent expert and solicitor in 1881, retiring to his home in Great Barrington, Massachusetts, a year later. In the basement of that house he had installed transformers for the local waterpower plant, which he had switched from a steam-powered operation, to simplify his work. Going down to the basement in 1895 to investigate a problem, Pope was killed accidentally. His other publications include *The Telegraphic Instructor* (1871) and *The Electric Incandescent Lamp* (1889).[3]

Thirty-two years after Alaska attained statehood, a telegraph line was completed that connected Fort St. Michael with Seattle, Washington. Only several hundred miles of it followed the route pioneered by Kennicott, Ennis, Adams, and Dall. After reaching Forty Mile in the Yukon Territory, it angled southwest to the coast, where a submarine cable connected it to Seattle.

Three years after his return from Alaska, William H. Dall was appointed to the United States Coastal Survey, in which job he continued his Alaskan studies and those of the North Pacific littoral. In 1884 he joined the U.S. Geological Survey as a paleontologist, a position he held until 1925. In the interim he had been appointed as honorary curator of the U.S. National Museum's Mollusk Division. Besides his book *Alaska and Its Resources*, he published a six-volume work titled *Contributions to the Tertiary Fauna of Florida* and a biography of Spencer Fullerton Baird. His numerous honorary degrees included a doctor of science from the University of Pennsylvania and doctor of laws from George Washington University. He died in 1927.[4]

We know very little about the postexpedition career of William H. Ennis except that he made a trip to the Pribilof Islands as purser aboard the *Caldera* in 1868, was married to Susan D. Coates of San Francisco that same year, and in 1869 shipped out on the brig *Commodore* as Norton Sound regional agent for Parrott and Waterman.[5]

The irrepressible George Russell Adams lived to be ninety-three years old. And what a life it was. Upon returning from Alaska, he joined Ennis for the schooner *Caldera's* Pribilof cruise, writing a description of rival commercial interests there titled *Pioneer Sealing in Alaska*. He then became a mining engineer, traveling around the world to such places as Siberia, Europe, Asia, and Africa. The only record extant on those years consists of a 393-page manuscript describing two and one-half years (1903–5) devoted to developing southern Congo mines. He married San Franciscan Lillian Hinckley, with whom he had five children, two of whom survived to maturity. One of them, Oliver, following his father's death, carried out his wishes and cast his ashes over the Pacific Ocean between San Francisco and Los Angeles.[6]

Dan Libby returned to Port Clarence in 1898 to search for gold, which remained as elusive as that which he had sought in previous years elsewhere in the territory. He seems to have dropped out of sight at the turn of the century. Then in 1925 a roughly dressed stranger identifying himself as Dan's son walked into the Juneau, Alaska, law offices of James Wickersham. Dan Jr. produced photographs of Bulkley, Lebarge, Ketchum, and Whymper, plus old Western Union orders for his father. Dan Jr. hoped to sell these items to purchase steerage passage to the Copper River country, where a job was waiting. Asked about his father, he told Wickersham that he was staying with his father down in Seattle, where the senior Libby was living in destitute circumstances. The lawyer, a Pioneers of Alaska organization member, was moved to action. He wired Western Union president Newcomb Carlton, asking him to send a trusted employee to Howe Street in Seattle to help eighty-five-year-old Dan Libby in any way possible. Here the Good Samaritan story ends. One can only hope it turned out well.[7]

Of the Siberian expeditioneers we know something of Bush's later life and quite a bit about Kennan's. Bush settled in the San Francisco area and became a fairly well-known California artist, working mostly in oils. His paintings were exhibited in various venues, including the Oakland Museum of California, which owns some of his works.[8]

Norwalk, Ohio-born George Kennan went to New York after his delayed return to America, where he held jobs in banks and law offices. More to his liking were the lectures he gave on his Siberian adventures. After a stint selling books for D. Appleton and Company, he moved to Washington, where he became night manager for the Associated Press. G. P. Putnam and Sons published his *Tent Life in Siberia* in 1870. He used proceeds from its sales to finance a return to Russia, traveling to the Caucasian Mountains between the Black and Caspian Seas and crossing them twice. His experiences produced material for more lectures and several articles. Through the 1870s, sketchy but dramatic information about government police repression in his old haunt, Siberia, prompted Kennan to defend publicly what he believed were unjust attacks on the tsarist regime. Following the assassination of Tsar Alexander II in 1881, masses of Russians were sent to Siberia for penal servitude and so-called administrative exile. In view of this situation, Kennan was determined to go and see and judge it for himself. Americans were becoming more and more interested in Russian matters; their curiosity about Siberia was stirred by news of survivors of the fated *Jeanette* reaching Moscow.

The ship, financed by newspaper tycoon James Gordon Bennett and crewed by U.S. Navy personnel, departed San Francisco July 1879 on an expedition attempting to reach the North Pole via the Arctic Ocean. Captain DeLong and his men were doomed to drifting, icebound, for twenty-one months. Eventually they stood on that same ice and watched *Jeanette* sink. Half of the party stayed; the rest struck out for the Siberian mainland by boats and sleds. Those who stayed perished. Of the rest, only a few survived to tell the grim story.

And so it probably didn't take much convincing for *Century Magazine* to sponsor Kennan's investigative trip to Russia which was authorized by a government aware of his favorable disposition towards it. Kennan, accompanied by Boston artist George A. Frost, arrived in St. Petersburg in 1885, thus beginning a fifteen-thousand-mile, sixteen-month journey into the terrible truth of Siberia. Towards the end of his stay, Russian authorities became aware that Kennan was now a critic of their regime. They decided to employ bureaucratic harrassment when he sought to leave the country and told him that he could not do so without permission from the governor-general of eastern Siberia. He sought assistance from the American charge d'affaires in St. Petersburg, who wrote a note to the passport bureau.

I delivered it in person in order that I might take the bull by the horns. . . . [T]he chief read the note, scrutinized me, crossed the room and consulted his clerk. Returning, he asked if I had ever before had a resident's permit. Yes, I answered. When? In March, 1868. He then called his clerk and ordered him to find the permit. Four minutes later the clerk returned with the *original* [emphasis mine] I had taken out 18 years before!

Kennan's previous Siberian experience proved to be the fortuitous key to his escape from potential ordeal by administrative detention, a cell-less prison with disappearing exits. The mollified official told Kennan all he needed now was a letter from the charge d'affaires, which was immediately forthcoming. After four more days of classic bureaucratic run-around, the exit visa was granted. Kennan and Frost went home. Kennan's account of the massive human rights abuses he witnessed were first published, serially, in *Century Magazine*, then in an 1891 book, *Siberia and the Exile System.*

The now-famous author, who had married Emaline Wells in 1879, continued his travels and writing through, and beyond, the turn of the century. He covered the Spanish-American War and the Russo-Japanese War. He also went to Martinique to study its Mt. Pelee volcano. Among his subsequent books was a two-volume biography of railroad magnate Edward H. Harriman, father of Averill, who envisioned a tracked version of Collins's North Pacific telegraph.

George Kennan died, at eighty years of age, in his Medina, New York, home, on May 10, 1924.[9]

The commander of Siberian operations, that single-minded practitioner of colorful language, Serge Abasa, seems to have disappeared into the mists of history upon his return to St. Petersburg. Suffice it to say that without his iron will, fierce determination, and leadership, telegraph army work in that hostile environment would not have succeeded to the degree that it did.

The San Francisco to which expeditioneers returned in October 1867 had no doubt changed in their eyes after what must have seemed a lifetime away. They had changed too as families, friends, and acquaintances surely noticed. And though expedition headquarters in the Cosmopolitan Hotel might have looked the same, it had weathered a minor storm, a local version of the North Pacific's contrary winds and violent weather.

Readers may remember that Captain Charles M. Scammon's Western Union service was granted in the form of a leave of absence from Revenue Marine duty; that he was relieved from duty with the telegraph expedition's navy in December 1866, handing over command of the *Nightingale* to Lieutenant John O. Norton. Scammon must have assumed he would soon be given command of another Revenue Marine ship or cutter. He could not have foreseen what rough seas lay ahead before it sailed into his life.

The first inkling he had of them took the form of a letter from Russell Glover, a junior officer who had served aboard the *Shubrick* and the *Golden Gate*. He informed Scammon that he had heard that Bulkley was glad that Scammon had been relieved of duty by Western Union, that he was no "scientific man" as he had represented himself. There is no record that Scammon ever had done so. He had signed on to command the telegraph navy. His relations with Bulkley had been professional and correct. So why this animosity? What prompted Bulkley to write that terse note on January 14, 1867 stating, "You can transact your business with Col. F. Wicker, who is delegated to confer with you"?

Scammon wanted answers to these puzzlements and went to Bulkley's office to try to discuss matters with him. He may have been at his desk, but he was not there for Scammon. The issue subsided for several months and Scammon probably thought and hoped it was over. He was wrong. On March 19 came the shocking letter from Captain Howard, senior customs inspector, that "serious charges have been preferred against you by Col. Bulkley and the Russian-American Telegraph Expedition." The charges included drunkenness, smuggling furs, and command incapacity. Howard suggested that Scammon demand a Court of Inquiry to prove his innocence regarding the charges.[10]

This bolt from the blue could not have come at a worse time. Scammon had just been given command of the U.S. Revenue schooner *Joe Lane*, a ship he had rated highly in a previous assessment of Revenue Marine vessels. Her size and speed, three boats with twelve-man crews, made her the efficient ideal for executing assigned missions.

Scammon wasted no time in securing letters of commendation from former officers and men who had served with him aboard *Shubrick*, *Golden Gate*, and *Nightingale*. Testimonials to his faithful service, soberness, and competency were forthcoming. One of the most telling came from James Black, who had been Bulkley's personal secretary when he sailed on Western Union navy flagships, who praised his seamanship, command bearing, and "gentlemanly deportment." Others noted that he had been "strict but fair."

Whether it was the strength of these testimonials or Bulkley's failure to follow through on his charges, no Court of Inquiry was ever held. Captain Scammon was exonerated and continued in command of the *Joe Lane* for two more years, at which time he was given the Revenue Marine steamer *Wayanda*.[11]

Ironically, Bulkley and Scammon met fourteen months later . . . in the Congressional Record. The sale of Alaska prompted, as we have seen in the case of Michael Lebarge and his Pioneer American Fur Company, intense interest on the part of trappers and traders, not to mention sealers and fisherman. Some of that interest focused on St. Paul's Island in the Pribilofs, now part of Alaska. The former Russian American Company outpost boasted a huge population of fur seals. A group of Californians wanted to sail there and occupy the island as a base for harvesting them. Governor Haight, knowing that Western Union personnel had explored Alaska and visited the island, requested a report on the commercial and natural resources of the new territory. Bulkley was only too happy to oblige, providing "a synopsis of my own observations and the report of the exploring parties under my charge during the past three years."

His report contained pertinent information on Sitka, Cook's Inlet, New Archangel, St. Paul's and the Pribilofs, Kodiak Island, the Aleutians, Norton Sound, Fort St. Michael, and the Yukon River. His concluding remarks contained some interesting comments.

> Permit me to say that I consider the acquisition of this territory of the greatest importance, and not to be measured by the dollars paid. The fur production is probably the most valuable in the world. As before remarked, the island of St. Paul alone, properly managed, will produce fur seal enough to pay the cost of the territory in a few years.

He appended another report on Alaska's ports and harbors which had already appeared in New York newspapers, one "obtained from my office without authority by a clerk formerly in our employ" that he described as having "but little interest." The identity of the clerk is unknown, but the author of the report "of little interest" is: Charles Scammon. Titled "Notes on the Russian American Company's trading posts," it contained information not found in Bulkley's survey and data invaluable to mariners.

This comprehensive document found its way to the House Foreign Affairs Committee, chaired by Bulkley's old Civil War commander, Nathaniel P. Banks, who deemed it appropriate for inclusion in the Record along with other material relating to the new territory of Alaska.[12]

In later years Bulkley, having settled his wife Abbie and sons Charles Jr. and Howard in Stockton, California, traveled to what can only be assumed were engineering projects. One of them took him to Guatemala in the latter part of the nineteenth century. His will indicates he was a resident of that country as of 1892. He died there two years later.[13]

> The chief object of this work is to give as correct figures of the different species of marine mammals found on the Pacific Coast of North America as could be obtained from a careful study of them from life, and numerous measurements after death, whenever practicable. It is also my aim to give as full an account of the habits of these animals as practicable, together with such facts in reference to their geographical distribution as have come to my knowledge.

Thus in his preface did the middle-aged sea captain plot the course of his book *The Marine Mammals of the North-West Coast of North America,* which contained "an account of the American whale fishery."

While Charles Scammon continued his career with the Revenue Marine, he embarked on a second one. Writing came naturally enough to a man who had kept logs and diaries aboard ships for decades. Combined with his experiences as a whaler and years of observation sailing the Pacific, Scammon produced his magnum opus, illustrated with his own drawings, in 1874. It represented the culmination of writing begun after his Western Union service in the form of newspaper and magazine articles on topics such as the Revenue Marine, explorations of Baja, California, and Alaskan geography. There followed a series of pieces in the highly respected *Overland Monthly* on the Pribilof Islands, travel scenes, lumbering, cod fishing, and the story of Chief Seattle. The remainder dealt with marine mammals. Not being a scientist, he sought assistance from some of the most distinguished men of his day. Edward Drinker Cope, curator of the Philadelphia Academy of Natural Sciences, edited and contributed substantially to Scammon's article on West Coast cetaceans.

In San Francisco, Scammon met Louis Agassiz. The famous zoologist, in the last year of his life, must have inspired him; Scammon dedicated the book to Agassiz. His old expedition acquaintance, William H. Dall, was a helpful and supportive correspondent.

Marine Mammals was written at the home where Scammon and his wife had settled, a thirty-five-acre farm situated north of San Francisco in Sebastopol amidst the wine country of Sonoma County. The surroundings and view were therapeutic, for Scammon continued to suffer from that undisclosed illness that had plagued him a while on his last voyage aboard *Nightingale.* It had kept him ashore for periods of time during the rest of his Revenue Marine career, which lasted until 1895. By that time he and his wife, Susan, had moved to east Oakland, where the ill and aging mariner had a good view of ships plying his beloved Pacific Ocean. His equally beloved wife died in 1911, and so did he, aged eighty-six, following her to that final port of call.[14]

Scammon's modicum of immortality can be found on maps of Alaska that show Scammon Bay, so named by Dall, just southwest of Norton Sound, and in the Latin designation of one of the gray whales, *Globiocephalus Scammoni.*

And what of the two lead ships of Scammon's telegraph navy, the *George S. Wright* and the *Nightingale*? Following her telegraph expedition service, the *Wright* was sold to Jacob Kamm, who in turn sold her to the North Pacific Transportation Company. The Puget Sound-built, schooner-rigged steamer that had transnavigated the North Pacific would now carry mail and passengers and haul cargo on the Alaska route.

In January 1870, under the command of Captain Thomas Ainsley, she departed Portland, Oregon, bound for Sitka and other destinations along Alaska's southern coast. Under way for Nanaimo loaded with barrels of salmon and oil and bundles of skins, she disappeared. Family and friends of crew and passengers implored the government to institute a search for the missing vessel after weeks had passed with no word of her. In due course the steamer's owners sent a ship to investigate. Some pieces of wreckage were found near Cape Caution but that was all. Some months later two bodies from the *Wright* were discovered on a beach in that vicinity. Whether the boiler exploded, deemed unlikely since one of the bodies had on a life preserver, or the ship struck an unmarked rock was never determined.[15]

The *Nightingale* set sail from San Francisco in January 1868, arriving in New York nine months later. Her trip around the Horn was delayed by six thousand dollars' worth of repairs accomplished at Valparaiso, Chile. She continued service as a merchant trader, plying the seas between San Francisco, New York, and China through 1876. The North Pacific was never her friend. On a voyage across its stormy expanse in 1871, she arrived in San Francisco under bare poles. That same year, taking on too much water, she was forced to put into the Falkland Islands. Before getting under way again, some of her crew mutinied, and the mate died of knife wounds.

In 1876 she was sold at auction at San Francisco's Merchant Exchange for $11,500. Her new owner loaded the clipper with oil and sent her to New York, where she was sold again, this time for $15,000. Now sailing under Norwegian colors, *Nightingale* was rerigged as a bark. From clipper passenger ship, then slave ship, to telegraph expedition flagship, to merchant trader, her sailing career ended after forty-one years. Perhaps the once-proud clipper, wind singing in her sails, could no longer stand the ignominy to which her owners had brought her, a bark hauling lumber across the Atlantic. In April 1893 her captain and crew abandoned *Nightingale* at sea. Taken off by a passing vessel, they watched ship and cargo sink beneath the waves.[16]

Seven years later there appeared in New York and San Francisco newspapers an obituary notice: Perry MacDonough Collins, aged eighty-seven, died on January 18. The entrepreneurial visionary watched his project's demise from his vantage point as Western Union's managing director. He withstood what must have been acute disappointment as well as the company's ensuing financial storm. In the aftermath, Western Union issued $3,170,292 worth of bonds for the redemption of extension stock, which had been sold to finance the project. The majority of those who had eagerly purchased that stock in 1864 were also Western Union stockholders. That the company survived is a tribute to its strength and soundness, a faith further indicated by the fact that its market value remained steady.[17]

Collins had been paid one hundred thousand dollars for devising the Overland Line project and securing permissions from Great Britain and Russia to build it through their territory. Though it is not known what he did in the years immediately following cessation of work on the line, it can be assumed that he invested some of his money and increased the total. In 1876 Collins returned to New York and took up residence in the St. Denis Hotel. When not continuing his investments, especially in railroads, he lived the life of a wealthy bachelor and enjoyed himself until his death in 1900. He bequeathed the bulk of his fortune to his favorite niece, Kate Collins Brown. When she died seventeen years later, her will revealed a handsome bequest in her uncle's name of $550,000 to New York University, Columbia University, and Presbyterian Hospital.[18]

Collins himself never viewed the Atlantic cable that ended his overland line as competition, nor with animosity, but rather as a component of a global communications network.

> I do not deprecate other plans of telegraphic communications with Europe or any other country. . . . I say success and God speed to all telegraph lines on sea or on land. The world is broad enough and round enough to accommodate them all; commerce and intelligence active enough to give them employment and pay for their use.

His vision had no boundaries. It connected with commerce, of course, linking self-interest with national interests and transnational interests in a world "girded with steam and electricity."[19]

Had he lived in this century, Collins might have been a computer entrepreneur or perhaps an internet swashbuckler. He would not be surprised by e-commerce or instantaneous global communications that put California, British Columbia, Alaska, Siberia, and Europe at our fingertips as we stand on the banks of the river of time flowing into the new millennium.

NOTES

1. "Speech of Col. Charles S. Bulkley, Engineer-in-Chief," reprinted in *The Esquimaux*, 1867.

2. Corday Mackay, "The Collins Overland Telegraph," *British Columbia Historical Quarterly* 10 (1946): pp. 212–13.

3. *Dictionary of American Biography*, vol. 15, ed. Dumas Malone (New York: Scribner, 1935), pp. 75–76.

4. Smithsonian Institution Archives, William H. Dall Papers, Introductory Biographical Notes, July 1971.

5. "Journal of William H. Ennis, Member, Russian-American Telegraph Exploring Expedition," transcribed with intro. and notes Harold F. Taggart, *California Historical Society Quarterly* 33 (March 1954): concluding paragraph, p. 167.

6. Richard A. Pierce, introduction to *Life on the Yukon, 1865–1867* by George R. Adams (Kingston, Ontario, Canada: The Limestone Press, 1982).

7. Letter, James Wickersham to Newcomb Carlton, president, Western Union Telegraph Co., dated March 26, 1925, Wickersham Historical Site Collection Papers, Alaska State Library, MS 107, box 73, folder 2.

8. Richard J. Bush file data, Oakland Museum of California.

9. George Kennan, *Siberia and the Exile System*, abridged ed. (Chicago: Univ. of Chicago Press, 1958), pp. xi–xiii, 242–43, and *The Firelands Pioneer*, n.s., 23, The Firelands Historical Society, Norwalk, Ohio, April 1925, pp. 502–3.

10. Note, Charles S. Bulkley to Captain Scammon, dated January 14, 1867, and Letter, Captain Howard to Scammon, dated March 19, 1867, in the Charles M. Scammon Papers, Bancroft Library, Berkeley, Cal.

11. Letters from Russell Glover, John Davison, James Black, et al, in the Scammon Papers, and Lyndall Baker Landauer, *Scammon: Beyond the Lagoon, A Biography of Charles Melville Scammon* (San Francisco: J. Porter Shaw Library Associates, 1986), Pacific Maritime History Series, no. 1 pp. 102–3.

12. Miscellaneous Document no. 1317, 40th Congress, 2nd Session, Congressional Record Service.

13. Landauer, *Beyond the Lagoon*, p. 131, and Last Will and Testament, Charles S. Bulkley, February, 1892. Copy in British Columbia Archives.

14. Charles M. Scammon, *The Marine Mammals of the North-Western Coast of North America*, new intro. Victor B. Scheffer (New York: Dover Publications, 1968), pp. v–11, and Landauer, *Beyond the Lagoon*, pp. 133–34.

15. *Lewis and Dryden's Marine History of the Pacific Northwest*, ed. E. W. Wright (Seattle: Superior Publishing Company, 1967), pp. 204–5.

16. Octavius T. Howe and Frederick C. Matthews, *American Clipper Ships 1833–1858* (Salem, Mass., Marine Research Society, 1927), pp. 437–38.

17. James D. Reid, *The Telegraph in America* (New York: John Polhemus Publisher, 1886), p. 517.

18. "Perry MacDonough Collins, A Generous Benefactor of New York University," P. B. McDonald, in the Collins File, New York University Library Archives.

19. Collins speech in the "Origin, Organization, and Progress of the Russian-American Telegraph," Western Union Telegraph Company, Rochester, N.Y., 1866.

GLOSSARY

Back, as a sail: Trim (pull in) to the windward.

Bear away, or up: To change course, especially away from the wind.

Beat(ing): To sail as close to the wind as possible.

Block: A nautical pulley.

Bulwark: A ship's side above the upper deck.

Clew: The after lower corner of a mainsail, jib, or mizzen; either lower corner or spinnaker.

Clew up: To raise the lower corners of a square sail by its clewlines.

Close hauled: Sailing as close to the wind as is efficient; same as beating.

Cutter: A single-masted boat flying two jibs at the same time.

Draft: Depth of a ship's keel below the waterline.

Flying jib: A light sail extending beyond the jib attached to an extension of the jib boom.

Gig: A light ship's boat with sails and oars reserved for the captain. A fast, light rowboat.

Haul: To veer or shift direction clockwise.

Hauled her wind: Steering a ship away from an object.

Hawser: A cable or rope used in mooring or towing a ship.

Full rigged ship under all plain sail to skysails, with all staysails and all port studding sails, drawing by J. B. Dwyer.

1. flying jib
2. jib
3. fore-topmost staysail
4. foresail
5. lower fore-topsail
6. upper fore-topsail
7. fore-topgallant sail
8. fore royal
9. fore skysail
10. lower studding sail
11. fore-topmast studding sail
12. fore-topgallant studding sail
13. fore-royal studding sail
14. main staysail
15. main-topmost staysail
16. main-topgallant staysail
17. main-royal staysail
18. mainsail
19. lower main topsail
20. upper main topsail
21. main-topgallant sail
22. main royal
23. main skysail
24. main-topmast studding sail
25. main-topgallant studding sail
26. main-royal studding sail
27. mizzen sail
28. mizzen-topmast sail
29. mizzen-topgallant staysail
30. mizzen-royal staysail
31. mizzen sail (crossjack)
32. lower mizzen topsail
33. upper mizzen topsail
34. mizzen-topgallant sail
35. mizzen royal
36. mizzen skysail
37. spanker

Heave: To turn a ship pointing its bow into the wind.

Heave to: To head slowly into the wind; to stop.

Hook: Slang for anchor.

Jib: A triangular sail stretching from the foretopmast head to the bowsprit or the bow.

Kedge off: Using an anchor (kedge) to pull a grounded boat or ship back into deep water.

Port: The left side of a ship facing forward.

Reefing: Decreasing the size of a sail.

Scuppers: Deck drains.

Starboard: The right side of a ship facing forward.

Swell: A long wave created by prevailing winds or a distant storm.

Tacking: Changing a ship's direction so that the wind is coming from its other side.

Warping ship: To move a ship by hauling on a line fastened to or around a piling, anchor, or pier.

Wearing ship: To make a ship come about with the wind aft.

SELECTED BIBLIOGRAPHY

DOCUMENTS

Charles M. Scammon Papers, to include private journals. Bancroft Library, University of California, Berkeley, BANC MSS P-K 200-207.

"Journal of William H. Ennis, Member, Russian-American Telegraph Exploring Expedition." *California Historical Society Quarterly* 33 (March 1954).

Melnikoff letter and Sibley-Collins reply letter. University of Rochester, Rush Rhees Library, Hiram Sibley Papers, Department of Rare Books and Special Collections.

"Memorial of Perry McDonough Collins . . ." Documents authorized by Senate Commerce Committee chairman Zachariah Chandler on the Collins Overland Telegraph project transmitted to Secretary of State William H. Seward, April 14, 1864. The University Libraries, The Pennsylvania State University, University Park, Penn.

Miscellaneous Document No. 1317. 40th Congress, 2nd Session, May 1868, Congressional Record Service.

"Origin, Organization and Progress of the Russian-American Telegraph." Western Union Telegraph Company, Rochester, N.Y., 1866. Microfilm document from Pattee Library, Pennsylvania State University, University Park, Penn.

"Report of James L. Butler to Majors E. Conway and F. L. Pope on British Columbia Explorations." May 1, 1866, Smithsonian Institution Archives, Record Unit 7073, William H. Dall Papers.

"Report on Explorations of British Columbia from Victoria and Vancouver to the Stekine River." Frank L. Pope to Col. Charles S. Bulkley, May 5, 1866. Wemple Papers relating to the Russian-American Telegraph Project, 1865–1867, Special Collections, University Libraries, University of Washington, Seattle.

William H. Dall Papers. Smithsonian Institution Archives, Record Unit 7073.

BOOKS

Adams, George R. *Life on the Yukon, 1865–1867*. Kingston, Ontario, Canada: The Limestone Press, 1982.

Billington, Ray Allen. *Westward Expansion: A History of the American Frontier*. 3rd ed. New York: The Macmillan Company, 1967.

Bobrick, Benson. *East of the Sun*. New York: Henry Holt & Company, 1992.

Bush, Richard J. *Reindeer, Dogs, and Snowshoes: A Journal of Siberian Travel and Explorations*. New York: Harper and Brothers, 1871.

Coe, Lewis. *The Telegraph: A History*. Jefferson, N.C.: McFarland and Company, 1993.

Collins, Perry MacDonough. *Siberian Journey: Down the Amur to the Pacific, 1856–1857*. A New Edition of *Voyage down the Amur*. Ed. with intro. Charles Vevier. Madison: University of Wisconsin Press, 1962.

Dall, William H. *Alaska and Its Resources*. Boston: Lee & Shepard, 1870. Reprint ed. 1970. New York: Arno Press.

Durant, John and Alice. *Pictorial History of American Ships*. New York: A. S. Barnes and Company, 1953.

Ferrell, Ed, ed. *Biographies of Alaska-Yukon Pioneers, 1850–1950*. Vol. 2. Bowie, Md.: Heritage Books, 1947.

Horan, James D. *Mathew Brady: Historian with a Camera*. New York: Crown Publishers Inc., 1955

Howe, Octavius T., and Frederick C. Matthews. *American Clipper Ships*. Salem, Mass.: Marine Research Society, 1927.

James, James Alton. *The First Scientific Exploration of Russian America*. Evanston, Ill.: Northwestern University, 1942.

Jennings, John. *Clipper Ship Days: The Golden Age of American Sailing Ships*. New York: Random House, 1952.

Kennan, George. *Tent Life in Siberia*. New York: G. P. Putnam's Sons, 1893.

———. *Siberia and the Exile System*. Abridged edition. Chicago: University of Chicago Press, 1958.

Landauer, Lyndall Baker. *Scammon: Beyond the Lagoon, A Biography of Charles Melville Scammon*. San Francisco: J. Porter Shaw Library Associates, 1986.

MacKay, Douglas. *The Honourable Company: A History of the Hudson's Bay Company*. New York: Bobbs-Merrill Company, 1936.

Malone, Dumas, ed. *Dictionary of American Biography*. Vol. 7. New York: Scribner, 1934.

Malone, Dumas, and Basil Rauch. *Empire for Liberty: The Genesis and Growth of the United States of America*. Vol. 1. New York: Appleton-Century Crofts, 1960.

McDougall, Walter A. *Let the Sea Make a Noise: Four Hundred Years of Cataclysm, Conquest, War, and Folly in the North Pacific*. New York: Avon Books, 1993.

Neering, Rosemary. *Continental Dash: The Russian-American Telegraph*. Ganges, British Columbia: Horsdal & Schubart Publishers, 1989.

O'Brien, John Emmet. *Telegraphing in Battle: Reminiscences of the Civil War*. Scranton, Penn.: Raeder Press, 1910.

Ormsby, Margaret A. *British Columbia: A History*. Vancouver, British Columbia: The Macmillan Company of Canada, 1959.

Place, Marian T. *Cariboo Gold: The Story of the British Columbia Gold Rush*. New York: Holt, Rinehart and Winston, 1970.

Plum, William R. *The Military Telegraph during the Civil War in the United States*. New York: Arno Press, 1974.

Reid, James D. *The Telegraph in America*. New York: John Polhemus Publisher, 1886.

Roscoe, Theodore. *Picture History of the U.S. Navy*. New York: Charles Scribner's Sons, 1956.

Scammon, Charles M. *The Marine Mammals of the North-Western Coast of North America*. New Introduction by Victor B. Scheffer. New York: Dover Publications, 1968.

Stefansson, Vilhjalmur. *Northwest to Fortune*. New York: Duell, Sloan & Pearce, 1958.

Thompson, Robert L. *Wiring a Continent*. Princeton, N.J.: Princeton University Press, 1947.

Whymper, Frederick. *Travel and Adventure in the Territory of Alaska*. Ann Arbor: University of Michigan Microfilms, 1966.

Wright, E. W., ed. *Lewis and Dryden's Marine History of the Pacific Northwest*. Seattle, Wash.: Superior Publishing Company, 1967.

MAGAZINE ARTICLES

Mackay, Corday. "The Collins Overland Telegraph." *British Columbia Historical Quarterly* 10, 1946.

NEWSPAPER ARTICLES

"The Blank in our News from the Outside World." *The Esquimaux*, January 6, 1867.

"City Intelligence." *The Esquimaux*, November 4, 1866. Alaska State Library Historical Collections.

"Congratulatory Letter." *The Esquimaux*, December 9, 1866.

de Bendeleben, Otto. "Sketches of the First Telegraph Explorations in Russian America." *The Esquimaux*, April 4, 1867.

"Letter from Yankee Jim." *The Esquimaux*, April 7, 1867.

"Libbysville Items." *The Esquimaux*, July 14, 1867.

"Memoir of the Late Robert Kennicott." *The Esquimaux*, November 4, 1866.
"Our Arctic Home." *The Esquimaux*, July 7, 1867.
Romanoff, D. I. "The Russian-American Telegraph, Collins Line." *Russian Gazette*, St. Petersburg, February 1866, nos. 37, 41, and 44. Hiram Sibley Papers, Rush Rhees Library, University of Rochester.

Index

About the Author

JOHN B. DWYER is a Professional Military Historian. His main research interests include tactical deception, the Scouts and Raiders of World War II, and amphibious special warfare. Some of his numerous articles have appeared in magazines such as *Proceedings*, *Naval History*, and *Vietnam*.